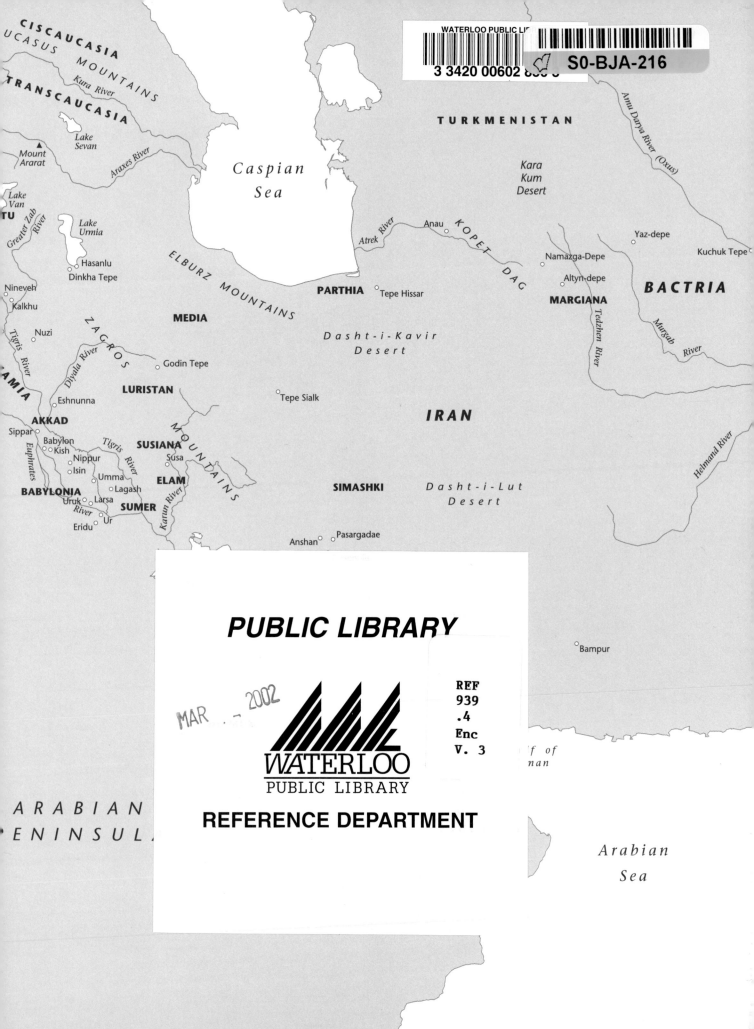

CISCAUCASIA

UCASUS MOUNTAINS

TRANSCAUCASIA

Kura River

Lake Sevan

Mount Ararat ▲

Araxes River

Lake Van

TU

Greater Zab River

Lake Urmia

Hasanlu

Dinkha Tepe

Nineveh

Kalkhu

ZAGROS

Nuzi

Tigris River

Diyala River

Godin Tepe

MEDIA

ELBURZ MOUNTAINS

Caspian Sea

TURKMENISTAN

Kara Kum Desert

Atrek River

Anau

KOPET DAG

PARTHIA

Tepe Hissar

Amu Darya River (Oxus)

Yaz-depe

Namazga-Depe

Kuchuk Tepe

Altyn-depe

BACTRIA

MARGIANA

Tedzhen River

Murgab River

Dasht-i-Kavir Desert

LURISTAN

AMIA

Eshnunna

AKKAD

Sippar

Tigris River

Babylon

Kish

Nippur

Isin

Umma

Lagash

SUSIANA

Susa

ELAM

MOUNTAINS

BABYLONIA

Euphrates

Uruk

Larsa

River

SUMER

Eridu

Ur

Karun River

Tepe Sialk

IRAN

SIMASHKI

Dasht-i-Lut Desert

Anshan

Pasargadae

Helmand River

Bampur

PUBLIC LIBRARY

MAR - 2002

WATERLOO
PUBLIC LIBRARY

REFERENCE DEPARTMENT

REF
939
.4
Enc
V. 3

f of
nan

ARABIAN

PENINSUL

Arabian

Sea

The Ancient Near East

An Encyclopedia for Students

Ronald Wallenfels, *Editor in Chief*

Jack M. Sasson, *Consulting Editor*

Volume 3

CHARLES SCRIBNER'S SONS
An Imprint of The Gale Group
NEW YORK   DETROIT   SAN FRANCISCO   LONDON   BOSTON   WOODBRIDGE, CT

Developed for Charles Scribner's Sons by Visual Education Corporation, Princeton, N.J.

For Scribners
PUBLISHER: Karen Day
SENIOR EDITOR: Timothy J. DeWerff
COVER DESIGN: Lisa Chovnick, Tracey Rowens

For Visual Education Corporation
EDITORIAL DIRECTOR: Darryl Kestler
PROJECT DIRECTOR: Meera Vaidyanathan
WRITERS: Jean Brainard, John Haley, Mac Austin, Charles Roebuck, Rebecca Stefoff
EDITORS: Dale Anderson, Carol Ciaston, Linda Perrin, Caryn Radick
ASSOCIATE EDITOR: Lauren Weber
COPYEDITING MANAGER: Helen Castro
COPY EDITOR: Marie Enders
PHOTO RESEARCH: Sara Matthews
PRODUCTION SUPERVISOR: Marcel Chouteau
PRODUCTION ASSISTANT: Brian Suskin
INTERIOR DESIGN: Maxson Crandall, Rob Ehlers
ELECTRONIC PREPARATION: Cynthia C. Feldner, Christine Osborne, Fiona Torphy
ELECTRONIC PRODUCTION: Rob Ehlers, Lisa Evans-Skopas, Laura Millan, Isabelle Ulsh

Library of Congress Cataloging-in-Publication Data

The Ancient Near East : an encyclopedia for students / Ronald Wallenfels, editor in chief; Jack M. Sasson, consulting editor.
         p.   cm.
     Includes bibliographical references and index.
     ISBN 0-684-80597-9 (set : alk. paper) — ISBN 0-684-80589-8 (vol. 1)
— ISBN 0-684-80594-4 (vol. 2) — ISBN 0-684-80595-2 (vol. 3) — ISBN 0-684-80596-0 (vol. 4)
     1. Middle East—Civilization—To 622—Dictionaries, Juvenile.
[1. Middle East—Civilization—To 622—Encyclopedias.] I. Wallenfels, Ronald. II. Sasson, Jack M.

DS57 .A677 2000
939'.4—dc21   00-056335

TABLE OF CONTENTS

VOLUME 1   Abraham–Cities and City-States

VOLUME 2   Clay Tablets–Inheritance

VOLUME 3   Inscriptions–Phoenicia and the Phoenicians

VOLUME 4   Phrygia and the Phrygians–Zoroaster and Zoroastrianism

MAPS & CHARTS

COLOR PLATES

A Time Line of the Ancient Near East

	Neolithic Period ca. 9000–4000 B.C.	Chalcolithic Period ca. 4000–3000 B.C.

Mesopotamia	Neolithic culture in northern Mesopotamia
	    Earliest permanent farming settlements, ca. 7000 B.C.
	    Earliest evidence of pottery, ca. 6500 B.C.
	Ubaid settlements in southern Mesopotamia
		Late Ubaid period
		Uruk and Jamdat-Nasr periods
		    Development of city-states
		    Invention of writing

Anatolia	Earliest permanent farming settlements, ca. 7000 B.C. Çatal Hüyük inhabited Earliest evidence of pottery, ca. 6300 B.C.	Development of agricultural and trading communities
Syria and the Levant	Agriculture first practiced, ca. 8500 B.C. Settlement of Jericho Domestication of animals, ca. 7300 B.C. Earliest evidence of pottery, ca. 6600 B.C.	Development of agricultural and trading communities
Egypt	Earliest permanent farming settlements in northern Egypt, ca. 5200 B.C. Earliest evidence of pottery in northern Egypt, ca. 5000 B.C. Evidence of predynastic graves in southern Egypt, suggesting the existence of permanent settlements, ca. 4000 B.C.	Predynastic period Invention of hieroglyphics
Arabia	Earliest evidence of pastoralism and pottery in western Arabia, ca. 6000 B.C. Contact between eastern Arabia and southern Mesopotamia	Permanent settlements established Contact between western Arabia and Syria and the Levant Continued contact between eastern Arabia and southern Mesopotamia
Iran	Earliest permanent farming settlements in southwestern Iran, ca. 7000 B.C. Earliest evidence of pottery in southwestern Iran, ca. 6500 B.C. Susa founded	Proto-Elamite culture
Aegean and the Eastern Mediterranean	Earliest permanent farming settlements on Crete, ca. 7000 B.C. Earliest permanent farming settlements on the mainland, ca. 6700 B.C. Earliest evidence of pottery on the mainland, ca. 6300 B.C. Earliest evidence of pottery on Crete, ca. 5900 B.C.	Development of agricultural and trading communities

A Time Line of the Ancient Near East

	Late Bronze Age ca. 1600–1200 B.C.	Iron Age ca. 1200–500 B.C.
Mesopotamia	Hittites invade Babylon Dark Age Middle Babylonian (Kassite) period Hurrian kingdom of Mitanni Middle Assyrian period	Second Dynasty of Isin Neo-Babylonian period Neo-Assyrian empire 　Sargon II (ruled 721–705 B.C.) Late Babylonian period (Chaldean dynasty) 　Nebuchadnezzar II (ruled 605–562 B.C.) Persians conquer Babylonia
Anatolia	Hittite empire 　Shuppiluliuma I (ruled ca. 1370–1330 B.C.) 　Hittite wars with Egypt Destruction of Khattusha	Dark Age Rise of Neo-Hittite states Kingdoms of Urartu and Phrygia Cimmerian invasion Kingdoms of Lydia and Lycia Median expansion Greek city-states in western Anatolia Persians conquer Lydia
Syria and the Levant	Canaanites develop aleph-beth Egyptian domination Hittite invasions Hurrian domination Sea Peoples	Aramaean migrations Israelites settle in Canaan Philistine and Phoenician city-states Kingdoms of Israel and Judah Assyrian conquests Babylonian conquests
Egypt	Expulsion of Hyksos New Kingdom period Expansion into Syria, the Levant, and Nubia Invasion of the Sea Peoples	Third Intermediate period 　Libyan dynasty 　Nubian dynasties 　　Taharqa (ruled 690–664 B.C.) Assyrian conquest Late period 　Saite dynasty
Arabia	Decline of Dilmun Qurayya flourishes Arabia dominates aromatics trade	Qedar tribe dominates northern Arabia Syria dominates in the east Neo-Babylonians control trade routes Sabaean rulers
Iran	Middle Elamite period Aryans (Medes and Persians) enter Iran	Neo-Elamite period Median kingdom Zoroaster (lived ca. 600s B.C.) Persians overthrow Medes Cyrus the Great (ruled 559–529 B.C.) 　Conquest of Babylonia Persian empire established 　Darius I (ruled 521–486 B.C.)
Aegean and the Eastern Mediterranean	Decline of Minoan civilization Rise of Mycenaeans Mycenaeans colonize Aegean	Trojan War Dorian invasions Fall of Mycenae Dark Age Greek colonization Competition with Phoenician trade

Persian domination Alexander the Great (lived 356–323 B.C.) enters Babylon	Seleucid empire Parthian empire
Persian domination Macedonian conquest	Roman rule

Persian domination
   Jews return from Babylon
    Second temple of Jerusalem
Macedonian conquest
	Ptolemaic kingdom and Seleucid empire
	Maccabean Revolt
	Hasmonean dynasty
	Roman rule

Persian domination
Local dynasties of native Egypt
Macedonian conquest
	Ptolemaic dynasty
	   Ptolemy I (ruled 305–282 B.C.)
	   Cleopatra (ruled 69–30 B.C.)
	Roman rule

Nabatean kingdom in Jordan Persian domination	Trade with Hellenistic world Roman conquest
Persian empire dominates the ancient Near East Greek invasions Macedonian conquest Alexander the Great	Seleucid empire Parthian empire
Persian wars Classical period Peloponnesian War Macedonian conquest	Hellenistic dynasties Roman conquest

INSCRIPTIONS

* **scribe** person of a learned class who served as a writer, editor, or teacher

* **archaeologist** scientist who studies past human cultures, usually by excavating material remains of human activity

* **funerary** having to do with funerals or the handling of the dead

* **Levant** lands bordering the eastern shores of the Mediterranean Sea (present-day Syria, Lebanon, and Israel), the West Bank, and Jordan

* **cuneiform** world's oldest form of writing, which takes its name from the distinctive wedge-shaped signs pressed into clay tablets

* **second millennium** B.C. years from 2000 to 1001 B.C.

* **Semitic** of or relating to a language family that includes Akkadian, Aramaic, Arabic, Hebrew, and Phoenician

The term *inscription* refers to writing on a durable material that is meant to provide a permanent record. In the ancient Near East, inscriptions were usually made by scribes* and masons working on many different types of material. Inscriptions are found throughout the ancient Near East on palace walls, statues, and rock formations and on smaller, movable objects, including tablets and scrolls.

Kings often had inscriptions made to preserve their accomplishments for future generations to see. Inscriptions were also made by travelers who wanted to leave their mark on a place. As a result, the texts range from basic names and dates to accounts of almost fantastic tales and exploits of rulers.

Type. Inscriptions provide important data for reconstructing the history of the ancient Near East. They are the words of the people themselves. Although inscriptions are helpful to historians, they cannot be solely relied on because they only provide a one-sided and often exaggerated view of events. The monumental royal inscriptions archaeologists* have uncovered generally show kings portraying themselves in the best light possible. The pattern is the same no matter where the inscriptions were written or during which period. They were written in the first person, each naming the particular king and his ancestors, emphasizing his relationship to the gods, and telling of his achievements, both civic and military. Each royal inscription also specifies the king's current project and puts a curse on anyone who might steal or harm the monument. KING LISTS, texts containing the names of kings and details of their reigns, are another type of inscription that provide historical data, but these too are often biased.

Many other types of inscriptions exist, such as funerary*, celebrative, commemorative, and SEAL inscriptions, along with administrative records and school lessons. In Egypt, the Levant*, ANATOLIA (present-day Turkey), and parts of Iran, there are also "graffiti" inscriptions, which contain a person's name and a prayer. Such inscriptions serve to record that that person was passing along a road or route. Scholars suggest that these inscriptions are not found in Mesopotamia because the landscape there is flat and not as rocky as elsewhere in the ancient Near East. Therefore, there was little for a passerby to leave his mark on.

Format. Writing emerged around 3300 B.C. in Sumer and shortly thereafter in Egypt. Sumerians used a system of writing known as cuneiform*, which consisted of several hundred symbols that represented words and syllables. Egyptians used HIEROGLYPHICS, pictorial symbols similarly representing words and syllables. Later, other cultures of the ancient Near East developed their own systems of writing, which were often based on hieroglyphics and cuneiform. In the early second millennium B.C.*, people who spoke Semitic* languages in the Levant developed a system of writing based on an aleph-beth, which contained signs only for consonants. These scripts were written in different directions, some left to right, some right to left, and some top to bottom. In some inscriptions in South Arabic, Greek, and Semitic languages, each line takes the reverse direction of

𐤇𐤁𐤉𐤄𐤌𐤃𐤋𐤐𐤕𐤊𐤂𐤆𐤈𐤙𐤉𐤕𐤅𐤔𐤀𐤐𐤏𐤂𐤎𐤌𐤋𐤊𐤇𐤁𐤉𐤄𐤌𐤃𐤋𐤐𐤕𐤊𐤂𐤆𐤈

Inscriptions

* **literate** able to read and write

* **parchment** writing material made from the skin of sheep or goats
* **papyrus** writing material made by pressing together thin strips of the inner stem of the papyrus plant; *pl.* papyri

* **piety** faithfulness to beliefs

* **stela** stone slab or pillar that has been carved or engraved and serves as a monument; *pl.* stelae

the one before, much like the way an ox plows a field, a system known as boustrophedon.

Large public inscriptions, such as those on palace walls, contained text and pictures. Few people knew how to read, and the small literate* elite of one region often did not know the language of another area. Consequently, pictures recording a victory over enemies were an effective means of showing the greatness of a king because they could be "read" by everyone.

Materials and Methods. Scribes in the ancient Near East wrote on and carved in stone, clay, wax, wood, leather, parchment*, metal, ivory, and ostraca—flat stones or broken pieces of clay pottery; in Egypt, papyrus* was used. To carve inscriptions in damp clay, scribes used a stylus—a reed or metal tool with a pointed end for writing and a blunt "eraser" end for smoothing out errors. When the inscription was to be made in stone, scribes either inked or scratched the symbols and pictures into the stone, and then stoneworkers followed the marks using a chisel. The dry climate in Egypt allowed scribes there to use papyrus, a paperlike material on which scribes used pens or brushes and ink.

Smaller objects, such as pottery, seals, or metal and ivory personal items, including amulets and bowls, were also sometimes inscribed. Pottery inscriptions were either painted in or scratched in. Smaller luxury items might be inscribed with the owner's name as were seals.

Mesopotamia. Mesopotamian kings were concerned with "celebrative texts," which contained a record of their military victories and civil accomplishments. The earliest preserved inscriptions are brief, but there are longer texts dating from the time of the Akkadian empire (ca. 2350–2193 B.C.). They describe the kings' continued power and their greatness. For example, inscriptions about the kings SARGON I and NARAM-SIN placed in the major temples of the country tell of the wide-sweeping changes they instituted with their victories. The inscriptions also attribute the victories to the piety* of the kings, saying, "Sargon, the king, bowed down in prayer to Dagan in Tuttul, and [the god] gave him the Upper Country." These glorifications of kings proved to the gods that they had made wise choices in Sargon and Naram-Sin.

One of the longest inscriptions found in the ancient Near East appears on the seven-foot-tall stela* ordered by King HAMMURABI of Babylon. It shows Hammurabi standing, facing the enthroned sun god Shamash. Hammurabi appears to be listening to Shamash. Below the figures is a lengthy cuneiform text explaining how Hammurabi was chosen by other gods to care for the Mesopotamian people and to create a system of laws to ensure justice and well-being. The inscription goes on to list his 282 laws, known as the Code of Hammurabi. This inscription is addressed to Shamash to impress him with what Hammurabi did on his behalf. In keeping with the idea of leaving a permanent mark, it is also addressed to Hammurabi's people and the generations to come, and it curses anyone who tampers with the stela.

Mesopotamian kings also left "private" celebrative inscriptions that were not meant for the public. The kings intended these inscriptions for

This statue of the Sumerian governor Gudea was found at Tello, a site in southern Mesopotamia, and dates from around 2130 B.C. Gudea's hands are shown clasped in a pose of deference to a god. The inscription on his robe reveals the name of the god and the circumstances of the dedication of the statue to that god.

the gods and future kings. Such inscriptions were usually not illustrated and were placed in the foundation or some other out-of-the-way part of a palace or temple. They describe how well the king served the gods and contain instructions for future kings. Because temples were frequently rebuilt, a king could expect that a successor would find these inscriptions and be suitably impressed by his predecessor's accomplishments.

The most commonly preserved form of inscribed material from Mesopotamia is the CLAY TABLET. Some 500,000 clay tablets have been recovered to date. They span the period from about 3300 B.C. through at least the first century A.D. Most of the tablets are records of various kinds from palaces, temples, and private households. They include sales receipts, leases, accounts, letters, marriage contracts, wills, and court decisions. Another important group of tablets include the schoolwork of students and teachers, ranging from simple lists of signs and

Inscriptions

Sumerian and Akkadian words to mathematics problems, epics*, myths, and legends.

Egypt. Egypt is known for large inscriptions in tombs, monuments, and temples. The earliest inscriptions are displays of laws and decrees. Not until the establishment of the New Kingdom (ca. 1539–1075 B.C.) did pharaohs* inscribe their military exploits in detail. King Kamose commissioned three inscribed stelae to celebrate his military victories over the HYKSOS. King THUTMOSE III described 21 years of military campaigns, including a list of the spoils of war, which he offered to the god Amun-Ra. These inscriptions are found variously on stelae and on the walls of the Temple of Amun at Karnak. Those found at the temple were in recognition of Amun-Ra, who is believed to have granted the king his victory. This was also Thutmose's way of claiming his legitimacy as heir to the throne.

Inscriptions in tombs were very important to the ancient Egyptians because they helped guide the deceased in the AFTERLIFE. At first, inscriptions were carved into the walls of tombs; later, inscribed linen shrouds or papyrus scrolls buried with the body helped the soul reach its destination. Tomb inscriptions contained prayers, such as the one the deceased recited on his day of judgment, as well as a "road map" through the underworld—if he got lost, he could be stuck there for eternity. One especially helpful map was carved into the bottom of the coffin. It showed a safe route through the underworld, including tips on etiquette and advice on repelling snakes and crocodiles. During the Old Kingdom period (ca. 2675–2130 B.C.), only members of royalty had these guides along with autobiographical inscriptions, but by the New Kingdom period, many Egyptians were buried with inscribed spells for guidance.

Egyptians also left smaller and shorter graffiti inscriptions carved into rock throughout the kingdom. These served as markers to identify the person who visited or passed by or to record significant accomplishments, such as a military victory or a mining expedition that occurred there. The markers were situated on well-traveled routes, so many visitors would see them.

I Destroyed, I Felled, I Conquered

The following is an inscription describing a victory of the Assyrian king Ashurnasirpal II:

I besieged [and] conquered the city. I felled 3,000 of their fighting men with the sword. I carried off prisoners, possessions, oxen . . . from them. I burnt many captives from them. I captured many troops alive: I cut off some of their arms [and] hands; I cut off of others their noses, ears, [and] extremities. I gouged out the eyes of many troops. I made one pile of the living [and] one of the heads. I hung their heads on trees around the city. I burnt their adolescent boys [and] girls. I . . . destroyed, burnt, consumed the city.

Iran. The most important inscription in Iran was the BEHISTUN INSCRIPTION, carved into the cliffs in the Zagros Mountains. The carvings show Darius I's triumph over rebels and his ascent to the throne of the Persian empire in 521 B.C. The accompanying text was written in cuneiform in three languages: Old Persian, Akkadian, and Elamite. Darius arranged for smaller copies of the inscription to be circulated throughout his kingdom.

Various inscriptions in the Elamite language have also been found in Iran. One of the earliest is the Treaty of Naram-Sin, from around 2250 B.C., which was found at Susa. This treaty, a series of about 24 tablets, records an agreement between the Elamite king Khita and the Akkadian conqueror, King Naram-Sin. In the treaty, Khita states that Naram-Sin is his ally and promises to provide the Akkadians with troops. Several thousand cuneiform tablets, many containing Elamite inscriptions, have also been recovered at Persepolis, the capital of the Achaemenid empire from the 500s to the 300s B.C. These tablets record the distribution of food, clothing, and silver to various officials throughout the empire.

Anatolia. Inscribed royal pronouncements in Hittite Anatolia from around 1600 B.C. were meant to impress. Some detailed a king's military victories, or his "manly deeds," year by year. These were an early form of autobiography. Some texts looked back and explained a king's actions, justifying his unorthodox or failed activities. An inscribed apology of King KHATTUSHILI III contains his justification for usurping* the throne from a nephew and his thanks to the goddess Ishtar for being his guide and protector. This indicated to the people that it was the gods who wanted him to serve as king. These royal inscriptions, as well as several thousand clay tablets found in the palace archives, were written in a cuneiform script. However, the Hittites also developed their own form of hieroglyphics, which they used on seal inscriptions and monumental reliefs* that were carved on rock faces.

The Luwians and the Lycians, who lived in southern and southwestern Anatolia, also left inscriptions. They cut their inscriptions into the faces of rocks. Some are primarily artistic, showing a king engaged in some activity, with an inscription that is merely an identification. Others include long texts giving a context for the art. Luwian inscriptions use a form of Hittite hieroglyphics. Lycian inscriptions—written with a Greek-like alphabet—were carved into rock tombs and consist mainly of burial instructions and prayers. The most important Lycian inscription is the pillar of Xanthus, dating to 400 B.C., which details the military adventures of the Xanthian dynasty.

The Levant. In the ancient Near East, the Levant was a crossroads. Everyone traveling by land between Mesopotamia or Iran and Egypt passed through this region, which lies on the eastern border of the Mediterranean Sea. Some of these travelers liked what they saw and stayed. Consequently, inscriptions in every imaginable script appear in virtually every language spoken by these settlers: Luwian, Aramaic, Phoenician, Hebrew, Arabic, Egyptian, Akkadian, Canaanite, Greek, and Latin.

Very early inscriptions in Syria were used to dedicate statues, temples, and palaces. They contained the name of the king and his ancestors, assurances of his approval by the gods, and lists of his civic and military achievements. They also included colorful curses on anyone foolish enough to harm the monument. One such statue is that of Idrimi, king of the city of ALALAKH, in Syria. It is 41 inches tall and dates from the second millennium B.C. In this statue, Idrimi sits on a throne with his left hand in his lap and his right hand over his heart. His expression is serious. The inscription is written in Akkadian cuneiform, but the language reflects Hurrian and West Semitic influences. The 104 lines of inscription are carved into the figure itself. They are written in the first person: "Thirty years I was king. My achievements I have inscribed on my statue." Idrimi asks people to read this record of his life's work and "let them continually bless me." It includes the requisite curse: "Whoever alters . . . [this statue],

* **usurp** to wrongfully occupy a position

* **relief** sculpture in which material is cut away to show figures raised from the background

may the storm god, lord of heaven and earth, and the great gods annihilate his name and his seed from his land." (*See also* **Papyrus; Scribes; Semitic Languages; Writing.**)

IRAN

Located in southern Asia, south of Armenia, Azerbaijan, Turkmenistan, and the Caspian Sea, present-day Iran corresponds roughly to the same region as ancient Iran. It is bordered on the west by Iraq (ancient MESOPOTAMIA) and Turkey (ancient ANATOLIA), on the east by Afghanistan and Pakistan, and on the south by the Gulf of Oman and the Persian Gulf. Iran is known for the diversity of its cultures, both in ancient and in modern times.

Geography. The majority of Iran is made up of the huge central Iranian Plateau and its surrounding mountain ranges, the Elburz Mountains to the north and the Zagros Mountains to the west. The central plateau contains two large deserts, the Dasht-i-Lūt and the Dasht-i-Kavīr. Iran is divided into three main climatic regions. In the south, the coast is hot; the plateau is dry and has milder temperatures; the mountains, particularly the high regions of the northern Elburz, are much colder. Most of Iran receives little rainfall.

Human History. The availability of water and access to it have greatly determined the patterns of human habitation in Iran. Populations historically congregated at the edges of the region, in the mountains, and along the coasts, though later the oases* became populated as well.

Humans have lived in present-day Iran for many millennia*. The earliest evidence of human habitation, dating from around 10,000 B.C., has been found on the Iranian Plateau. From excavations at old farm sites in the Zagros Mountains, archaeologists* have determined that people were domesticating animals at least as early as 7000 B.C. Archaeologists know far more about human development in southwestern Iran, or present-day Khuzestan, a region that receives more rainfall than much of the rest of the country. Located next to ancient Mesopotamia, the region's development was linked to that of Mesopotamia.

Beginning in about 4000 B.C., cultural influences from southern Mesopotamia began to strongly influence local development in southwestern Iran, creating the Proto-Elamite culture. The descendants of the Proto-Elamite people, the Elamites, later dominated the region until 640 B.C. By the end of the third millennium B.C.*, Elam stretched from the borders of Mesopotamia in the south to the Caspian Sea in the north and included the great Iranian deserts. For much of its history, Elamite civilization was centered on the city of Susa (present-day Sush). However, evidence suggests that during the third and into the second millenia B.C., if not earlier, Susa was its own kingdom. Throughout their history, the Elamites were conquered at various times and controlled by the Babylonians and Sumerians, among others.

Much less is known about the cultures that thrived in northern Iran. What is known is that a tribe called the Manneans was among several

* **oasis** fertile area in a desert made possible by the presence of a spring or well; *pl.* oases

* **millennium** period of 1,000 years; *pl.* millennia

* **archaeologist** scientist who studies past human cultures, usually by excavating material remains of human activity

* **third millennium** B.C. years from 3000 to 2001 B.C.

The Treasure of Ziwiye

In A.D. 1947, antiquities dealers reported that a treasure of artifacts had been recovered from an Iron Age site in Ziwiye, in northwestern Iran. Hundreds of these objects were sold, and scholars published papers based on their conclusions about the artifacts. However, these conclusions were invalid because no one knew the actual place from which the objects had come. Archaeologists eventually investigated a site in Ziwiye and found nothing resembling the treasure that was said to have come from there. The artifacts themselves may be extraordinary, but much of their value to scholars has been lost.

different groups who had built cities and established distinct cultures there. The Manneans also controlled trade routes leading to the north and east of Iran.

Starting around 1000 B.C., a new group called the ARYANS entered Iran. The Aryan tribes were a nomadic* people who migrated from the steppes* of CENTRAL ASIA into Iran and India. Between the 800s and 600s B.C., two important Aryan tribes came to settle in Iran, the MEDES and the Persians. The Medes settled in the northwest, a region that became Media. The Persians settled on the southern plateau, which they named Parsamash (present-day Fārs). By the 600s B.C., the Medes had become the dominant tribe and controlled an empire stretching from India to Anatolia. The Persians were their vassals*.

All that changed when the Persian king CYRUS THE GREAT (ruled 559–529 B.C.) came to power. He rebelled against his grandfather, the Median king Astyages, and established Persia as an independent state. He successfully conquered most of the surrounding kingdoms, including Babylonia, and created the PERSIAN EMPIRE. With help from his sons, Cyrus expanded the empire to include Egypt and eastern lands in Central Asia. Cyrus's dynasty later became known as the Achaemenid dynasty.

In 331 B.C., the Persian empire was conquered by ALEXANDER THE GREAT (ruled 336–323 B.C.). When Alexander died, control of the core of the Persian empire passed to his general Seleucus I, who founded the Seleucid dynasty, which ruled Iran to the 260s B.C., when the Parthians took over.

Religion. The Elamites and the Persians had different religious beliefs. The Elamites, like other ancient Near Eastern peoples, worshiped many

* **nomadic** referring to people who travel from place to place to find food and pasture

* **steppe** large semiarid grassy plain with few trees

* **vassal** individual or state that swears loyalty and obedience to a greater power

See map on inside covers.

The chariot scene depicted on this silver beaker, excavated at Hansanlu in northwestern Iran, is comparable to scenes of warfare and hunting that are common in Assyrian art. Such themes were probably transmitted to Iran when the Assyrians held campaigns in that region in the mid-800s B.C., around the time this beaker was crafted.

* **cult** system of religious beliefs and rituals; group following these beliefs

* **prophet** one who claims to have received divine messages or insights

* **deity** god or goddess

* **lapis lazuli** dark blue semiprecious stone

gods and goddesses. Elamite religious cults* played an important role in society, and religious rituals included regular public feasts and OFFERINGS of animal blood to the gods. The Persians practiced a religion called Zoroastrianism. This religion was named for Zoroaster, a prophet* who lived during the 600s B.C. and taught that there was only one god, AHURA MAZDA. At first, Ahura Mazda was the only deity* and was worshiped as a sun god, the creator of all things, and called Wise Lord. Later he was seen as the chief god among others.

Trade. For much of its history, Iran served as the crossroads for the ancient Near East and central and south Asia. Various ancient Iranian kingdoms were involved in international trade throughout the region by the end of the fourth millennium B.C. (the years between 4000 and 3001 B.C.). Lapis lazuli* was very popular all over the ancient Near East and could be found only in what is now northeastern Afghanistan. Sumerian traders traveled through the Zagros Mountains of Iran to obtain lapis lazuli. In the third millennium B.C., the Proto-Elamites and Elamite kingdoms controlled areas with large supplies of tin, an essential product to the peoples of the Bronze Age. Later the Manneans to the north controlled the routes into the Ural Mountains, where copper and precious gems were mined and animal fur was obtained. (*See also* **Darius I and Darius III; Elam and the Elamites; Parthia; Persepolis; Persian Wars; Satraps; Zoroaster and Zoroastrianism.**)

Iraq

See *Mesopotamia.*

Iron

See *Metals and Metalworking.*

Iron Age

See *Chronology.*

IRRIGATION

Irrigation is the process of supplying WATER to land for AGRICULTURE. Natural irrigation depends on normal rainfall and flooding to irrigate land. Artificial irrigation uses human-made systems to irrigate land that would not otherwise get water. Irrigation by means of ditches, channels, CANALS, basins, and other methods was critical to successful agriculture and thus to the growth of cities. In the ancient Near East, civilizations grew because natural and artificial irrigation allowed people to establish settled communities and live off the land. Developing and managing irrigation contributed to social organization as societies defined their rights and responsibilities for water and land use.

Early Irrigation. Although cities were established along RIVERS, the earliest attempts at irrigation occurred away from the great rivers. Farming itself began in hill country or on plains where rainfall sustained crops—a method known as dry farming*. At first, the land near the NILE RIVER in Egypt and the TIGRIS RIVER and the EUPHRATES RIVER in MESOPOTAMIA was difficult to irrigate. The rivers, especially during flooding, were too large or too destructive for early societies to control. Consequently, the first attempts at irrigation took place where smaller streams spread out during flooding. These regions of streams, called alluvial* plains, or floodplains, were natural places to extend farming beyond a reliance on rainfall. Archaeological* site surveys reveal ancient systems of irrigation and field patterns, even in areas that are now barren. Artificial watering methods were developed in the Nile, Tigris, and Euphrates Valleys before 5000 B.C., long before the great settlement of southern Mesopotamia.

Large-Scale Irrigation. There are two basic ways to extend the reach of a river. The first is to draw water away from the banks of the river by means of channels. Each channel waters a specific area. Such channels run roughly perpendicular from the stream out to the intended area. The other way to extend the fertile area is to cut a channel parallel to the river, widening the river's floodplain. Although details of the earliest irrigation plans are unknown, site surveys suggest that networks of channels and small canals were the early means of large-scale irrigation.

As the population grew in Mesopotamia, so did the need for irrigation. In the north, the people were able to rely on rainfall, but in the south, the lands were dry and the people there depended on large-scale irrigation. Most of this effort was directed at the Euphrates River because it was easier to control than the Tigris. The Euphrates also tended to split into branches in the floodplain, which was helpful for irrigation.

By about 2500 B.C., larger and more permanent canals and channels began to replace smaller or temporary irrigation systems in Mesopotamia. Building and maintaining canal systems became important political concerns to developing societies. Some scholars believe that the need to construct, control, and administer waterworks directly led to the growth of larger kingdoms. Others disagree, noting that the actual control of the irrigation devices usually remained in the hands of local authorities.

Mesopotamians used irrigation to carry out four important tasks necessary for growing crops and avoiding harmful FLOODS. These four tasks were supply, storage, drainage, and protection from unwanted water. Canals, channels, basins, dikes*, and other water management systems performed these roles. Whether waterways ran out in small branches from the river or in larger courses parallel to the main stream, control devices were necessary. A sluice* diverted water to the intended area and could be as simple as a hole in the side of a channel blocked with a board when not in use. Regulators* held water back until it reached a great enough level to flow freely through sluices. Early regulators were as simple

* **dry farming** farming that relies on natural moisture retained in the ground after rainfall

* **alluvial** composed of clay, silt, sand, gravel, or similar material deposited by running water

* **archaeological** referring to the study of past human cultures, usually by excavating material remains of human activity

* **dike** embankment used to confine or control the flow of water

* **sluice** human-made channel or passage to direct water flow

* **regulator** gate or valve to control amount of water passing through a channel

Irrigation

as piles of brush or reeds, but large, permanent structures of baked brick were constructed as well.

Water supply was critical in the late autumn when planting occurred, but the Tigris and the Euphrates were at their lowest then. It was essential for the ancient Mesopotamians to distribute water efficiently and fairly to ensure that everyone got the water necessary for newly planted crops to grow. Rotating the irrigation of fields was the solution. Good timing and division of water were necessary for effective irrigation.

Location of crops depended on the irrigation system. Such plants as date palms do best with moist roots, and vegetables need daily watering. Cereal crops, such as wheat, require less frequent watering. Therefore, orchards and vegetable gardens were close to the waterways, while the cereal fields were farther away. The channels served to get water to the more distant cereal crops whenever necessary.

Maintenance of the irrigation channels was important to supply. Slow-flowing water left much of its silt in the channel. Silt, reeds, brush, and other debris clogged waterways further, slowing water flow and leading to evaporation. Other problems included salt buildup in the water and leaks. These problems necessitated constant maintenance of irrigation systems, which was the responsibility of officials and workers at the local or village level. In the case of large-scale projects, such as those constructed during the reign of SARGON I (ca. 2334–2278 B.C.), the upkeep depended on cooperation between city-states*.

Storing the water from annual floods was difficult. Around each field was a low bank to hold water in the fields. These earthen dikes not only prolonged floods, but also held water to be used during the ten-day to two-week interval between irrigations later in the year. Ancient Near Eastern people also built narrow basins alongside canals, but their purpose is not clear. The basins varied in size, but none was large enough to retain water through the Mesopotamian dry season. Perhaps these small reservoirs were for other crops growing nearby that needed to be watered more frequently than the cereal fields.

Draining excess water from the relatively flat land was another important task. If water remained on the land for too long, it would pull up salt from the ground below. This process, called salinization, ruined the fields. One way Mesopotamian farmers tried to avoid salinity was to let fields lie fallow* for a season, but they were often forced to abandon land. Other drainage strategies remain unknown. Protection against floods was a feature of Mesopotamian irrigation as well. In times of high water, the same sluices and regulators that diverted water to the fields were opened to allow as much water as possible to run off the land.

Natural Irrigation. In contrast to the hard work of large-scale artificial irrigation in Mesopotamia, Egypt depended mostly on natural irrigation, which consisted largely of working with the natural flow and drainage patterns of the Nile flood. The timing of the annual flood in Egypt was better suited to farming than it was in Mesopotamia. The flood ended in September, just before planting season. The floodplain itself was not flat but slightly rounded outward, allowing water to drain to its edges, carrying away harmful salts. Although marshy areas at the edges of the floodplain

* **city-state** independent state consisting of a city and its surrounding territory

* **fallow** plowed but not planted, so that moisture and organic processes can replenish the soil's nutrients

became salty, elsewhere the fields remained free of salt. Egyptians built channels to extend the reach of the floodwater, allowing it to flow into natural depressions or basins.

Irrigation efforts in Egypt consisted primarily of maintaining the Nile banks, the channels through which the water flowed, and dikes that surrounded natural basins. The favorable timing of the flood made the constant labor of irrigation less necessary in Egypt than in Mesopotamia.

In Upper Egypt, canals crossed the west side of the Nile Valley. They may have had a role in irrigation, probably directing the natural flood into basins. They could also have helped conserve water for irrigation in years when the Nile did not have a large flood. During the Middle Kingdom period (ca. 1980–1630 B.C.), a large royal project took place in the Faiyûm Depression, a lake and oasis* west of the Nile near the delta*, which is fed by a branch of the Nile called the Bahr Yusuf. Its purpose was to drain the marshes, resulting in the development of more farmland, which would mean more food and wealth. In the Ptolemaic period (305–30 B.C.), the Bahr Yusuf was redirected to fill a valley, creating a reservoir called Lake Moeris. The waters from the lake were used to water a second summer crop.

Intensive Artificial Irrigation. In Mesopotamia, Egypt, and elsewhere around the Mediterranean, some plants required water daily. Hand-drawn water was the only answer for them. Private GARDENS such as those in Egypt and pleasure gardens such as the HANGING GARDENS OF BABYLON used wells or ponds as sources. For large-scale agriculture, however, only high-value crops justified the cost and effort of carrying water by hand. Orchards, vineyards, and vegetable gardens were placed as close to water as possible. Combining certain crops also eased the task of irrigation. For example, fruit trees were grown beneath date palms, and vines were trained on trellises to form leafy shelters. This shading reduced water loss through evaporation.

Ancient Syria subsisted on dry farming. Most agriculture in the rest of the Levant*, however, depended on intensive artificial irrigation from springs and wells. JERICHO, one of the earliest urban sites, was near a perennial spring. JERUSALEM, Gibeon, and MEGIDDO used natural springs for their water supplies and developed wells and cisterns, or underground tanks, to conserve them. Protecting the water supply against attackers was crucial to a city. Defenders built increasingly complex systems of camouflage, tunnels, and shafts to protect the water supply. At Megiddo, a shaft went straight down, then joined a tunnel that came from a spring. The tunnel was pitched slightly downward to allow water from the spring to form an underground pool. A similar tunnel discovered in A.D. 1838 near Jerusalem was 1,750 feet long.

Another ancient Near Eastern irrigation technique that used tunnels was the *qanat* system. This system involved using underground mountain water sources—the water was channeled through a series of tunnels. The *qanat* system originated in Oman in the late second millennium B.C.* It was used in Iran in the early first millennium B.C., and its use spread to the rest of the ancient Near East shortly thereafter. The *qanat* system is still used in regions with an arid climate. (*See also* **Climate; Floods.**)

* **oasis** fertile area in a desert made possible by the presence of a spring or well; *pl.* oases

* **delta** fan-shaped, lowland plain formed of soil deposited by a river

* **Levant** lands bordering the eastern shores of the Mediterranean Sea (present-day Syria, Lebanon, and Israel), the West Bank, and Jordan

* **second millennium B.C.** years from 2000 to 1001 B.C.

Isaiah

ISAIAH

lived ca. 700s B.C.
Jewish prophet

* **prophet** one who claims to have received divine messages or insights

* **prophecy** message from a deity; also, the prediction of future events

* **exile** person forced to live away from his or her homeland for a long period of time

saiah (eye•ZAY•uh) was a priest and prophet* in the kingdom of Judah. Around 742 B.C., he was called to prophecy* when he had a vision in which he saw the god YAWEH and angels in a heavenly temple. Isaiah then began to urge the people of Judah to observe the worship of Yahweh. Isaiah also criticized social injustice.

Isaiah made his prophecies at a time when Judah was at risk of attack by foreign powers, especially Assyria. Believing that the threat was a warning from Yahweh, Isaiah advised the rulers of Judah to show their faith in Yahweh because that, and not their attempts to thwart Assyria by entering into foreign alliances, would deliver their people.

Between about 740 and 700 B.C., Isaiah, or one of his followers, wrote the first 39 chapters of the Book of Isaiah, which is included in the Hebrew BIBLE. During the captivity of the Jews in Babylon between 587 and 539 B.C., later writers added several chapters, which they also attributed to Isaiah. Modern scholars attribute chapters 40 through 55 to a "second Isaiah," and chapters 56 through 66 to a "third Isaiah."

The authors of the later chapters wrote to inspire hope in the Jewish exiles*, who had been removed to Babylon when the Babylonians conquered Judah. The authors claimed that Yahweh would help the Jews and looked to the rise of the Persians as a sign of Yahweh's favor. This proved correct when the Persian king CYRUS THE GREAT conquered Babylon and allowed the Jews to return home to Judah. (*See also* **Hebrews and Israelites; Israel and Judah; Oracles and Prophecy.**)

ISHTAR

* **city-state** independent state consisting of a city and its surrounding territory

shtar was the most important goddess in ancient MESOPOTAMIA. She was known as Ishtar by the Akkadians; as Inanna, which means "lady of heaven," by the Sumerians; and as Astarte in Syria. Although best known as a goddess of LOVE and fertility, Ishtar was also revered as a fierce goddess of war, especially by the Assyrians.

Near Eastern myths reveal different aspects of Ishtar's personality, ancestry, and life. In some, she is the daughter of the sky god ANU or the moon god Nanna; in others, she is the daughter of either ENLIL or EA. In Babylonian mythology, Ishtar is the wife and sister of Tammuz, known as Dumuzi by the Sumerians. In other myths, she has no spouse, and Tammuz is her lover.

One popular myth about Ishtar tells of her yearly descent into the netherworld, a realm ruled by her sister Ereshkigal. Ishtar went there in search of Tammuz, who had been forced into the netherworld. His return from the netherworld and reunion with Ishtar became associated with fertility and were linked to the seasons and to the agricultural cycles. Another well-known myth, embedded in the *Epic of Gilgamesh,* tells how Ishtar offers herself in marriage to the mortal hero GILGAMESH. However, he refuses, insulting her. She then unleashes the fierce Bull of Heaven against him, but Gilgamesh and his friend Enkidu manage to kill the bull.

Ishtar's most important center of worship was at the city-state* of URUK, which contained a shrine dedicated to her known as E-anna (House of Heaven). Her equivalents were the Greek goddess Aphrodite and the Roman goddess Venus. (*See also* **Cults; Gods and Goddesses.**)

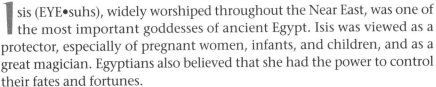

* **hieroglyphic** referring to a system of writing that uses pictorial characters, or hieroglyphs, to represent words or ideas

See color plate 10, vol. 1.

Isis (EYE•suhs), widely worshiped throughout the Near East, was one of the most important goddesses of ancient Egypt. Isis was viewed as a protector, especially of pregnant women, infants, and children, and as a great magician. Egyptians also believed that she had the power to control their fates and fortunes.

Symbolically, Isis was considered the mother of the Egyptian king. To reflect this role, her name was always written with a hieroglyphic* sign that represented a throne. In art and architecture, Isis usually was portrayed wearing the throne symbol on her head or wearing a crown of cow horns with a sun disk between them.

Isis was believed to be the sister and wife of OSIRIS, the king of the Egyptian gods. According to Egyptian mythology, Osiris's brother SETH murdered Osiris to take over his position as king of the gods. Seth scattered pieces of Osiris's body throughout Egypt, but Isis found them and put him back together again. Then Isis became pregnant by Osiris and gave birth to a son named HORUS. She raised Horus in secret in the marshes of the Nile Delta, so that he might grow up to avenge the death of Osiris and take the throne from Seth. Isis guarded Horus closely and used her magic to protect him from such dangers as scorpions, spiders, and crocodiles. When Horus became an adult, Isis helped him fight for his rightful inheritance. She convinced the other gods to support him, and Horus became the new king of the gods. (*See also* **Egypt and the Egyptians; Gods and Goddesses; Religion.**)

* **Semitic** of or relating to people of the Near East or northern Africa, including the Assyrians, Babylonians, Phoenicians, Jews, and Arabs

The kingdoms of Israel and Judah were founded by the Israelite people in the highlands of CANAAN. The kingdoms, which had once been parts of a larger unified kingdom of Israel, were both later overcome by more powerful Near Eastern empires. Because many events in Jewish history occurred in Israel and Judah, modern Jews consider these regions their Holy Land. Christians and Muslims, whose religions are derived in various ways from Judaism and who have their own connections with the regions, also consider several sites there sacred.

Origins of the Kingdoms. There are few sources for the early history of the Israelites outside the Hebrew BIBLE, the sacred book of Judaism. However, historians debate the reliability of the Bible as a source of history because much of it was composed many centuries after the events it describes and because of the lack of other supporting sources. Moreover, the editors who compiled the Bible may have been attempting to strengthen national and religious unity by emphasizing the shared past of the Israelite people.

The Israelites were a Semitic* people who settled in the highlands of Canaan sometime during the Late Bronze Age (ca. 1500–1200 B.C.). According to the Bible, they called themselves the children of Israel, or Israelites, after their ancestor Jacob, whom their god YAHWEH had renamed Israel. The Bible also notes that on occasion, outsiders referred to the Israelites as "Hebrews," which remains a common synonym for them. The Israelites were divided into 12 tribes, each named for one of Jacob's sons

Israel and Judah

* **famine** severe lack of food due to failed crops

* **Promised Land** land promised to the Israelites by their god, Yahweh

or grandsons (other tribes not attached to Jacob's descendants are also mentioned in the Bible). These tribes lived in Canaan for several generations until a famine* forced them to leave. They went to Egypt, where they eventually became slaves until a leader named MOSES freed them and led them back to Canaan—the Promised Land*.

After returning to Canaan, the Israelites gradually expanded their territory. They established the kingdom of Israel and amassed great wealth under their kings DAVID and SOLOMON. After Solomon's death, however, tensions grew between the northern and southern tribes in the kingdom. Ultimately, around 925 B.C. Israel was split into two smaller kingdoms—Israel in the north and Judah in the south. Although the people remained united in the worship of Yahweh and in their shared religious and historical traditions, the kingdoms fought over territory for about 50 years.

No other source recovered to date from the time in which David and Solomon were said to have lived mentions either of the two kings or the

In about 925 B.C., the Israelite kingdom split into two kingdoms: Israel in the north and Judah in the south. Jerusalem remained the capital of Judah, but the capital of Israel was moved several times until it was finally established at Samaria. The two kingdoms flourished until the Assyrians began to invade the region. In 722 B.C., they attacked and captured Israel, bringing that kingdom to an end. Judah was soon forced to acknowledge Assyrian dominance and became a vassal state of Assyria in the 600s B.C.

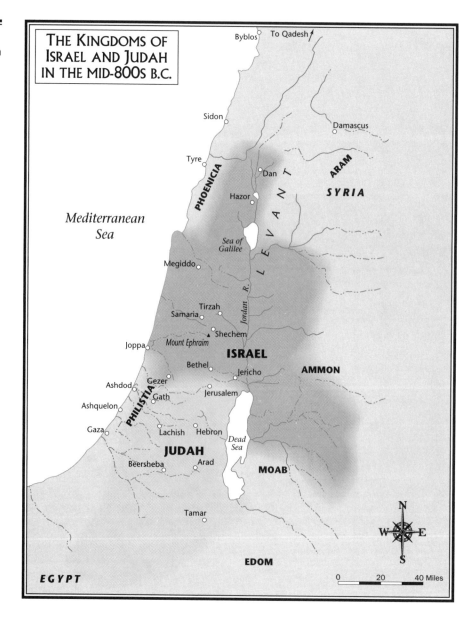

THE KINGDOMS OF ISRAEL AND JUDAH IN THE MID-800s B.C.

* **stela** stone slab or pillar that has been carved or engraved and serves as a monument; *pl.* stelae

* **archaeological** referring to the study of past human cultures, usually by excavating material remains of human activity

* **city-state** independent state consisting of a city and its surrounding territory

* **Levant** lands bordering the eastern shores of the Mediterranean Sea (present-day Syria, Lebanon, and Israel), the West Bank, and Jordan

* **vassal** individual or state that swears loyalty and obedience to a greater power

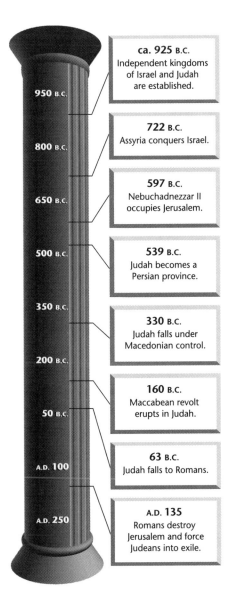

ca. 925 B.C.
Independent kingdoms of Israel and Judah are established.

722 B.C.
Assyria conquers Israel.

597 B.C.
Nebuchadnezzar II occupies Jerusalem.

539 B.C.
Judah becomes a Persian province.

330 B.C.
Judah falls under Macedonian control.

160 B.C.
Maccabean revolt erupts in Judah.

63 B.C.
Judah falls to Romans.

A.D. 135
Romans destroy Jerusalem and force Judeans into exile.

empire they created. The earliest known reference to David occurs on a recently excavated fragment of a victory stela* written by an Aramaean king in the 800s B.C. The near lack of historical evidence about David and Solomon suggests to some scholars that their achievements may have been more modest than described in the Bible. A few other scholars even question whether the united monarchy existed. Relying on archaeological* evidence, they suggest that the kingdoms may have emerged separately—Israel around 900 B.C. and Judah around 800 B.C.

History of Israel. Israel was the larger and the more populated of the two kingdoms. It consisted of 10 of the 12 tribes: Asher, Dan, Ephraim, Gad, Issachar, Manasseh, Naphtali, Reuben, Simeon, and Zebulun. Centered in the region around Mount Ephraim and the Sea of Galilee, Israel possessed good agricultural land, and its people produced grain, wine, and olive oil for export and local use. Israel also controlled major north-south and east-west trade routes and had many contacts with ancient Near Eastern powers. These economic advantages led to rapid population growth.

In 886 B.C., Omri became king of Israel. The first Israelite king to be mentioned in sources outside the Bible, Omri established a new capital called Samaria, a city that eventually gave its name to the whole kingdom. During his reign, Omri engaged in several conflicts with the Moabites, neighbors and enemies of the Israelites. He reconquered lands that had previously been lost when Israel split into two kingdoms. Omri was succeeded by AHAB (ruled ca. 875–854 B.C.), who fought against DAMASCUS, an increasingly powerful city-state* in Syria. In 853 B.C., however, Ahab joined forces with the king of Damascus and with other nearby kingdoms to fight an invading army of Assyrians led by their king, SHALMANESER III. They won that battle, but the small states of the Levant* could not hold back the Assyrian empire for long. The Assyrians continued to seize more of Syria and Israel until 722 B.C., when they captured Samaria and brought the kingdom of Israel to an end.

Assyrian policy called for the relocation of captured populations to minimize the possibility of revolts. The Assyrians shifted large numbers of Israelites into other parts of the Assyrian empire, where they gradually merged with other peoples and disappeared from history. As a result, the Israelites came to be called the Ten Lost Tribes of Israel. The Assyrians settled people from Mesopotamia in Samaria. Later a cult of Yahweh arose there among a group known as SAMARITANS.

History of Judah. The kingdom of Judah consisted of the tribes of Judah and Benjamin and their land. It was smaller and less fertile than its northern neighbor, but it included JERUSALEM, the city that had been the capital of the united Israel. Founded by King David, Jerusalem was the site of the Temple of Solomon, the Israelites' religious center.

From the late 900s to the 700s B.C., Judah achieved periods of stability under the kings Asa, Jehoshaphat, and Uzziah (Azariah). The kingdom was later forced to acknowledge the dominance of Assyria in the 700s B.C., becoming its vassal*. After the Assyrian empire's collapse in the late 600s B.C., the Babylonian empire expanded westward. In 597 B.C., Babylonian

Israelites

The Moabite king Mesha erected this black basalt stela in about 830 B.C. to commemorate his victories over the kingdom of Israel. Carved in Phoenician script, the stela specifically honors Chemosh, the patron god of the Moabite dynasty, for aiding in these victories. The stela was excavated in Dhiban in present-day Jordan in A.D. 1868 by a German missionary.

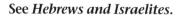

* **sack** to loot a captured city

Israelites

* **Levant** lands bordering the eastern shores of the Mediterranean Sea (present-day Syria, Lebanon, and Israel), the West Bank, and Jordan

See color plate 1, vol. 4.

armies under King NEBUCHADNEZZAR II occupied Jerusalem and forced the Judeans to submit to their rule. Ten years later, Judah rebelled, and Babylonia responded by destroying Jerusalem and the temple. The Babylonians dissolved the kingdom of Judah, made the region a Babylonian province, and forced many Jews (as the Judeans became known) into exile in Babylonia.

In 539 B.C., the Babylonians were conquered by the Persians, whose leader CYRUS THE GREAT allowed the Jews to return to Jerusalem and rebuild the temple. The former territory of Judah became a Persian province called Yehud, which the Greeks called Judaea. Judah remained a part of the Persian empire for several hundred years. Generally, this was a peaceful time.

In 330 B.C., Judah became part of the Macedonian empire, when ALEXANDER THE GREAT overthrew the Persian empire. After Alexander's death, Judah was ruled by his successors—first by the Ptolemies and later by the Seleucids. When the Seleucids prohibited the practice of Judaism, the Judeans, led by Judas Maccabeus, revolted in the 160s B.C. After the Maccabean Revolt, Judah enjoyed a brief period of independence.

In 63 B.C., the region came under the control of Rome. The Jews revolted against Roman rule in A.D. 66, and the Romans sacked* Jerusalem and destroyed the second temple shortly thereafter. Another Jewish uprising occurred between 132 and 135, ending with the destruction of Jerusalem. The Romans forced the Jews of Judah into exile in other regions of the Roman Empire and gave Judah the name Syria-Palestina. (*See also* **Assyria and the Assyrians; Babylonia and the Babylonians; Hebrews and Israelites; Judaism and Jews; Patriarchs and Matriarchs of Israel.**)

Israelites

See *Hebrews and Israelites.*

IVORY

Ivory, a rare and expensive material recovered from the tusks of elephants and hippopotamuses, was used for decorative arts throughout the ancient Near East. Most elephant ivory was imported from India, although there were elephants in SYRIA from about 3000 B.C. to about 800 B.C., when they became extinct due to hunting. Hippopotamuses lived in and near the Nile River in Egypt and also in the Levant*.

Ivory was used to make luxury items, such as finely carved cosmetics containers, perfume jars, and combs. The carvings contained the images of gods, animals, or plants. Other objects made from ivory included small statues of people and animals, ivory dolls, ornamental panels for chair backs, and headboards for beds. Carved ivory also appeared on chair legs and as the decorative tops of bedposts.

A large number of ivory objects were excavated from tombs and palaces in the Levant, especially at UGARIT, MEGIDDO, and SAMARIA. The objects include boxes with hinged or pivoting lids and several plaques depicting hunting and conquest scenes. The carvings on these objects reflect styles and images prevalent in Egyptian, Mesopotamian, and Hittite art. In Egypt during the New Kingdom period (ca. 1539–1075 B.C.), a technique known as cloisonné was popular among ivory carvers. In this technique, carvers made small hollows in the ivory and filled them with stones. This technique was also used in the Levant by the Phoenicians and Syrians after 1000 B.C. This is evident from the large numbers of Syrian and Phoenician ivory carvings found at Assyrian palaces. In Assyria, artisans* also connected flat pieces of wax-coated ivory with hinges to make writing boards.

* **artisan** skilled craftsperson

lived ca. 650–570 B.C.
Jewish prophet

* **prophet** one who claims to have received divine messages or insight

Born to a family of priests, Jeremiah (jer•uh•MY•uh) was a prophet* and social critic in Judah during the turbulent period when the Babylonians captured JERUSALEM and took many Jews to BABYLON. His deeds and words are preserved in the Book of Jeremiah in the Hebrew BIBLE.

Around 627 B.C., Jeremiah emerged as a prophet. His messages were chiefly criticisms of the Jews' religious and social faults. Sometime after 609 B.C., Jeremiah delivered a sermon in which he attacked the Jews for emphasizing worship in the Temple of Solomon in Jerusalem. This temple was the religious center of the Jews, and Jeremiah felt that Jews relied on worshiping there rather than truly observing their god Yahweh's religious laws. This made him unpopular, and his popularity did not improve when Babylonia seized Jerusalem in 597 B.C. Jeremiah wrote that Babylonia's domination of Judah was Yahweh's will, and he counseled the people to surrender and to submit quietly. He believed that the Jews would earn the chance to regain their homeland by obeying Yahweh's will.

Jeremiah was eventually imprisoned for attempting to desert Jerusalem. However, he was freed by the Babylonians who appointed Gedaliah, their governor in Judah, to look after him. When Gedaliah was assassinated, a group of Jews who feared that the Babylonians would come to avenge his death took Jeremiah to Egypt. According to legend, Jeremiah annoyed his fellow Jews so much with his unpopular views that they stoned him to death in about 570 B.C. (*See also* **Israel and Judah; Judaism and Jews; Oracles and Prophecy.**)

* **artifact** ornament, tool, weapon, or other object made by humans

* **archaeologist** scientist who studies past human cultures, usually by excavating material remains of human activity

Jericho (JER•i•koh) is an ancient town located in the Palestinian West Bank. Settled as early as 9000 B.C., it is perhaps the oldest permanent settlement in the world. Artifacts* found at the site have enabled archaeologists* to learn more about the development of the first settlements and civilizations in the Near East.

Beginnings of Urban Civilization. Jericho may have first served as a camp to nomadic* hunters who stopped there because it was located near the Jordan River and a spring, both of which provided water in an otherwise arid region near the Dead Sea. Between 9000 and 8000 B.C., people began to establish permanent settlements in Jericho. They built

Jerusalem

* **nomadic** referring to people who travel from place to place to find food and pasture
* **mud brick** brick made from mud, straw, and water mixed together and baked in the sun
* **obsidian** black glass, formed from hardened lava, useful for making sharp blades and tools
* **cult** formal religious worship

Did the Walls Come Tumbling Down?

According to the Book of Joshua in the Hebrew Bible, the Israelites captured Jericho with trumpet blasts and a loud war cry that made the city's defensive walls collapse. Modern scholars debate whether the Israelites conquered Jericho militarily or took over the city gradually and peacefully. During the A.D. 1950s, Kathleen Kenyon of the British School of Archaeology in Jerusalem excavated the site and found no evidence of a city wall from what is believed to be Joshua's time, about 1200 B.C. However, erosion has left almost no trace of Jericho from that period. Is the Joshua story an exaggerated account of a real battle? Archaeology cannot yet answer that question.

round, one-room houses with mud bricks*. For protection, they surrounded the town with a 5-foot-thick stone wall that included a watchtower about 30 feet high.

By around 7500 B.C., about 2,000 people were living in Jericho and practicing AGRICULTURE. Researchers have found cultivated grain in Jericho, evidence that the people there might have been among the earliest farmers. They grew wheat and barley and may have been the first to build IRRIGATION channels to water their crops. Moreover, tools made from obsidian* found in the ruins show that Jericho had established trade with places as far away as ANATOLIA (present-day Turkey), the source of the obsidian.

Around 7000 B.C., the people of Jericho began building rectangular houses centered on courtyards that contained fireplaces. Bodies buried beneath these houses suggest that the people practiced ancestor worship. Archaeologists have also found collections of human skulls, suggesting the presence of an ancestor cult*. The facial features of the skulls were reconstructed in plaster with seashells for eyes.

Between 6000 and 3000 B.C., Jericho was abandoned periodically for reasons not yet known. Thereafter, it once again became a permanent settlement. Its people traded salt, which they collected from the nearby Dead Sea, for goods from Anatolia, SYRIA, and Egypt. Using this wealth, the town rebuilt its walls. Then, sometime after 2300 B.C., the AMORITES—nomadic peoples from Syria—settled in the region.

New Inhabitants. By around 1900 B.C., Jericho had again become a fortified city, this time occupied by the Canaanites. Furnishings and tools found in tombs from this period have provided archaeologists with information about Canaanite life. Around 1550 B.C., Jericho was destroyed by a fire that may have been caused by an earthquake or an attack. Jericho's history after that time is not as well known as its earlier history because erosion wore away the ruins before archaeologists could study them. Historians do know, however, that the Israelites probably gained control of Jericho and other parts of Canaan around 1200 B.C.

Jericho was the site of later settlements, notably during the 600s B.C., when it was part of the kingdom of Judah. Later powers that occupied the region during the ancient period included Persia and Rome. (*See also* **Israel and Judah; Hebrews and Israelites.**)

JERUSALEM

* **archaeologist** scientist who studies past human cultures, usually by excavating material remains of human activity

The city of Jerusalem is located amid rocky hills about 25 miles from the shores of the Mediterranean Sea. Its most important role in the ancient world was as the capital of the united Israelite monarchy, later of the Judean state, and as the center of the religion known as Judaism. Today it is the capital of the modern nation of Israel. The name *Jerusalem* appears to have come from Canaanite words possibly meaning "[the god] Shalem is its founder," or "the foundation of Shalem." Texts from the city of UGARIT in Syria mention Shalem as a god of night.

The Canaanite City. Much of what is known about Jerusalem's early history comes from the work of teams led by archaeologists* Kathleen

Kenyon and Yigal Shiloh in the middle to late A.D. 1900s. Shiloh uncovered the oldest known traces of human occupation at Jerusalem at sites on a hill called Ophel. Those traces consist of pits dug in the late fourth millennium B.C.* and pottery from the third millennium B.C.*

During the 1700s B.C., Jerusalem became a fortified city ringed by a stone wall up to ten feet thick. By the 1300s B.C., the Canaanites, whose culture extended across much of the Levant*, occupied Jerusalem. Evidence of this has been found in several Egyptian texts that mention Jerusalem.

During the 1000s B.C., people called the Jebusites, members of a Canaanite culture group, occupied Jerusalem. However, little is known about them, and few artifacts* of their residence in Jerusalem have survived.

Biblical Jerusalem. The Hebrew BIBLE describes Jerusalem during the reigns of DAVID and his son SOLOMON, kings of the unified kingdom of Israel. However, no other surviving text from the period mentions the two kings or their kingdom, although a later inscription found at Tel Dan mentions the "House" (dynasty) of David.

According to the Bible, in the late 1000s B.C., the Israelites were united under David. One of David's greatest successes as king was the capture of Jerusalem from the Jebusites around 1000 B.C. David wisely incorporated Jerusalem into his kingdom and made it his capital. The city had a spring to provide water, its hilltop location gave it some protection against attack, and it lay along the main north-south trade route between Phoenicia and Egypt.

David captured Jerusalem for the Israelites, but his son Solomon gave the city its most impressive and important features. Solomon expanded the administrative functions of the Israelite state and created new royal institutions in Jerusalem, including a court and the Temple of Solomon, constructed in the Phoenician style.

The Temple of Solomon, also known as the First Temple, stood on the Temple Mount. The structure is known from descriptions in the biblical Books of Kings, Chronicles, and Ezekiel. No direct archaeological evidence of it exists, but researchers have found buildings at other Phoenician-Canaanite sites that resemble the biblical descriptions.

Solomon borrowed the basic design of his temple from his Phoenician neighbors and adapted it to the worship of the Hebrew god YAHWEH. For example, Phoenician temples featured thrones on which stood statues of the deities. Reflecting the invisible spirit of Yahweh, the throne in Solomon's temple was empty, except for an ark—a box of acacia wood, which contained the tablets of the Covenant. The Israelites not only accepted the new structure, they willingly paid for it with increased taxes. As a highly visible, impressive monument in the capital, the temple became the focus of religious life, which was closely linked to national identity. This royal state religion was a departure from the traditions of worship outside Jerusalem. Over the years, tension would occasionally develop between those who wanted the temple to be at the center of religious life and those who resisted the authority of the temple priests.

During the rule of Solomon's son Rehoboam, the kingdom of Israel broke up into two kingdoms: Israel in the north and Judah, including

* **fourth millennium B.C.** years from 4000 to 3001 B.C.

* **third millennium B.C.** years from 3000 to 2001 B.C.

* **Levant** lands bordering the eastern shores of the Mediterranean Sea (present-day Syria, Lebanon, and Israel), the West Bank, and Jordan

* **artifact** ornament, tool, weapon, or other object made by humans

 See map in Israel and Judah (vol. 3).

Focus of Three Faiths

Jerusalem is a holy city for three of the modern religions that originated in the Near East: Judaism, Christianity, and Islam. To Jews, Jerusalem symbolizes their continued identity over thousands of years. It was the capital of their ancient state and the site of their most sacred temple. Christians honor Jerusalem as the site of Christ's teachings and miracles and of his death, burial, and resurrection. Muslims believe that the prophet Muhammad, the founder of Islam, began a journey to heaven from a rock on the Temple Mount. The mosque, or Muslim house of worship, built there in the A.D. 680s, is one of the oldest surviving Islamic buildings.

Jewelry

* **siege** long and persistent effort to force a surrender by surrounding a fortress or city with armed troops, cutting it off from supplies and aid

Jerusalem, in the south. In the centuries that followed, the Temple of Solomon was the center of Jewish religious movements and reforms.

In the late 700s B.C., the Assyrians attacked Israel and Judah, but Jerusalem's thick city wall enabled it to survive an Assyrian siege*. By 597 B.C., however, the Babylonians had occupied Judah, including Jerusalem. When the Judeans (people of Judah) rebelled ten years later, the Babylonians destroyed Jerusalem and its temple.

Exile, Return, and Exile Again. After the destruction of Jerusalem, the Babylonians carried many Judeans off to exile in Babylonia. Around 538 B.C., CYRUS THE GREAT of Persia conquered the Babylonians and permitted the Jews, as the Judeans later became known, to return to Jerusalem. There the governor Nehemiah and the scribe* and prophet* Ezra tried to rebuild civic and religious institutions. They also rebuilt the temple at a somewhat smaller scale.

* **scribe** person of a learned class who served as a writer, editor, or teacher
* **prophet** one who claims to have received divine messages or insights

During this time of resettlement and rebuilding, Jerusalem took on additional importance to the Jews. It became the symbol of a people who had suffered but whom Yahweh was now lifting to a new level of glory. Yet, Jerusalem was smaller than it had been before the Babylonian exile. The city did not regain its importance until the 100s B.C., when King Herod rebuilt the temple and built a lavish palace and other structures there.

The Jews who resettled Jerusalem may have dreamed of creating a new and greater kingdom of Israel, but in the centuries that followed, Jerusalem passed into the hands of a series of outside powers: first the PERSIAN EMPIRE, then the SELEUCID EMPIRE, and finally the Roman Empire. The Romans destroyed Jerusalem and the second temple in A.D. 70 and took many Jewish captives to Rome. The Jews who remained in Jerusalem revolted against Rome in 132 but were defeated by the Roman emperor Hadrian in 135. After this defeat, Hadrian ordered that the Jews could no longer live in Jerusalem, so they were forced into a second, much longer, exile. Hadrian renamed the city Aelia Capitolina. (*See also* **Canaan; Hebrews and Israelites; Israel and Judah; Judaism and Jews.**)

JEWELRY

* **deity** god or goddess
* **amulet** small object thought to have supernatural or magical powers

In the ancient Near East, jewelry was—as it is now—a sign of status. Because jewelry was expensive, it was generally worn only by royalty and the elite. However, jewelry was used for more than personal beautification. Ancient Near Eastern peoples adorned the statues of gods and goddesses with bracelets, rings, necklaces, and other items. People wore jewelry bearing images of their deities* to show their devotion. They also wore amulets* to protect themselves from evil spirits or to enlist the aid and support of favorable ones. The rareness of the material, the beauty of the design, and the artisan's skill also made jewelry a valuable gift for weddings or royal exchanges. Finally, jewelry was an investment as well as a currency.

Materials for Jewelry. Many materials were used to make jewelry in ancient times. The base of much jewelry was gold and, less commonly,

silver or copper. Gold is an easy metal to work with—when heated; it can be molded into any shape or thickness. It also lasts and does not tarnish as do silver and copper. The Egyptians favored gold for symbolic reasons; its yellow color and long-lasting quality reminded Egyptians of the sun and the sun god Amun-Ra.

Jewelry was decorated with many semiprecious stones. Among the most popular GEMS were lapis lazuli*, carnelian, turquoise, agate, and obsidian*, but many others were used as well. Valuable natural materials, such as ivory and bone, seashells, ostrich eggshells, and amber were also set in jewelry. Manufactured products such as faience* were used, too, because they were less expensive and could be sold to common people. Around 1400 B.C., craft workers in the Levant* developed great skill in making faience and, later, glass. This skill supported a lively export trade in many goods.

The Development of Jewelry. The earliest jewelry was simple. Finds from the seventh millennium B.C.* in MESOPOTAMIA have yielded jewelry made of bones or shells strung together. Over the years, artisans* perfected their craft and produced magnificent jewelry for rulers and people of wealth. Records from as early as 2100 B.C. in Mesopotamia reveal the practices of jewelers' workshops. One text describes a workshop divided into eight different specialists: metalworkers, goldsmiths, stonecutters, blacksmiths, leather workers, felt workers, carpenters, and reed workers.

Some of the jewelry produced by artisans in the ancient world was placed in tombs as part of burial practices. This is evident from the excavations of the Sumerian royal tombs at UR, dating from about 2600 B.C. There archaeologists* found a queen's jewelry, including gold earrings and necklaces. They also found chokers strung with beads in a variety of shapes made of gold, lapis lazuli, and carnelian. The jewels found in the tomb of the Egyptian king TUTANKHAMEN further reveal the skill and talent of ancient crafts workers—and the great wealth of the rulers. Such excavations are still under way at many sites. The royal tombs of the Assyrian queens in the city of KOLKHU were discovered only in the A.D. 1980s. Archaeologists uncovered large quantities of jewelry there. The intricate designs of the pieces—which include delicate gold flowers and tiny grapes made of lapis lazuli—show that Assyrian goldsmiths were highly skilled workers.

Types of Jewelry. Common items in ancient Near Eastern jewelry included diadems (ornamental crowns or headdresses), necklaces, pectoral (chest) ornaments, bracelets, armlets, and rings. Ancient peoples wore diadems around the head, across the forehead. In Mesopotamia, archaeologists found one royal diadem made of lapis beads with carved gold animals, fruit, and flowers and another with large interlocking rings that extended down and over the forehead. In Egypt, they have excavated a diadem in gold and copper with a carving of a papyrus nest for two ibises, a bird linked to Thoth, the god of learning, and another with 15 flowers inlaid with carnelian and faience. In King Tutankhamen's tomb, archaeologists found a gold diadem with a snake in the front and back and details in carnelian, obsidian, and colored glass. A Sumerian queen's

* **lapis lazuli** dark blue semiprecious stone

* **obsidian** black glass, formed from hardened lava, useful for making sharp blades and tools

* **faience** decorated object made of quartz and other materials that includes a glaze

* **Levant** lands bordering the eastern shores of the Mediterranean Sea (present-day Syria, Lebanon, and Israel), the West Bank, and Jordan

* **seventh millennium B.C.** years from 7000 to 6001 B.C.

* **artisan** skilled craftsperson

* **archaeologist** scientist who studies past human cultures, usually by excavating material remains of human activity

Buried Treasure

Archaeologist Leonard Woolley led the excavation at the Royal Cemetery of Ur, which dates from about 2900 B.C. Among his finds was the magnificent tomb of Queen Pu-abi, whose body was adorned with jewelry that required great skill to create. Covering her upper body was a garment of gold, silver, and beads made from blue, red, white, and multicolored stones. Near her head were three diadems, two of which were decorated with delicate leaves made of faience attached to a gold band. Necklaces of semiprecious stones circled her neck. She wore amulets made of gold and lapis lazuli. Even the horses buried with her were decorated with jewelry.

Jewelry

This magnificent headdress, made in about 2600 B.C., belonged to Queen Pu-abi of the Mesopotamian city of Ur. Made of gold, lapis lazuli, and carnelian—three materials commonly found in ancient Near Eastern jewelry—the headdress ex-hibits the remarkable workmanship of Mesopotamian jewelry makers. It was ex-cavated from the queen's tomb at the Royal Cemetery of Ur.

gold, lapis, and carnelian headdress had tall stemmed flowers on the top, with leaves, hoops, and other shapes covering the forehead and dan-gling all around. In Egypt, one of the queens of THUTMOSE III wore a head-dress of flower-shaped gold disks that covered the hair like a wig and extended down past the shoulders.

Men and women wore earrings, usually made for pierced ears. Most were large and long. The earrings contained gold filigree, carvings with stone inlays, or dangling beads. In the Levant, earrings were shaped like birds, beans, pomegranate buds, and lotus flowers.

Beaded necklaces of precious stones were also worn throughout the region. They ranged from simple chokers to multistrand necklaces of stones and beads in many shapes and colors, interrupted by carved gold. Egyptian jewelry included the *wesekh*, a collar that covered the entire breastbone and was worn by men and women. It consisted of many rows of stone or faience beads in geometric or floral patterns.

Egyptian and Mesopotamian men and women also wore pectorals on the upper chest (the location of the pectoral muscles). One Egyptian example shows two large birds, two snakes, two ankhs*, and a scarab*, all inlaid with amethyst, turquoise, feldspar, lapis, garnet, and carnelian. Another contains papyrus plants, two lionlike animals, defeated enemies, and the god HORUS. A third, of gold, silver, and stones, has flowers, fish, snakes, and a scarab with large wings.

Men and women wore bracelets at the wrists and armlets on the upper arms. They were decorated with lion heads, trees, and winged creatures. A frequent and useful feature was the metal hinge, which served a decorative purpose as well as a practical one. An armlet with hinges fit snugly around the upper arm, whereas a bangle-type bracelet was large and could get past the elbow. An Egyptian statue shows a woman wearing 11 bracelets on one arm and 12 on the other.

Rings, worn on many fingers, were common. They might be of carved gold, silver, bronze, or iron; plain or engraved or with stone settings. Sometimes attached to the band was a gold wire, at the end of which a precious stone dangled. Many Egyptian rings contained a stone scarab, some of which swiveled, and the other side was carved. This allowed the ring also to be used as a SEAL. (*See also* **Faience; Metals and Metalworking.**)

* **ankh** cross with a loop at the top; Egyptian symbol of life

* **scarab** representation of the dung beetle, held as sacred by Egyptians

See color plate 8, vol. 4.

Jews   See *Judaism and Jews.*

Jezebel   See *Ahab.*

Judah   See *Israel and Judah.*

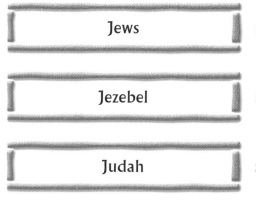

JUDAISM AND JEWS

Judaism—the religion of the Jews—is a monotheistic* faith that developed over hundreds of years among the ancient Israelites. The religion is centered on the worship of YAHWEH, the god also known as EL, a Semitic* term that means god. Many ancient texts deal with the legends, history, laws, prophecies*, and teachings of Judaism, but the sacred book of the religion is the Hebrew BIBLE.

The name *Jew* comes from the Old French word *Jiu,* which referred to the people of Judah, the ancient name of their homeland. The ancient Jews were united by their religious beliefs and by their strong tradition of religious education and customs. For a time, they had lived together in Israel—a land with which they identified deeply. However, conquest and deportation* caused the Jewish population to spread out across the Near Eastern landscape. Separated from old institutions such as the Temple of Solomon, the place of worship in their holy city of

* **monotheistic** referring to the belief in only one god

* **Semitic** of or relating to a language family that includes Akkadian, Aramaic, Arabic, Hebrew, and Phoenician

* **prophecy** message from a deity; also, the prediction of future events

Judaism and Jews

* **deportation** forced movement of individuals or groups of people from one place to another

* **patriarch** male leader of a family or tribe

* **famine** severe lack of food due to failed crops

JERUSALEM, they interacted with other people and absorbed new influences. Their religion developed further as a result of political and social changes.

Origins of Judaism. Jews trace their history to the patriarch* Abraham (also called Abram), who lived in Ur of the Chaldees (a city and district in ancient Sumer). According to the Hebrew Bible, Yahweh made a covenant, or solemn agreement, with Abraham. Yahweh promised him the land of CANAAN (known as the Promised Land) and many descendants. (These descendants called themselves the children of Israel after Abraham's grandson Jacob, whom Yahweh had renamed Israel.) The Israelites then lived in Canaan for several generations, until a famine* forced them to leave. Thereafter, they went to Egypt, where they eventually became enslaved.

Another important figure in Judaism was MOSES, a leader who brought the Israelites out of slavery in Egypt and back into Canaan. This journey, known as the Exodus, lasted 40 years. During the Exodus, Moses gave the Israelites a new understanding of Yahweh. A key element of this new understanding was the renewal of the Covenant. The Israelites vowed to follow Yahweh's laws so that the promises he made to them, the ones he promised Abraham, might be fulfilled. The covenant meant that they were a "chosen people" who had a special relationship with Yahweh. It also made them responsible for living in accordance with Yahweh's will as interpreted in laws and rules, such as the TEN COMMANDMENTS, which Yahweh had revealed to Moses during the Exodus.

Conflict, Reform, and Change. When the Israelites arrived in Canaan, Moses was not allowed to enter the Promised Land because he had not followed one of Yahweh's orders exactly. Nevertheless, his followers entered Canaan, and there they eventually founded the kingdom of Israel, which endured in various forms for more than 400 years. King DAVID established Israel's capital at Jerusalem. SOLOMON, his son and successor, built a magnificent temple, which was the center of the Israelite religion, in Jerusalem. Solomon placed the ARK OF THE COVENANT—a sacred chest made of acacia wood and gold—in the temple. The ark contained tablets of the covenant between Yahweh and the Israelites from the time of the Exodus.

* **cult** system of religious beliefs and rituals; group following these beliefs

Religion and the government were closely linked in Israel. The state cult*, which centered on institutions such as the Temple of Solomon, was headed by the king. He had supreme authority over the cult and performed duties such as offering animal sacrifices and ordering the people to religious meetings. Kings, administrators, and the urban priesthood worked to make temple rituals the focus of the religion. The state cult helped fuse the Israelites' religious and national identity.

Some Israelites resisted the trend toward centralized authority. They criticized royal laws and policies and emphasized the importance of moral purity, justice, and individual worship that was not based on participating in functions of the state cult.

Another trend influenced Israelite religious life during the period of the monarchy: the attraction to other gods and cults, such as the fertility cults of the Canaanites. Soon Israelites began to worship deities other than Yahweh, and prophets* began to criticize them for falling away from the sole worship of Yahweh. They claimed that Yahweh would punish those who continued to worship foreign gods. The prophets' words became part of the Bible and sometimes inspired such reforms as the destruction of shrines to other gods.

The Exile. In about 925 B.C., Israel separated into two kingdoms—Israel in the north and Judah in the south. Although the kingdoms achieved some stability at first, they were both eventually overcome by other Near Eastern empires. The people of the kingdom of Israel disappeared from history after they were conquered and deported by the Assyrians in 722 B.C. Nevertheless, Judaism continued to develop with the Judeans (the people of Judah, who later became known as Jews), even after the Babylonians conquered Judah, destroyed Jerusalem and the temple, and forced many Jews into exile in Babylonia in the early 500s B.C.

The period of Babylonian exile is known as the Diaspora, as were all subsequent periods when Jews lived scattered outside of Israel, even to this day. The exiled Jews considered their plight a test of their faith in Yahweh. They developed a belief in a future when Yahweh would restore Israel to its former glory.

While they were in exile, the Jews had also developed a reliance on rituals and rules about prayer and dietary laws to keep themselves pure in Yahweh's eyes. This body of practices became associated with their identity as Jews. Thus, the Babylonian exile changed Judaism from a local

Before monotheism became firmly established in Judaism, the Israelites worshiped deities other than just Yahweh. This copy of an inscription that decorates a Samaritan storage jar from the 700s B.C. suggests that they worshiped the goddess Asherah. The inscription reads, "I bless you by Yahweh of Samaria and by his Asherah," reflecting a close relationship between Yahweh and the goddess.

faith, tied to its place of origin, into a universal or world religion based on following a code of laws.

After the Exile. In 538 B.C., after the Persian empire had conquered Babylonia, the Persian emperor CYRUS THE GREAT allowed the Jews to return to Jerusalem and Judah, which had become part of Persian territory. The Persians called this province Yehud, which was known in Greek as Judaea. The Jews who returned to Jerusalem focused on building the second temple and on organizing and publishing the traditional texts dealing with Jewish law, which became established as the constitution within their province.

Two important figures in Judaism during the 400s B.C. were Nehemiah, a leader and Persian official who helped rebuild Jerusalem, and Ezra, a scribe* and priest. Both men felt that Jews in Judah had fallen away from traditional worship and set about to reform and reorganize the people. Nehemiah issued many reforms and worked to strengthen the Jews' observance of religious laws. Ezra brought together the most important traditional writings in the TORAH, the first five books of the Hebrew Bible. In doing this, Ezra made the law a central fixture of Judaism and linked observance of the laws with preserving Jewish identity. As a result of his efforts, Ezra is considered responsible for reestablishing Judaism after the exile.

Another important development after the exile was in the role of the scribe. Scribes had always been important as transmitters of the Israelite religion, but with the new emphasis on the law brought by Ezra, they became the recognized experts on religious and other issues.

The issue of who was a Jew also became important after the exile. Jews who had returned from Babylonia to Jerusalem considered themselves more faithful to Yahweh and more observant than those who had not been forced to leave Judah. This feeling caused a rift between Jews who had returned and those who had not been exiled. As a result, Jewish leaders, scribes, and priests, such as Ezra and Nehemiah, tried to prevent these "pure" Jews from mixing with other cultures, including Jews who had remained in Judah.

By this time, Jews' experiences had led them to believe that Yahweh directed the destinies of all nations and peoples, which meant that Judaism was now completely monotheistic. They also believed in the immortality of the human soul, punishment after death for those who chose sin, and a heavenly reward for those who chose righteousness.

Judaism During the Hellenistic Period. Around 330 B.C., the Macedonian army of ALEXANDER THE GREAT overthrew the Persian empire and Judah passed into Alexander's control. After Alexander's death, his successors, the Ptolemies of Egypt and the Seleucids of Syria and Mesopotamia, fought over Judah and the other territories that Alexander had conquered. During the Hellenistic* period, as many as a million Jews may have lived in each of the four major sites of the Diaspora: Babylonia, Egypt, SYRIA, and ANATOLIA (present-day Turkey). Alexandria, a Greek city in Egypt, became a center of Jewish learning, and the Jews there adopted the Greek language. During the Diaspora, the emphasis on education and

* **scribe** person of a learned class who served as a writer, editor, or teacher

The Issue of Intermarriage

Judaism is not just a religion but also an ethnic and national heritage or identity. After their return from the exile, Jewish leaders in Judah took steps to preserve that identity. They discouraged marriages between descendants of returned exiles and descendants of people who had not been exiled. The scribe Ezra, to whom the Persians had given considerable power in Judah, set up a court that examined marriages and dissolved those that did not meet his standards. Not all Jews appreciated Ezra's high standards. The marriage court made him unpopular. As a result, the Persians took away Ezra's authority.

* **Hellenistic** referring to the Greek-influenced culture of the Mediterranean world and western Asia during the three centuries after the death of Alexander the Great in 323 B.C.

the transmission of knowledge helped preserve and spread the Jewish traditions and beliefs. Jewish culture itself developed in new directions, producing rival schools of thought and sects*.

* **sect** group of people with a common leadership who share a distinctive set of religious views and opinions

The Jews also absorbed aspects of the local cultures into their religion. For example, a common Mesopotamian belief in healing through magic was adopted by the Jews of Babylon. The Persian religion known as Zoroastrianism and Egyptian beliefs shared some common features with Judaism, especially the idea that the immortal human soul receives punishment or reward based on a person's actions in life.

The Israelites originally spoke Hebrew, a Semitic language. In the second half of the first millennium B.C.*, Hebrew, like some other Near Eastern languages, was replaced in daily life by another Semitic language, Aramaic, the language of the ARAMAEANS. The exiles* who returned from Babylonia brought Aramaic with them. The Jews continued to use Hebrew as a literary and scholarly language, but by the Hellenistic period, they were speaking Aramaic and Greek.

* **first millennium** B.C. years from 1000 to 1 B.C.

* **exile** person forced to live away from his or her homeland for a long period of time

Jerusalem and the Jews enjoyed a brief period of independence in the 100s B.C., but in 63 B.C., they came under the control of yet another foreign power—Rome. When the Jews revolted against Roman rule, the Romans destroyed the second temple and Jerusalem in A.D. 70. Jerusalem had been partially rebuilt and repopulated when the Jews revolted again in 132. After this revolt, the Romans dispersed the Jewish inhabitants of Judah to other regions of the Roman Empire and renamed Judah Syria-Palestina. Jewish religion and culture remained alive, however, in this second exilic period.

Further Developments. After the destruction of the second temple, synagogues—places of assembly and worship—became important centers of Jewish life. Synagogues date back to the 200s B.C. and possibly as far as the 580s B.C., when the Temple of Solomon was destroyed. The earliest synagogues may have been homes that were used for religious instruction. In the first century A.D., synagogues existed in the Levant*, Rome, Greece, Egypt, Babylon, and Asia Minor. Synagogues remain as places of worship by Jews today.

* **Levant** lands bordering the eastern shores of the Mediterranean Sea (present-day Syria, Lebanon, and Israel), the West Bank, and Jordan

After the destruction of the second temple, Judaism was further changed with the emergence of rabbis as religious leaders. Rabbis were spiritual guides and teachers who organized around separate houses of worship or synagogues. They devoted themselves to studying the scripture, or sacred writings, and teaching it to their communities. They were considered interpreters of Jewish law. Rabbis took on even greater importance after A.D. 135, when the Jews were forced to leave Jerusalem. This began what is referred to as Rabbinic Judaism, when the rabbis and their centers of learning were looked to for religious leadership. The rabbis emphasized the study of the sacred writings of Judaism, prayer, and faithfulness over centralized worship in a temple. This reemphasized the idea that had emerged during the Babylonian exile that Judaism could be practiced anywhere.

The rabbis arranged and set an order for Jewish laws during the first centuries A.D. in a compilation of ancient sacred teachings known as the Talmud. The Talmud contains explanations of and commentaries on the laws that Yahweh told to Moses. Talmudic schools were established where scholars could study the Talmud. Between the A.D. 500s and 900, scholars at these schools devoted themselves to retrieving and arranging the Hebrew scriptures and recording them in Hebrew. This version of the Bible, known as the Masoretic text, was carefully transcribed when it was compiled, and was first printed in the late 1400s. Today rabbis and scholars around the world consider the Masoretic text to be the authentic Hebrew Bible. (*See also* **Assyria and the Assyrians; Babylonia and the Babylonians; Hebrews and Israelites; Israel and Judah; Monotheism; Mosaic Law; Patriarchs and Matriarchs of Israel.**)

KALKHU

* **archaeologist** scientist who studies past human cultures, usually by excavating material remains of human activity

* **tribute** payment made by a smaller or weaker party to a more powerful one, often under the threat of force

* **vassal** individual or state that swears loyalty and obedience to a greater power

* **provincial** having to do with the provinces, outlying districts, administrative divisions, or conquered territories of a country or empire

Kalkhu (KAL•hoo), present-day Nimrud, was a city located on the banks of the TIGRIS RIVER in northern MESOPOTAMIA. Kalkhu was established in the 1200s B.C. and during the reign of ASHURNASIRPAL II (ca. 883–859 B.C.), became the capital of the Assyrian empire.

Archaeologists* have found temples dedicated to the city god Ninurta and another to Nabu, the god of writing. They have also found the Northwest Palace built by Ashurnasirpal, which contained stone sculptures describing important events in the king's reign. The palace was guarded by stone statues of lions and bulls. In addition, archaeologists have discovered the "tombs of the queens," where important women in the Assyrian empire were buried. Among the many objects found in the tombs are golden jewelry and pottery and alabaster containers.

One of the most important buildings found at Kalkhu was built in the mid 800s B.C., during the reign of SHALMANESER III. The building was an arsenal (military structure) and contained items of tribute* that the Assyrians received from their vanquished enemies and vassal* states. Objects found there include ivory carvings, figurines, tools, jars, and furniture panels.

In 721 B.C., King SARGON II moved Assyria's capital to Khorsabad. Thereafter, Kalkhu became a provincial* capital. In the late 600s B.C., the city was destroyed by the invading armies of the MEDES. A small village remained until the 100s B.C., when the site was finally abandoned. (*See also* **Cities and City-States.**)

KARKAMISH

* **city-state** independent state consisting of a city and its surrounding territory

* **Neolithic period** final phase of the Stone Age, from about 9000 to 4000 B.C.

Karkamish (KAHR•kuh•mish), also known as Carchemish, was a Hittite city-state* on the west bank of the upper EUPHRATES RIVER, near the border of present-day Turkey and Syria. It was inhabited from the Neolithic period* but flourished during the Neo-Hittite period.

Karkamish first appears in written records dating from the 2500s B.C. Its location made it an important part of the trading network of the ancient Near East. Caravans from ancient SYRIA, MESOPOTAMIA, and ANATOLIA all crossed the Euphrates near Karkamish. The city was known as a trading center for wood, which was shipped down the river to be sold to desert peoples who had little access to this rare and useful material. During the Late Bronze Age (ca. 1600–1200 B.C.), the city was ruled by the Hittite king's governor.

Karkamish contained buildings that attested to its prosperity, including a temple dedicated to the storm god Teshub, a gatehouse, and the King's Gate. Much of the architecture and sculpture is inscribed in Luwian hieroglyphics* with details of rulers' successes and blessings from the gods.

These blessings could not protect the region from the mighty Assyrians, however. Tiglath-pileser III and Sargon II conquered several Neo-Hittite cities including Karkamish in 717 B.C. Karkamish remained a province of the Assyrian empire until Assyria fell in 612 B.C. In 605 B.C., Karkamish was the site of the final battle between the Babylonians and the Egyptians. The Babylonians, under Nebuchadnezzar II, prevailed and drove the Egyptians out of Syria. Thereafter, Karkamish disappeared from history. (*See also* **Hittites; Neo-Hittites.**)

* **hieroglyphics** system of writing that uses pictorial characters, or hieroglyphics, to represent words or ideas

See map in Syria (vol. 4).

KARNAK

See map on inside covers.

Located near the ancient city of Thebes in Lower Egypt, Karnak was among the most important religious sites in ancient Egypt. The site began as a small shrine but developed into a massive temple complex over a period of 2,000 years. Karnak was home to Amun, the chief god of Thebes.

Begun by Sesostris I, the founder of the Twelfth Dynasty, the temple was enlarged by many later kings, each eager to show his devotion to the god. It evolved into a huge T-shaped structure surrounded by four walls enclosing more than seven acres. Within the walls, six monumental pylons, or gateways, lead from the west to the main temple, which was set near the center. Four more pylons lead to the temple from the south.

One of the temple's most striking features is a hall with 134 columns carved to look like huge papyrus plants. The columns are laid out in 16 rows with up to 9 columns in each row. The complex also contains many smaller temples, chapels, and a sacred lake. In ancient times, the high priest washed and purified himself in the waters of the sacred lake each morning before entering Amun's temple and worshiping the god. It was here that pharaohs prayed to Amun for victory.

Two other brick-walled enclosures comprise the rest of the ruins at Karnak. To the north of the enclosure of Amun is the enclosure of Montu, the original local god of the Theban area. To the south is the enclosure of Mut, another god of Thebes. (*See also* **Egypt and the Egyptians; Palaces and Temples.**)

KASSITES

* **dynasty** succession of rulers from the same family or group

The Kassites, a tribal people of unknown origin, began arriving in Mesopotamia by way of the Zagros Mountains around 1800 B.C. They lived in the countryside surrounding the cities of Babylonia and worked as farm laborers, construction workers, and soldiers. Shortly after 1595 B.C., when Hittite king Murshili I raided Babylon and weakened the ruling dynasty* there, the Kassites seized power. They ruled Babylonia for about 400 years—the longest-ruling dynasty in the ancient Near East.

During Kassite rule, there were political stability, economic prosperity, and achievements in culture and literature. The Kassites also undertook

Khabiru

* **assimilate** to adopt the customs of a society

* **lapis lazuli** dark blue semiprecious stone

* **relief** sculpture in which material is cut away to show figures raised from the background

public building projects, encouraged trade, and improved international relations. The Kassites brought about a lasting period of political unification in Babylonia. The ruling classes also adopted traditional philosophy, according to which the ruler was responsible for the land and was to ensure the basics of life for all.

The Kassites assimilated* Babylonian culture and integrated themselves into mainstream society. They worshiped the Babylonian gods as well as two of their own—Shuqamuna and Shumaliya—who were sometimes called the gods of the king. The Kassites also favored the Sumerian god Enlil, and they adopted the language of Babylonia. Consequently, little is known about the native Kassite language and customs.

During the Kassite period, Babylonia engaged in trade with Egypt, Afghanistan, and the peoples of the Aegean. Babylonian textiles, horses, and chariots and imported lapis lazuli* were traded for gold, precious stones, and varieties of wood. The Kassites invented a type of boundary stone called the *kudurru,* which recorded areas of land given by the king to people he favored. These stones were inscribed with writing about the land and its recipient and were elaborately carved with images of the gods who witnessed its being given by the king. The Kassites also brought horse breeding, horse riding, and new technology in chariot making to Babylonia, and they invented molded bricks to form figures in relief*.

In addition to the ruling dynasty in Babylon, Kassite tribal groups inhabited regions east of the Tigris River. These tribes remained there long after the Kassite dynasty lost power around 1158 B.C., when they were attacked by Elamites.

Khabiru

See *Hebrews and Israelites.*

KHATTI

* **indigenous** referring to the original inhabitants of a region

* **decipher** to decode and interpret the meaning of

See map in Anatolia (vol. 1).

Throughout the history of the ancient Near East, the term *Khatti* (HAT•ti) was used to refer to different groups or states in different periods. Before the 1600s B.C., the term referred to the indigenous* peoples who inhabited ANATOLIA (present-day Turkey) before the arrival of the HITTITES. During the Late Bronze Age (ca. 1600–1200 B.C.), the term referred to the Hittite kingdom with its capital at KHATTUSHA (present-day Bŏgzköy). During the Iron Age (ca. 1200–500 B.C.), Khatti referred to north Syria probably because that region contained several NEO-HITTITE settlements, such as KARKAMISH.

The indigenous people of Khatti, sometimes called the Proto-Khattians, spoke Hattic, a language that has not been deciphered*. Consequently, the land and people of Khatti will remain a mystery until scholars are able to read the Hattic tablets. However, historians know that they were skilled metalworkers from evidence (sophisticated metal objects) excavated at tombs in northeastern Anatolia. After the arrival of the Hittites, the people of Khatti were absorbed into the Hittite state, and their history became intertwined with that of the Hittites.

KHATTUSHA

* **city-state** independent state consisting of a city and its surrounding territory

See map in Hittites (vol. 2).

* **archaeologist** scientist who studies past human cultures, usually by excavating material remains of human activity

* **cuneiform** world's oldest form of writing, which takes its name from the distinctive wedge-shaped signs pressed into clay tablets

The ancient city of Khattusha (HAT•tu•sa) was located in north-central ANATOLIA (present-day Turkey). It was the capital of the empire of the HITTITES. Known today as Boğazköy, the site was first settled shortly before 2000 B.C. and became the empire's capital around 1650 B.C.

Khattusha was located at a great distance from a group of city-states* near the Euphrates River and seemed an unlikely place for a capital. However, the site had practical and strategic advantages because it was situated on a hill at the junction of two smaller rivers. This gave the city's inhabitants access to water and a means of transportation. Moreover, the city fulfilled the Hittites' need for a strategic location from which they could safely wage war.

Khattusha reached the peak of its power around the 1300s B.C. At that time, it covered an area of more than 400 acres. The city had a population of about 20,000 and was protected by a wall and a moat. Seven gateways, including the famous King's Gate, Lion Gate, and Sphinx Gate, led into Khattusha. The city also contained 30 temples, administrative and royal buildings, and an audience hall.

Around 1200 B.C., there was unrest on all sides of the Hittite empire and dissent within. Enemies from the north captured and burned Khattusha. Not all was lost, however. Archaeologists* have found more than 10,000 cuneiform* tablets in the ruins at Khattusha. They offer valuable and detailed information about Hittite history and culture.

KHATTUSHILI I

**ruled ca. 1650–1620 B.C.
Hittite king**

Khattushili I (hat•too•SEE•li) was the founder of the Hittite Old Kingdom. He made the city of KHATTUSHA—atop a hill and at considerable distance from other major Hittite cities—the kingdom's capital. Surrounded by a tall, thick wall, Khattusha was well defended from invaders and an excellent location for launching military campaigns.

Khattushili concentrated on extending the Hittite kingdom. He decided to take over powerful cities on the trade routes because they would ensure a steady supply of metals, such as tin, to his empire. His aim was to conquer all the regions south of Khattusha so that he would have access to the Mediterranean Sea. From there, he planned to sail to northern SYRIA, a region that could bring the HITTITES great wealth because most trade routes met there.

Khattushili decided to attack the powerful Syrian cities of ALALAKH and Halab (present-day Aleppo). He carried out this plan and conquered Alalakh, robbing Halab of an outlet to the sea. Then instead of moving on to Halab, he turned west toward Arzawa, a powerful state in western Anatolia bordering on the Aegean Sea. After the success of this campaign, he turned his attention back to Halab. However, the Halab campaign was again postponed when HURRIANS attacked the Hittites from the east. It took Khattushili more than a year to push them back across the Euphrates River. He attempted one more attack on Halab but was unable to conquer the city. Some historians believe that Khattushili may have been killed during this attempt, but no one is certain how he died.

During most of his reign, Khattushili was away from his kingdom. In his absence, the kingdom experienced civil strife, and his three rebellious sons competed for power. In retaliation, Khattushili disowned them and named his grandson Murshili I his successor. Murshili successfully conquered Halab, realizing Khattushili's plans.

KHATTUSHILI III

ruled ca. 1275–1250 B.C.
Hittite king

K hattushili III (hat•too•SEE•li), ruler of the HITTITES for 25 years, was an accomplished soldier and an expert in diplomacy and peacemaking. He was a younger son of Murshili II. When his father died in about 1306 B.C., Khattushili's older brother, Muwattalli II, became king, and Khattushili was appointed governor of a region in northeastern ANATOLIA. There he repelled the Gasga people who invaded from the region of the Pontic Mountains. He also recovered Hittite territory that had been previously lost, including the capital, KHATTUSHA.

When King Muwattalli II died around 1282 B.C., his son Urkhi-Teshub became king, taking the name Murshili III. Khattushili continued his military campaigns in the north, but he resented his nephew, who began to undermine Khattushili's power. Finally, after seven years, Khattushili assembled an army and marched against Murshili. He overthrew the king and exiled him.

Knowledge of the events of Khattushili's reign comes from his autobiography, entitled *Apology,* a document written largely to justify the new king's actions and his right to rule. His rule was generally one of peace and prosperity. However, the growing power of Assyria and of the Kassites in Babylonia had become a problem. Khattushili used his powers of persuasion to work out agreements with both empires. With Babylonia, he signed a treaty by which each party would help the other in times of war or crisis. Khattushili had in mind a Hittite-Babylonia force in case Assyria did not remain friendly.

In light of Assyria's growing power, Khattushili forged good relations with the Egyptian king RAMSES II, with whom his father had previously waged war. A peace treaty with Egypt was signed around 1258 B.C.— a significant diplomatic feat. The treaty was originally inscribed on two silver tablets (one tablet for each party). Although these tablets are lost, archaeologists* have unearthed an Akkadian language cuneiform* copy on clay from Khattusha. They have also recovered hieroglyphic* Egyptian copies that were carved on stelae* at the KARNAK temple and at Ramses' mortuary temple. The treaty marked the beginning of a national and personal friendship. For example, the Egyptians sent medicine for Khattushili's eye disease and offered the king other medical advice as well. Around 1245 B.C., Khattushili arranged a dynastic marriage between one of his daughters and Ramses II.

Khattushili spent the last years of his reign securing the throne for his son Tudkhaliya IV against threats from other family members, including descendants of his nephew Murshili III. In his autobiography, Khattushili credited the goddess ISHTAR with all his success. Years earlier, she had said: "Hand him over to me and let him be my priest, then he will live." Khattushili was thus ordained a priest of Ishtar and remained devoted to her: "In times of fear the goddess, My Lady, never abandoned me. . . . [She] shielded me in every way, favored me." Khattushili was more than 70 years old when he died.

* **archaeologist** scientist who studies past human cultures, usually by excavating material remains of human activity

* **cuneiform** world's oldest form of writing, which takes its name from the distinctive wedge-shaped signs pressed into clay tablets

* **hieroglyphic** referring to a system of writing that uses pictorial characters, or hieroglyphs, to represent words or ideas

* **stela** stone slab or pillar that has been carved or engraved and serves as a monument; *pl.* stelae

KHEPAT

* **pantheon** all the gods of a particular culture

Khepat (HE•pat), the Queen of Heaven, was the chief goddess of the HURRIANS and companion of the storm god TESHUB. In art, Khepat is usually represented as standing on a lion or on a leopard as well as seated on a throne.

A member of the Hurrian pantheon*, Khepat was also the city goddess of Halab (present-day Aleppo). Along with Teshub and ISHTAR, she formed the triad of gods worshiped at the city of ALALAKH. In the 1300s B.C., when the Hurrian pantheon was incorporated into the Hittite state religion, Khepat became identified with the Hittite sun goddess of Arinna, the traditional protector of the king and queen.

In mythology, Khepat appears in the Kumarbi Cycle, which tells the story of KUMARBI's attempt to destroy his son Teshub and keep him from power. In the end, the stronger and wiser gods prevail, and Teshub and Khepat keep their thrones in heaven.

KHUFU

ruled ca. 2585–2560 B.C.
Egyptian king

* **sarcophagus** ornamental coffin, usually made of stone; *pl.* sarcophagi

Khufu (KOO•foo), also known as Cheops, ruled ancient Egypt during the peaceful and prosperous Old Kingdom period (ca. 2675–2130 B.C.). He is remembered mainly as the builder of the Great Pyramid at GIZA. Khufu succeeded his father, Sneferu, who founded the Fourth Dynasty (ca. 2625–2500 B.C.). He reigned for about 25 years and was succeeded by his sons, Redjedef and Khafre.

After Khufu ascended the throne around the age of 25, he ordered his overseer of royal works to begin building the Great Pyramid as his tomb. He chose Giza as the site for the pyramid, and construction continued throughout his reign. When finished, the Great Pyramid at Giza was the largest of all of Egypt's pyramids. It is still the largest stone structure in the world, covering more than 570,500 square feet and rising to a height of about 1,500 feet. Located nearby are three smaller pyramids, one each for Khufu's mother and his two principal queens, the mothers of Khufu's sons and successors. In addition, Khufu ordered the Great Sphinx to be carved out of a large stone outcropping nearby. In this massive statue, the king's head is carved atop the body of a lion. Khufu also ordered the building of a ship that is known today as the Royal Ship of Khufu. The ship imitates the papyrus craft that Egyptians believed transported the sun god Amun-Ra across the heavens.

When Khufu died, his mummified body may have been transported on the Royal Ship from his palace at MEMPHIS to the burial site in a funeral procession. His attendants carried his coffin through a temple at the base of the pyramid and then climbed through a cavernous gallery to the king's burial chamber high inside the pyramid. The location of the chamber reflects the belief that after death, the king would rise to the sky and become one with Ra. The attendants placed the king's mummy in a stone sarcophagus* and closed off the chamber with huge boulders. Notwithstanding these precautions, robbers later found their way into the burial chamber and stole its contents.

In order for Khufu to have built his Great Pyramid, he must have had the state's resources completely under his control. This indicates the power of Egyptian kings during the Old Kingdom period. Building the

King Lists

* **bureaucracy** system consisting of officials and clerks who perform government functions

Great Pyramid also is evidence of a complex and efficient government bureaucracy* at that time. (*See also* **Egypt and the Egyptians; Kings; Pharaohs.**)

KING LISTS

* **second millennium B.C.** years from 2000 to 1001 B.C.

* **cuneiform** world's oldest form of writing, which takes its name from the distinctive wedge-shaped signs pressed into clay tablets

* **dynasty** succession of rulers from the same family or group

* **city-state** independent state consisting of a city and its surrounding territory

The baked clay prism shown here is the best-preserved version of the Sumerian king list. This version of the list traces the reigns of rulers from "before the flood" to King Sin-magir of Isin (ruled ca. 1827–1817 B.C.). However, because this list, like others found in the region, is both idealized and biased, it is not a completely reliable source of information about Sumerian history.

In the ancient Near East, king lists were texts that contained the names of kings and details of each ruler's accomplishments and exploits as well as important events in the history of an empire. Few king lists have survived to modern times, and those that have provide only a fragmentary picture of ancient history. Nonetheless, king lists have greatly aided modern historians in establishing a CHRONOLOGY for ancient Near Eastern history and determining the origins of kingship in that region.

Mesopotamian King Lists. Several king lists from ancient MESOPOTAMIA have helped historians piece together the history of kingdoms in that region. Among the oldest is the Sumerian king list. Composed in the early second millennium B.C.*, the list is preserved in several versions on cuneiform* tablets. It served as the basis for later king lists developed by the Babylonians, and at least one version of the list was used in BABYLON as late as the 300s B.C.

In its oldest form, the Sumerian king list describes how kingship was established in the city of KISH. It also lists the dynasties* that ruled city-states* in Mesopotamia and traces the transfer of power from one city to another. Later versions of the Sumerian king list extend back to even earlier times, attempting to reach back to the origins of human life. These versions name semidivine kings who reigned for very long periods at the beginning of Sumerian civilization.

Much of the early history presented in the Sumerian king list is more myth than fact, portraying an idealized view of the establishment of Sumerian civilization. It is also highly biased, ignoring some cities and dynasties and focusing on others, such as the city of URUK and the first dynasty of LAGASH. This is possibly because the scribes* who created the king list were trying to justify the dominance of a particular city and its kingship over other cities.

The Babylonian king lists trace the chronology of Babylon from the time of King HAMMURABI (ruled ca. 1792–1750 B.C.) through the period of the KASSITES to the time when Assyrians dominated the region (ca. 1200s B.C.). These lists were based on year lists, which identified each year by a unique name based on important events, such as the accession of a new king to the throne. Although there are gaps in the surviving king lists, historians have been able to piece together a chronology by comparing the lists with other Babylonian texts and chronicles and to Assyrian king lists that cover the same periods.

The most important Assyrian king list dates from the 700s B.C. Produced by royal scribes, it was based on texts, INSCRIPTIONS, and the so-called Synchronistic History. This chronicle listed the kings of Assyria and Babylonia in a comparable sequence over hundreds of years. The Assyrian list traces the kings of Assyria from about 1700 B.C. until the 700s B.C. The

* **scribe** person of a learned class who served as a writer, editor, or teacher

list suggests that Assyria had been an independent state from the beginning, but that is historically untrue.

Egyptian King Lists. The earliest surviving Egyptian king list is a text known as the Palermo Stone. Compiled from earlier sources in about 2400 B.C., it originally contained the names of all the kings from the earliest periods of Egyptian history and summarized the significant events in each year of their reigns. The Palermo Stone became an important source for later Egyptian king lists and texts and was used as a type of calendar to date events in Egyptian history.

Among the most important of these later Egyptian king lists is the Turin Canon of Kings, a fragmentary papyrus, which lists the names of kings from earliest times to the reign of RAMSES II (ruled ca. 1279–1213 B.C.). Considered the most detailed and reliable Egyptian king list, the Turin Canon not only lists the kings but also the years, months, and days of each of their reigns. It further divides Egyptian history into three major periods, a system that later historians adopted and labeled the Old Kingdom, Middle Kingdom, and New Kingdom periods. Another important feature of the Turin Canon was that it listed gods and demigods* as the earliest rulers of Egypt, thus supporting the idea that the kingship was a divine institution. The Turin Canon and other king lists served as sources for Manetho, a Greco-Egyptian writer of the 200s B.C., who compiled a complete chronology of Egyptian history up to his time.

* **demigod** partly divine being

Other King Lists. The HITTITES do not appear to have had an interest in long-range chronologies or king lists. However, the rulers of Persia and CANAAN did create such lists to record their history and to provide a basis for their kingship.

An important source for late Mesopotamian history is a king list produced in Egypt during the time of the Roman Empire. Called Ptolemy's Canon, it was written in Greek by the astronomer Claudius Ptolemy. It lists kings from 747 B.C. through the period of the PERSIAN EMPIRE and the empires of ALEXANDER THE GREAT and his successors. (*See also* **History and Historiography; Kings; Record Keeping; Scribes.**)

KINGS

* **secular** nonreligious; connected with everyday life

Throughout ancient times, kingship was the predominant institution of government in the Near East. Kings filled both sacred and secular* roles. Although their power and prestige changed from time to time and place to place, they remained at the center of government and society.

The Rise of Kingship. Kingship emerged in the ancient Near East when strong leaders began to gain power and authority over cities and states. Their authority came from the military power they held and from the belief that they were chosen by the gods to rule.

According to the traditions of most Near Eastern societies, the roots of kingship stretched back to the beginning of time, when gods ruled the earth. Kings were the chosen successors of the gods, and in some cases,

Kings

This relief from Assyrian king Ashurbanipal's palace at Nineveh dates from the 600s B.C. It illustrates the luxuries that many ancient Near Eastern kings enjoyed during their reigns. As the king reclines comfortably on a couch, his queen sits atop an ornate chair in front of him. Both are adorned in richly ornamented clothes and surrounded by several mindful attendants.

Egyptian Royal Titularies

Egyptian kings had several royal titularies, or titles. Among these were names of gods, which symbolized the king as the earthly embodiment of a particular god. The first titulary of Egyptian king Amenemhet III, for example, was The Horus: Great of Might. Sometimes, the titles might include a throne name, such as the King of Upper and Lower Egypt, Nimaatre, and a birth name, such as the Son of Ra: Amenemhet. The throne name and birth name usually appeared inside a cartouche— a hieroglyphic symbol that indicates that the person named is an Egyptian ruler and symbolizes the king's authority over the entire world.

* **third millennium B.C.** years from 3000 to 2001 B.C.

* **deity** god or goddess

See color plate 4, vol. 1.

particularly in ancient Egypt, they were considered divine themselves. The link between kings and gods was often reflected in kings' official titles and their roles and responsibilities.

Roles and Responsibilities. Some scholars suggest that kings were originally chosen as temporary leaders, especially during times of war or emergency. As warfare became more common during the early third millennium B.C.*, however, kingships became permanent. As kingships developed in the ancient Near East, kings gained increasing power. They became absolute monarchs who reigned with seemingly unlimited power. Nevertheless, most citizens still had certain basic rights, and it was the responsibility of kings to guard these rights and to serve and protect their people.

Ancient Near Eastern kings had many roles and responsibilities to fulfill. Among a king's most important roles was to act as the chief priest of the state religion or national deity*. As priest, the king stood at the point of contact between the realm of the gods and that of humans. He served as both a symbol of divine power on earth and a mediator between humans and the gods.

In fulfilling his role as the chief priest, a king had several practical responsibilities, including building and maintaining temples, performing religious rites and ceremonies, attending religious festivals, and supporting the worship of the gods. The performance of these duties directly affected the society, bringing either prosperity or hardship, depending on whether the king had gained the favor of or caused displeasure to the gods.

A king might also serve as the chief justice for his society. Considered the source of all laws (through the divine inspiration of the gods), a king made and enforced laws and served as the foundation of morality. Although a king rarely dispensed justice himself, he served as the ultimate legal authority of the state, bound only by the higher authority of the gods.

Legitimacy from the Gods

Kings often expressed their relationship to the gods in prayers and official texts. The Hittite king Muwattalli II addressed his patron:

O storm-god of lightning, my lord! . . . [You] took me from [my] mother and raised me. You made me a priest for the sun goddess of Arinna and for all the gods and installed me in kingship for the Land of Khatti.

In this prayer, Muwattalli not only expresses gratitude toward the god but also justifies the legitimacy of his rule by saying that the storm god installed him as king.

* **scepter** ceremonial baton or staff carried by a ruler to show his authority

* **pharaoh** king of ancient Egypt

* **cult** system of religious beliefs and rituals; group following these beliefs

Hierarchy of Rulers

All kings of the ancient Near East were not equal in status or power. The rulers of large kingdoms and empires had much more power and prestige than the kings of smaller states. These differences created a hierarchy of kingship. The Great Kings of Egypt, Babylonia, Assyria, and Khatti were considered the most superior. Next came the rulers of smaller kingdoms and states, many of whom were subordinate to the Great Kings. The lowest levels of the kingship hierarchy consisted of the rulers of local city-states. These relationships were reflected in the administration of empires as well as in the titles and powers of different rulers.

The king was head of the government. As the most superior of officials, kings had overall responsibility for running the government. In practice, however, kings generally wielded their authority through a host of appointed officials. This was especially true in large empires, where the king could not possibly personally oversee all aspects of government.

The foremost role of a Near Eastern king was that of military leader and protector of the kingdom. As commander of the armies, the king was responsible for the organization, maintenance, and direction of the troops. Although these tasks were delegated generally to subordinates, the king was ultimately responsible for military decisions. Some kings, such as NARAM-SIN, ASHURNASIRPAL II, and SHALMANESER III, actually led troops into battle and distinguished themselves as warriors. SARGON II was killed defending his kingdom against an invasion of nomadic Cimmerians.

Symbols of Power and Kingship. The power and authority of kings was represented by various titles and visual symbols. Among the most obvious symbols of kingship was a king's titulary, or titles. While these differed from society to society, they often included references to the king's relationship to the gods, the territory he controlled, and terms of honor and respect. The title Great King applied only to the rulers of the greatest states, including Egypt, Assyria, Babylonia, and the Hittite kingdom of KHATTI.

Other symbols of kingship included crowns, scepters*, thrones, and palaces. In ancient Egypt, the pharaoh* wore several crowns, each representing the regions of Egypt. Scepters, such as a mace, generally served as symbols of authority. Thrones represented the social differences between the king and his subjects. Royal palaces, designed and decorated to awe visitors, also served as powerful symbols of kingship.

Such symbols of kingship were bestowed on kings during important and elaborate ceremonies, such as the king's accession to the throne and his coronation. It was also during these ceremonies that the power and authority of the gods were transferred to the king.

Succession to the Throne. In most cases, kingship was a hereditary institution in the ancient Near East, usually passed from the king to a male relative. This was often a son, but kings sometimes chose other male relatives to succeed them, including brothers, nephews, brothers-in-law, and sons-in-law. When there was no male heir, a woman might rise to the throne, as in the case of Nefrusobek of the Twelfth Dynasty in Egypt. She took the royal titles and reigned as king. Sometimes, to avoid disputes over succession, kings established a co-regency, in which they ruled alongside a chosen successor to help establish that individual's legitimacy and gain support for him.

Women rulers were rare in the ancient Near East. Although women from royal families usually played only a minor role in governing, some gained a great deal of power or became the head of a religious cult*. Others ruled as regents*, wielding authority on behalf of heirs too young to rule themselves. For instance HATSHEPSUT was regent for her stepson, but she soon seized power, declaring herself to be pharaoh by an oracle* for AMUN. (*See also* **Ahab; Ahmose; Akhenaten; Artaxerxes I, II, and III;**

Kish

* **regent** person appointed to govern while the rightful monarch is too young or unable to rule

* **oracle** priest or priestess through whom a god is believed to speak; also, the location (such as a shrine) where such utterances are made

Ashurbanipal; Cambyses II; Cyrus the Great; Darius I and Darius III; Djoser; Dynasties; Esarhaddon; Government; Hammurabi; Khattushili I; Khattushili III; Nabonidus; Nabopolassar; Nebuchadnezzar II; Necho II; Pharaohs; Ptolemy I; Ramses II; Ramses III; Sargon I; Sennacherib; Sety I; Shalmaneser V; Shamshi-Adad I; Shulgi; Shuppiluliuma I; Taharqa; Thutmose III; Tiglath-pileser III; Tutankhamen; Ur-Nammu; Wars and Warfare; Xerxes; Zimri-Lim.)

KISH

* **city-state** independent state consisting of a city and its surrounding territory

* **fourth millennium B.C.** years from 4000 to 3001 B.C.

* **ziggurat** in ancient Mesopotamia, a multistory tower with steps leading to a temple on the top

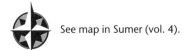

See map in Sumer (vol. 4).

Kish, located in present-day Iraq, just east of BABYLON, was an ancient Mesopotamian city-state*, inhabited as early as the fourth millennium B.C.* The city declined in importance later but remained occupied until the A.D. 600s. Kish was important throughout Mesopotamian history. According to Sumerian texts, it was the seat of the first Sumerian kings. The title King of Kish was a high-ranking one, and some Mesopotamian kings took this title to make others acknowledge their supremacy.

The excavations at Kish have yielded the remains of many structures, including two of the earliest-known Mesopotamian palaces. The two palaces, which testify to the importance of the king of Kish, were separated from the rest of the city by solid defensive walls. In one of the palaces, the main wing contained long corridors that formed a double enclosure around the royal rooms and courts.

The city also contained two ziggurats* and two temples, probably dedicated to the god Zababa and the goddess ISHTAR, patron gods of the city. King HAMMURABI and his son SAMSU-ILUNA both ordered reconstruction of the Zababa temple in the 1700s B.C., making it stronger and more elaborate. An inscription on the temple announced that Samsu-iluna was the god ENLIL's "favorite king," and that the god ordered him to rebuild a temple worthy of Zababa and Ishtar.

The cemeteries at Kish have yielded POTTERY, SEALS, and sophisticated metal objects, such as chariots and carts. The number of tombs and the valuable objects buried in them indicate that Kish had a large, wealthy population.

KNOSSOS

* **second millennium B.C.** years from 2000 to 1001 B.C.

* **Neolithic period** final phase of the Stone Age, from about 9000 to 4000 B.C.

* **colonnade** row of regularly spaced columns or pillars

Knossos (NAHS•suhs) was the chief city of CRETE during the second millennium B.C.* Its ruins lie about five miles inland from the present-day city of Heraklion, located on Crete's north coast. The site of Knossos was first occupied by a Neolithic period* culture from Anatolia (present-day Turkey) before the year 6000 B.C. New immigrants arrived at the beginning of the Early Bronze Age, in about 3000 B.C. Around 2000 B.C., an early palace with a large, rectangular central court was built at Knossos, but it was destroyed by an EARTHQUAKE around 1700 B.C.

A second, more magnificent palace was constructed on the ruins of the first, with staircases, colonnades*, and walls decorated with colorful frescoes*. The palace also had an elaborate drainage system, built with clay pipes, and rooms with large urns that may have been used to store oil, grains, and other foods.

* **fresco** method of painting in which color is applied to moist plaster so that it becomes chemically bonded to the plaster as it dries; also, a painting done in this manner

The palace is considered the most magnificent artifact of the MINOAN CIVILIZATION. Evidence suggests that power over Knossos may have shifted from the Minoans to the Mycenaeans from mainland Greece during the 1400s B.C. Palaces in Crete were destroyed by fires of unknown origin around 1400 B.C. After the destruction of its palace, Knossos was no longer a major city, but it remained in existence as a small town under Mycenaean control.

Excavation of the site of Knossos was begun in the late A.D. 1800s by the English archaeologist* Sir Arthur Evans. Evans worked at excavating Knossos for more than 30 years. The main building he unearthed was huge, and its features are astounding. The palace appears to have been three stories high and to have contained several dozen rooms arranged around a courtyard. Evans reconstructed many parts, some in ways that modern archaeologists believe are incorrect. (*See also* **Mycenae and the Mycenaeans.**)

* **archaeologist** scientist who studies past human cultures, usually by excavating material remains of human activity

Kumarbi was known as the father of the gods in the pantheon* of the HURRIANS, peoples who dominated northern SYRIA and MESOPOTAMIA in the 1400s B.C. He was the central figure in a series of mythological narratives known as the Kumarbi Cycle. In the late 1400s B.C., the HITTITES of ANATOLIA (present-day Turkey) translated the Kumarbi Cycle from Hurrian into their own language, inscribing it on clay tablets. These tablets were later found at KHATTUSHA, the capital of the Hittite empire.

* **pantheon** all the gods of a particular culture

The Kumarbi Cycle was apparently recited aloud for the entertainment and education of the Hittite people. The stories served to help the Hittites understand the personalities of their gods so that they could behave in a manner that would please the deities and ensure their continued blessing. The narratives in this work, including such stories as *Heavenly Kingship* and the *Song of Ullikummi,* describe the battles for power among the gods, including Kumarbi's struggles to achieve and then retain his control over other deities.

In these stories, Kumarbi dethrones ANU from his position as king of the heavens by biting off his genitals, just as Kronos did to Uranos in Greek mythology. In revenge, Anu causes Kumarbi to give birth to the storm god TESHUB and two other gods. Teshub quickly overpowers Kumarbi and banishes him. Kumarbi seeks revenge by fathering a monster, named Ullikummi, who temporarily dethrones Teshub. This monster grows out of the ocean until his head reaches the heavens, threatening all the gods. At first, Teshub is unsuccessful in his battle against Ullikummi. Eventually, however, he descends into the ocean in his chariot and defeats Kumarbi and his monstrous son in a great battle.

The kingdom of Kush was located in Upper Nubia (present-day northern central Sudan). Around 2000 B.C., Egyptian armies began to move south into Nubia, conquering the land. The Egyptians valued Kush because it was located along trade routes that ran to the Red Sea. Along these routes, merchant caravans carried ivory, gold, emeralds, and slaves.

Kush and Meroë

Meroë (MER•uh•wee), located on the east bank of the NILE RIVER, became the kingdom's most prosperous city.

During the early years of Egyptian control, Kush was governed by an Egyptian viceroy* and other officials, including Nubians. The Egyptians wanted to spread their culture, while Kushites attempted to preserve Nubian culture. Both succeeded. Kushites used Egyptian hieroglyphics* but had their own spoken language. They worshiped Egyptian gods, such as AMUN, but continued to worship their own gods as well. They built pyramids as tombs, but not in the Egyptian style.

By the 900s B.C., Egyptian control over Kush had greatly weakened. An independent kingdom of Kush developed around 850 B.C., with its capital at Napata. By around 725 B.C., the Kushites had regained control of the land, conquered Egypt, and reigned over Egypt during its Twenty-Fifth Dynasty. However, the Kushites did not rule Egypt for long. By around 657 B.C., they were driven out by invading Assyrians (conquerors from northern Mesopotamia). Nevertheless, Kush remained independent. Soon after fleeing Egypt, the Kushites moved their capital from Napata to Meroë, farther south.

Meroë had many natural advantages. The small amount of rain it received annually was enough to grow grass for raising animals such as Nubian horses, which were famous throughout the ancient Near East for their strength. The region also had sandstone for building material and clay, from which the Kushites made distinctive white and black pottery. The city also had iron ore for a robust smelting* industry and timber to fuel it. All this enabled Meroë to prosper.

The citizens who prospered in Meroë built temples, palaces, homes, and tombs. The area of Meroë where the rulers lived contained two large palaces, audience halls, living quarters for the palace staff, and a Roman-

* **viceroy** one who governs a country or province as a monarch's representative; royally appointed official

* **hieroglyphics** system of writing that uses pictorial characters, or hieroglyphs, to represent words or ideas

* **smelt** to heat ore for the purpose of extracting pure material

This stela of King Amanikhabale of Meroë was excavated at the Amun temple in Meroë. It contains a fragment of Merotic writing that has not been deciphered to date. Although the meaning of the writing is unknown, scholars have been able to interpret the names of rulers.

style bath connected by channels to a nearby well. A temple dedicated to Amun was typical of the combination of Egyptian and Nubian influences that dominated the culture. The walls of the temple were covered with Egyptian-style reliefs* of such Egyptian gods as Amun, OSIRIS, ISIS, and HORUS. However, the faces of the sculptures look Nubian rather than Egyptian.

* **relief** sculpture in which material is cut away to show figures raised from the background

Meroë continued to prosper for many years. Yet, its location along important trade routes and its rich iron ore deposits and gold and emerald mines attracted conquerors. In the A.D. 200s, Axum, a city in the highlands of northern Ethiopia, began to dominate the region. The final collapse of Meroë came when Axum invaded and conquered the city in the A.D. 300s. (*See also* **Nubia and the Nubians; Sudan.**)

* **nomadic** referring to people who travel from place to place to find food and pasture

In ancient times, the advancement from hunting and gathering to farming and herding allowed formerly nomadic* people to stay in one place over long periods of time. This shift to living in villages and later, in towns and cities concentrated the population and allowed for the development of new kinds of labor. People needed to perform different tasks in order for society to function.

In the ancient Near East, the great advances in ART, ARCHITECTURE, and AGRICULTURE could not have occurred without the work of thousands of organized laborers. Whether laborers were involved in building monuments or in growing food on the ruler's land, they were probably employed, for at least part of the year, by a temple or a palace.

Types of Laborers. The types of laborers in the ancient Near East can be divided into free, forced, semifree, and slave. The number of people in each category depended on the society and time period in which they worked. Free laborers probably existed in all societies to some degree, but they were the rarest type of workers in each society. These workers were paid wages, in either grain or silver, for their work. They probably were at the highest skill levels and had some freedom to choose for whom they worked and when they worked.

See color plate 12, vol. 2.

Forced laborers were free people who were required to give the palace or the temple a certain amount of their time each year. This was the earliest form of TAXATION; instead of taking money, the government demanded the people's time. Forced laborers were given rations of food and wool in exchange for their work. Almost all working members of a society were required to participate in forced labor.

In the most general sense, semifree labor included people who went into debt and had to work for the palace or temple to pay off their debt. They were also paid in rations, not wages.

Slaves were people who could be bought and sold. They were usually foreign-born captives, although they could also be indigenous*. Slaves generally worked inside households, which allowed their owners to keep an eye on them.

* **indigenous** referring to the original inhabitants of a region

Whatever their status, most workers were paid in the same "currency": wool and grain. There was also often little difference in the

Labor and Laborers

* **thresh** to crush grain plants so that the seeds or grains are separated from the stalks and husks

* **artisan** skilled craftsperson

* **scribe** person of a learned class who served as a writer, editor, or teacher

* **diviner** person who foretells the future

* **ziggurat** in ancient Mesopotamia, a multistory tower with steps leading to a temple on the top

Payment for Work Done

The Hittite Laws from the second millennium B.C. (years from 2000 to 1001 B.C.) were among the most detailed in the Near East. Law 158 describes the wages paid an unskilled laborer:

If a man hires himself out for the harvest (on the understanding) that he will bind the sheaves, (that) the bound (sheaves) will get on the wagon, (that) he will bring it into the barn, and (that) they will clear the threshing floor, his wages for three months shall be 30 parisu [390 gallons] of barley. If a woman hires herself out for the harvest, her wages for two months shall be 12 parisu [156 gallons] of barley.

This law reflects the fact that women in the ancient Near East were not paid the same wages as men.

amount laborers were paid, although wages, which were paid by the day, were worth more than monthly rations.

Most of the laborers in the ancient Near East were PEASANTS who worked in agriculture. They also performed most of the manual labor and might find themselves working as carpenters, miners, tanners, bricklayers, or millers. If the crops did not need to be sowed, weeded, harvested, or threshed*, then a laborer might repair the irrigation system or help build a new one. Generally, labor was highly specialized only among the most advanced artists and artisans*, such as metalworkers and stone carvers and those in the "intellectual" sphere, such as scribes*, physicians, and diviners*.

Mesopotamia. Most of the labor records from ancient Mesopotamia come from the palaces and the temples. The state was the largest employer, and the system of forced labor enabled the state to construct enormous public works projects such as the IRRIGATION system. This system was probably built by thousands of workers, both forced and semifree. After it was built, the state continued to employ manual laborers to maintain and repair the canals.

Large numbers of workers were also involved in the construction of buildings, including palaces, temples, and ziggurats*. When building a new capital city or rebuilding an old one, the state employed thousands of workers to construct city walls, gates, administrative buildings, and living quarters.

Generally, in early Mesopotamian society, if women and children were recorded as workers, it meant that they were semifree labor and among the poorest members of society. They were commonly put to work preparing and weaving cloth. For instance, during the Third Dynasty of Ur (ca. 2112–2004 B.C.), there is evidence of a textile factory that employed 6,000 workers, mostly women and children. Women were also employed to grind grain. In addition to these tasks, records of the time reveal that women also had to clear canals, tow boats, and gather and carry reeds.

Egypt. In ancient Egypt, the majority of organized labor was controlled by the state, although there were private landowners who hired or bought laborers. The greatest task for which labor was employed apart from farming was to build tombs for the kings and members of their households. Most of the laborers who helped build the great Egyptian monuments such as the PYRAMIDS at GIZA were peasants. They were used as forced labor by the government during the seasons between planting and harvesting, when there was less farmwork to be done.

Throughout ancient Egyptian history, women seem to have had some flexibility when it came to work. In addition to farming and the traditional household tasks, they worked as millers, bakers, spinners, weavers, musicians, and dancers. Some even held high offices.

Anatolia. The HITTITE empire of ANATOLIA (present-day Turkey) was made up of large cities dominated by government, where specialized labor thrived, and small villages, where labor was more a communal activity. As in the rest of the Near East, people were required to provide the

Dating from around 1900 B.C., this Old Babylonian clay plaque shows a wood-worker carving a wooden table leg. Wood-workers who achieved a high degree of skill and mastery were in demand, partly because there was a shortage of them. Royal courts attempted to secure the best artisans, which sometimes required going far from the local area. Often specialized artisans were lent by one ruler to another, especially when certain regions became well known for skilled work in certain fields.

government with their labor for a portion of the year. Very little evidence of independent enterprise exists.

The Hittites had very specific laws governing labor and payment, and unlike many other Near Eastern societies, some of those laws favored the worker. For example, if a worker was injured, the responsible party was required to take care of the worker while he recovered and to pay the physician's fees and an additional fee once the worker recovered. Wages were paid to workers either in silver or in grain. Wages were fixed for certain forms of labor.

Most occupations were male dominated, but there is evidence that women served as weavers, farmworkers, cooks, innkeepers, millers, musicians, singers, dancers, and medical workers.

The Levant. As was true elsewhere in the Near East, the rulers of the Levant* used forced labor. In the city of UGARIT, men were forced to spend a portion of each year in service to both Ugarit's king and his Hittite overlord.

According to the Hebrew BIBLE, King Solomon employed 30,000 Israelites for four months each year for forced labor. After around 1100 B.C., the majority of laborers were free, although they still paid taxes in the form of work. The Israelites, particularly the religious leaders, disliked forced labor. This has caused historians to speculate that forced labor was

* **Levant** lands bordering the eastern shores of the Mediterranean Sea (present-day Syria, Lebanon, and Israel), the West Bank, and Jordan

Lagash

imposed only on non-Israelites such as Canaanites. However, this was probably not true because during the reigns of Solomon and DAVID, at least, forced labor probably included Israelites as well. (*See also* **Land Use and Ownership; Markets; Mining; Nomads and Nomadism; Palaces and Temples; Servants; Slaves and Slavery; Work.**)

* **city-state** independent state consisting of a city and its surrounding territory

* **archaeological** referring to the study of past human cultures, usually by excavating material remains of human activity

* **fourth millennium** B.C. years from 4000 to 3001 B.C.

* **reservoir** place where water is collected and stored for future use

* **cuneiform** world's oldest form of writing, which takes its name from the distinctive wedge-shaped signs pressed into clay tablets

* **stela** stone slab or pillar that has been carved or engraved and serves as a monument; *pl.* stelae

Lagash (LA•gash) was a city-state* of ancient Sumer, a region located between the Tigris and Euphrates Rivers in southern MESOPOTAMIA. Archaeological* discoveries indicate that Lagash was inhabited as early as the fourth millennium B.C.*, but it did not flourish until around 2400 B.C.

Lagash was known for its building projects. The city's inhabitants built irrigation works to bring water from the surrounding rivers and even built reservoirs* to preserve the valuable water supply. These works were sophisticated for the time and included devices that controlled the water's direction and flow.

The people of Lagash believed that water was provided by deities, such as their patron god, Ningirsu. They built a temple complex called the Bagara to honor him. Another oval temple complex was dedicated to the goddess ISHTAR (Inanna). There also was a temple dedicated to the high god ENLIL.

Lagash was also well known for its warfare. Royal INSCRIPTIONS and cuneiform* tablets provide accounts of wars between Lagash and other city-states in Sumer, especially UR and UMMA. One of the most famous monuments found at Lagash is a stela* known as the Stela of the Vultures, which celebrates the military victory of Lagash over Umma.

Around 2300 B.C., Lagash fell to SARGON I, the king of Akkad, a city-state in central Mesopotamia. However, around 2100 B.C., Lagash revived and prospered under the leadership of its governor, GUDEA, who restored peace and prosperity during his rule. Sculptors in Lagash created many statues of Gudea with cuneiform inscriptions proclaiming his achievements. (*See also* **Sumer and the Sumerians.**)

Lamps

See *Furnishings and Furniture.*

* **domestication** adaptation for human use

In the ancient Near East, humans began taming wild land when they began farming. They chose areas where there was enough water and where they could easily turn the soil. AGRICULTURE was closely followed by the domestication* of animals and herding. Therefore, early humans settled near lands that also served as good pastures for their animals. The earliest societies were probably organized as simple, communal villages, where the people grew food to feed themselves.

As society became more complex, the purpose and organization of farming and herding changed. People began to gather around the regions

44

where farming was most successful. The settlements became large, leading to the growth of towns and cities. Soon not all people grew their own food. Grain, the most basic food, became a source of wealth, and ownership of land became important. For these reasons, ancient Near Eastern peoples began to draw boundaries around their property, and land was bought, sold, and held, with some people acquiring more than others.

Land Use. Water and the control of it have been key to the use of land. Humans began to control the water supply to their crops before 5000 B.C. This first occurred along the TIGRIS RIVER and the EUPHRATES RIVER in MESOPOTAMIA and along the NILE RIVER in Egypt. As agriculture developed and advanced, cities came into being. The existence and stability of cities, in turn, provided farmers with the protection to move into uncharted territory and therefore to increase their lands. Cities also provided large, centrally controlled workforces that could carry out huge public improvement projects such as irrigation and canal systems.

Still, most land in the ancient Near East was left wild because it was either unsuited for farming or was too far away from where people lived. This wild land was used by herders to graze their animals. The largest amount of farmland was used for growing grain. People used small plots of land for private gardens and vegetable plots. Land was also used for planting a relatively small number of orchards.

Landownership. Most of the information about landownership in the ancient Near East comes from excavations of tax records at the great temples and palaces. However, scholars have found that it is difficult to tell the difference between a palace's tax records (which would mean someone else owned the land) and its rental records (which would mean the palace owned the land). In addition, these excavations have yielded almost no information on the lands owned by small farmers. Notwithstanding, scholars believe that most ancient Near Eastern societies had private land ownership. This was probably even true in Egypt, where historians once believed that the rulers owned everything.

In most societies, there were many types of landowners—peasant farmers, large landowners, and rulers and priests. The rulers and priests generally owned more land than most others. Therefore, they required more people to work the land. They used two main methods to gather labor. One was forced labor, in which PEASANTS were required to work for the palace or temple as a form of TAXATION. Another was semifree labor, in which individuals gave themselves and their labor to the palace or temple for a period of time (perhaps their entire lives) to repay a debt or because they could not support themselves. Slave labor was less common than previously thought. Occasionally, the palaces and temples might even hire free laborers.

As with the temples and palaces, large landowners employed semifree and slave laborers to work their fields. (Forced laborers were generally only used on state lands.) Peasant farmers worked on land that they owned or on land owned by someone else. The latter form of farming is called sharecropping. In this system, the peasant retained a portion of the crop, and a portion went to the landowner. If the farmer provided all the

The Life of an Egyptian Farmer

Many school texts in ancient Egypt described the everyday life of a farmer. The descriptions were often satirical and poked fun at the farmer. They were written to encourage students to stay in school. In one of these texts, a farmer goes through a series of unfortunate experiences. First, his oxen are eaten by jackals, and he has to sell his clothes to buy a new team. Then as he plants his crop, all the seeds are eaten by a snake. He replants the crop, using borrowed seeds. Still, it seems that at the harvest, he has no grain. He and his wife are beaten up, and their children are taken away in chains.

Land Use and Ownership

tools, animals, and seed, he received two-thirds of the crop, and the landowner received one-third.

Mesopotamia. The Sumerians and Babylonians of southern Mesopotamia used the floodwaters of the Tigris and Euphrates Rivers to cultivate their crops. However, they had to devise a system to control the floodwaters because they came in when the crops were planted. The Mesopotamians built an elaborate system of levees* and canals to control and save the floodwaters and to divert water from the rivers in the dry months. Soon Mesopotamian farmers became expert in preventing flood damage to their crops and were often the most productive in the region.

From 5000 to 1595 B.C., more northern Mesopotamians owned land than did southern Mesopotamians. Moreover, land management practices differed between Akkad in the north and Sumer in the south. Mesopotamians bought and sold land until the time of the Third Dynasty of Ur (ca. 2112–2004 B.C.), when land sales seem to have ended abruptly. Many scholars believe that this was simply because land sales were not reported during that period. After the Third Dynasty of Ur, however, the sale of land began again (or began to be reported again). When the Kassites controlled the region, between about 1595 and 1158 B.C., the king began to award grants of land as gifts. The boundaries of such land grants were marked by stone monuments called *kudurrus*.

In Egypt. The Nile River was the source of agriculture in Egypt. Unlike the flooding in Mesopotamia, the Nile floods were predictable. Each year, the waters spread over the plains, depositing a thick layer of rich silt* on the land. After the waters subsided, the Egyptians could plant their crops in the moist floodplain, which remained wet until the harvest, about three months later. They planted their grains at the edge of the floodplain and used other lands for gardens and orchards. Lands that did not drain properly were used as pasture.

Modern scholars agree that private individuals owned some land and that land was consistently cheap. However, public institutions (the state and the temples) owned the majority of land. Throughout ancient Egyptian history, women could own land and rent it out to tenants.

Syria and the Levant. Using dry farming*, the people of ancient SYRIA and the Levant* cultivated such crops as barley and planted orchards. By the second millennium B.C.*, Levantine farmers began to manipulate the region's hilly land by building terraces.

In ancient EBLA, the palace owned most of the land and could give gifts of land to loyal subjects. The Canaanites and Israelites believed that all land belonged to god, who then allocated it among various families or clans. By the late 700s B.C., however, landowners began to buy enormous amounts of land, leaving many peasants poor and landless. Canaanite and Israelite kings also owned large amounts of land, which they often gave as a reward to high officials.

Anatolia. Most land in ANATOLIA (present-day Turkey) was owned as small farms or was used for herding. Palaces and temples also owned a

* **levee** embankment or earthen wall alongside a river that helps prevent flooding

* **silt** soil or other sediment carried and deposited by moving water

* **dry farming** farming that relies on natural moisture retained in the ground after rainfall

* **Levant** lands bordering the eastern shores of the Mediterranean Sea (present-day Syria, Lebanon, and Israel), the West Bank, and Jordan

* **second millennium** B.C. years from 2000 to 1001 B.C.

good deal of land, but they were not nearly as powerful as those in Egypt and Mesopotamia. Anatolian farmers and herders were organized into villages. In free villages, farmers owned the land, the village owned it communally, or the villagers sharecropped palace lands. In another type of village, people worked the land belonging to the king or a landowner. In a third type of village, the people worked for and belonged to state institutions, including palaces, temples, or royal tombs. (*See also* **Animals, Domestication of; Canals; Cereal Grains; Environmental Change; Irrigation; Slaves and Slavery.**)

LANGUAGES

* **dialect** regional form of a spoken language with distinct pronunciation, vocabulary, and grammar

* **diplomacy** practice of conducting negotiations between kingdoms, states, or nations

* **Semitic** of or relating to a language family that includes Akkadian, Aramaic, Arabic, Hebrew, and Phoenician

* **Levant** lands bordering the eastern shores of the Mediterranean Sea (present-day Syria, Lebanon, and Israel), the West Bank, and Jordan

* **third millennium** B.C. years between 3000 and 2001 B.C.

The people of the ancient Near East spoke hundreds of languages and dialects* over a period of several thousand years. Even during a short period of time, a region's population could include speakers of many languages, and people were generally aware of the multitude of tongues used by other peoples. For example, an inscription of the Babylonian king HAMMURABI (ruled ca. 1792–1750 B.C.) mentions the people of lands to the east "whose land is far and whose tongue is confused." Sometimes, however, one particular language became commonly spoken in large regions, perhaps because it was brought by a conquering kingdom.

A language that is widely used for communication among speakers of different languages is called a lingua franca. In the modern world, English is a lingua franca. Several languages served the same function in the ancient Near East. These languages—used for trade, diplomacy*, or literature—spread across large areas, replacing other tongues or becoming a region's second language.

Language experts called linguists have divided the world's ancient and modern languages into several large categories called families. A few languages, however, bear no relation to the recognized families, and their origins remain a mystery.

Major Language Families. Most of the ancient Near Eastern languages belong to one of two major language groups. The first is the Afro-Asiatic family, which is also called the Hamito-Semitic or Semito-Hamitic family. The other is the Indo-European family.

Many important languages of the ancient and modern Near East belong to the Afro-Asiatic family. This large family can be divided into Semitic* languages and Hamitic languages.

The Semitic subfamily includes the dominant languages spoken in MESOPOTAMIA, the Levant*, and Arabia since at least the middle of the third millennium B.C.* At various times, a Semitic language served as a lingua franca for the whole region; Akkadian was the lingua franca during the second millennium B.C. (years from 2000 to 1001 B.C.), Aramaic from around 700 B.C. to around A.D. 600, and Arabic since then.

The Semitic subfamily of languages can be further divided into East Semitic and West Semitic languages. The Old Akkadian, Assyrian, and Babylonian dialects for the Akkadian language of Mesopotamia, and perhaps the Eblaite language of Syria belong to the East Semitic group. The

𐤏𐤁𐤉𐤅𐤄𐤃𐤂𐤁𐤀𐤊𐤆𐤈𐤘𐤖𐤀𐤅𐤘𐤓𐤏𐤑𐤌𐤋𐤊𐤁𐤏𐤁𐤉𐤅𐤄𐤃𐤂𐤁𐤀𐤊𐤆𐤈𐤘

Languages

* **archaeologist** scientist who studies past human cultures, usually by excavating material remains of human activity

West Semitic group includes the languages of Ethiopia, Arabia, and the Levant. The Phoenician and Hebrew tongues are West Semitic, as is Aramaic, which was an official language of the PERSIAN EMPIRE. Some of the Hebrew BIBLE was written in Aramaic. Archaeologists* have found Aramaic texts from Egypt to Afghanistan.

The Hamitic subfamilies include ancient Egyptian, Berber, Cushitic, and Chadic. The ancient Egyptian language, which existed in different forms over at least 4,000 years, can be subdivided into Late Egyptian, demotic Egyptian, and Coptic. The languages of the Berber, Cushitic, and Chadic subfamilies include many modern languages and dialects spoken by millions of people.

The INDO-EUROPEAN LANGUAGES are thought to have originated in the region north of the Black Sea. Most modern European languages, and some of western and central Asia, belong to this family. People in various parts of the ancient Near East spoke languages belonging to three Indo-European branches, or subfamilies: Anatolian, Indo-Iranian, and Greek.

The Anatolian subfamily is one of the oldest Indo-European language groups in the Near East. These languages—now extinct—were spoken in ANATOLIA (present-day Turkey) and northern SYRIA at least as early as the second millennium B.C. Hittite—the language of the ancient HITTITES—is a well-known example of this subfamily. Other Anatolian languages include Luwian, Palaic, Lydian, Lycian, Pisidian, Sidetic, and Carian.

The Indo-Iranian subfamily of languages includes Avestan, the sacred language of Zoroastrianism, and Old Persian. These languages are known to have been spoken in IRAN during and after the first millennium B.C. (years from 1000 to 1 B.C.) They are related to some of the ancient and

Many of the languages of the ancient Near East belong to the Afro-Asiatic or Indo-European families. The Afro-Asiatic languages are further divided into Hamitic languages—spoken in Africa—and Semitic languages—spoken in Mesopotamia, Syria, the Levant, and the Arabian peninsula. Indo-European languages were spoken in Anatolia, Syria, Iran, and Greece. Although Afro-Asiatic languages were more widely spoken in the ancient Near East, today Indo-European languages are among the most widely spoken languages in the world. Both language families include groups that are not listed on this chart.

LANGUAGE FAMILIES OF THE ANCIENT NEAR EAST

Afro-Asiatic Languages

Hamitic Languages	Semitic Languages		
Egyptian	West Semitic		East Semitic
Late Egyptian	Central Semitic	South Semitic	Akkadian
demotic Egyptian	Amorite	South Arabic	Babylonian
Coptic	Canaanite	Ethiopian	Assyrian
Berber	Moabite		Eblaite
Cushitic	Phoenician		
Chadic	Hebrew		
	Aramaic		
	Arabic		

Indo-European Languages

Anatolian	Greek	Indo-Iranian
Hittite	Greek	Avestan
Luwian	Arcadian	Old Persian
Lydian	Aeolic	
Lycian	Doric	
Carian	Ionic	
	Attic	

modern tongues of India and Pakistan, many of which also belong to the Indo-Iranian subfamily.

Greek, which survives today in modern form, has existed in written form since the 1400s B.C. Greek dialects were spoken in western Anatolia and on the islands of the AEGEAN SEA as well as in Greece. The far-ranging conquests of ALEXANDER THE GREAT in the 300s B.C. spread the Greek language throughout the Mediterranean region and western Asia and made Greek the lingua franca of the Hellenistic* era.

Languages Outside Major Families. Some ancient Near Eastern languages, including several important ones, do not fall into either the Indo-European or the Afro-Asiatic language family. Linguists are still working to interpret these languages fully and to determine to which family they belong. Many of these languages survive in a large body of texts, whereas there is only fragmentary evidence for others, increasing the difficulty for the linguists who wish to study them.

The SUMERIAN LANGUAGE is the oldest language in the world for which written texts survive. The earliest documents in this language date from before 3000 B.C. Sumerian, the language of the rulers of southern Mesopotamia, was spoken along with Akkadian and other languages during the third millennium B.C. Akkadian became the official tongue after the conquests of SARGON I of Akkad (2334–2278 B.C.). However, rulers decided to continue to use Sumerian as a written language for scholarly, literary, and religious texts in the same way that Europeans during the Middle Ages used Latin long after they had stopped speaking it.

The language of the Elamites is another tongue with no known ties to other ancient or modern languages. Although Elam was located in southwestern Iran near Mesopotamia, its language—which existed in various forms from around 3500 B.C. to the 300s B.C.—developed independently.

Some ancient Near Eastern languages are known only from names or references in other languages. The language of the KASSITES falls into this category. The Kassites occupied Babylonia from the mid-1500s B.C. until the mid-1100s B.C., but they adopted the Sumerian and Babylonian languages. Their original tongue appears to bear no relation to any other language.

The HURRIANS came to northern and eastern Mesopotamia in the late third millennium B.C. Although speakers of the Assyrian and Hittite languages borrowed many words from Hurrian, the Hurrian language itself has only one known relative, the language of URARTU, a kingdom north of Assyria. The Hurrian and Urartian languages appear to belong to a small language group unrelated to all others. In fact, they may have been closely linked dialects of the same parent language.

Although Hittite belongs to the Anatolian subfamily of Indo-European languages, modern linguists have realized that Hittite texts also contain words or passages in a different language—Hattic. Hattic was spoken by the people who lived in the city of KHATTUSHA before the Hittites made it their capital. The Hittites preserved some traces of Hattic in their religious rituals.

Deciphering Lost Languages. Modern Western scholars have learned the languages of the ancient Near East in three ways. Some languages,

* **Hellenistic** referring to the Greek-influenced culture of the Mediterranean world and western Asia during the three centuries after the death of Alexander the Great in 323 B.C.

Aramaic: Then and Now

The Aramaic language, once the lingua franca of the ancient world, has been in use for thousands of years. The first textual evidence of the Aramaic language, known as Old Aramaic, dates from the 800s B.C. Today modern Aramaic can be subdivided into four branches: Western Aramaic, spoken in three Syrian villages; Central Aramaic, spoken in southeastern Turkey; Eastern Aramaic, spoken in various dialects in and near Kurdistan; and Neo-Mandaic, which is spoken by a small group of people in western Iran.

Lapis Lazuli

* **decipher** to decode and interpret the meaning

including Hebrew and Greek, have been used and studied in Europe since ancient times. Such languages as Arabic and Persian survived and are spoken today. Some languages became extinct, but scholars are sometimes able to decipher* these languages if they were preserved in texts on materials durable enough to survive the passing of centuries.

Many decipherers of ancient languages owe their success to bilingual inscriptions, a term referring to documents that contain the same text in two languages. If one of the languages is known, it can be used as a starting point for a researcher to identify words in the unknown text. Often the first words to be identified are names or terms repeated throughout the text. Deciphering from bilinguals is not simply a matter of substituting new words for known words one by one. Sentence structure and other elements of grammar may differ greatly between the two languages, making the text difficult to interpret.

One of the most famous of all bilingual archaeological texts is the ROSETTA STONE, which provided the key to the decipherment of the ancient Egyptian language in the early A.D. 1800s. The stone contains inscriptions in the Greek language and script, everyday Egyptian from the Hellenistic period in the demotic script, and ancient Egyptian, written in hieroglyphics*. Another famous text used by modern scholars to understand ancient languages is the BEHISTUN INSCRIPTION, a trilingual inscription written in the Old Persian, Akkadian, and Elamite languages. (*See also* **Decipherment; Hamitic Languages; Semitic Languages.**)

* **hieroglyphics** system of writing that uses pictorial characters, or hieroglyphs, to represent words or ideas

* **inlay** fine layer of a substance set into wood, metal, or other material as a form of decoration

* **entrepôt** intermediary center of trade, usually on a caravan or sea route

* **artifact** ornament, tool, weapon, or other object made by humans

Lapis lazuli is a rare, semiprecious stone of deep blue color, sometimes speckled with gold-colored minerals. Greatly prized in the ancient Near East, lapis lazuli was used in making beads, cylinder SEALS, inlays*, JEWELRY, and other decorative objects. The main sources of the stone lay in CENTRAL ASIA, just outside the Near East, and the demand for lapis lazuli helped stimulate interregional trade.

Ancient Mesopotamians and Egyptians believed that lapis lazuli had the power to protect against evil. The stone became popular for jewelry, and trade in lapis lazuli became well established by about 4000 B.C. The main sources of lapis lazuli were in Badakhshan, a mountainous region of Afghanistan far to the northeast of Mesopotamia. A number of sites in eastern IRAN served as entrepôts* where the stone was processed and prepared for distribution to areas throughout the Near East. By about 3500 B.C., an interregional trading network based on lapis lazuli extended from India in the east to Egypt in the west and from Central Asia in the north to the Persian Gulf in the south.

Lapis lazuli was especially prized by Mesopotamian rulers, including the Sumerians, and artifacts* from royal cemeteries at UR demonstrate its use in elite Mesopotamian life. It was often used in combination with gold and carnelian, especially in Sumerian jewelry. Even some Mesopotamian myths mention the importance of lapis lazuli. Wealthy Egyptians also greatly valued the stone for its rarity and beauty, and the finest Egyptian jewelry often contained lapis lazuli. Much of the lapis lazuli that reached Egypt before 3000 B.C. came through the city of UGARIT

in northern SYRIA. Although lapis lazuli never became very popular among the HITTITES, a number of Hittite texts contain references to the beautiful blue stone.

See color plate 5, vol. 1.

LAW

The people of the ancient Near East believed that laws were established by their gods. The king was chosen by the gods as their representative, and he was responsible for communicating the gods' laws to the people and ensuring that they were obeyed. In turn, the people put their faith in the king to protect the weak from the strong and to ensure that they were pleasing the gods. In this capacity, the king served as the supreme legal authority of the land.

Although the king had the most authority, he was not the only source of laws and legal decision making in the ancient Near East. In many societies, the male head of household—usually the father—had a number of legal rights and did not have to defer to the state or the temple for approval of his judgments. After the family, the next legal authority was the village council or town assembly. At this level, legal decisions were based on custom or tradition, not laws.

The final level of the law was the state and its law codes. These codes, however, were not strict rules to be followed. Rather, they were suggestions to the judges on how to decide different types of cases. Even as law codes became more complex, many legal matters, such as that of inheritance, were left up to local customs, because a large segment of the population was illiterate and therefore unable to consult the codes.

Throughout the ancient Near East, many legal transactions took place between people using contracts as a means to document events such as land sales or marriage or divorce agreements. In the Levant* and Mesopotamia, the contract was witnessed and often impressed with seals or fingernail marks. The contract could then be referred to in case of a dispute.

Judicial System. The court systems throughout the ancient Near East shared several characteristics. Trials were usually led by a group of judges. For minor crimes and disputes, such as those over property rights or inheritance, the judges were village or city elders. More serious crimes, such as murder or treason, were referred to a higher court, where decisions were made by state judges appointed by the king. Usually, the final judge was the king himself.

Evidence presented at trials often consisted of the testimony of the witnesses and participants, who testified under oath. If the defendant was convicted at the end of the trial, punishment was usually immediate. Depending on the nature of the crime, the types of punishment included fines, beatings, mutilation, banishment, terms of forced labor, or death. Certain societies punished not only the criminals but also their families or communities, especially in cases of treason.

Mesopotamia. Evidence of laws from the ancient Near East survives in the form of law codes, contracts, and court decisions. Historians know more about the law in ancient Mesopotamia than in other Near Eastern lands

* **Levant** lands bordering the eastern shores of the Mediterranean Sea (present-day Syria, Lebanon, and Israel), the West Bank, and Jordan

Law

This copy of the Code of Hammurabi from the library of Assyrian king Ashurbanipal was excavated at the site of the ancient city of Nineveh. The original code, dating from the 1750s B.C., contained 282 laws and was written by Hammurabi, king of Babylon. The Code of Hammurabi is one of the best-known artifacts of Mesopotamia and perhaps the most famous legal code of antiquity.

* **first millennium** B.C. years from 1000 to 1 B.C.

because the clay tablets on which Mesopotamians wrote have survived very well. Not only are there records of the numerous law codes from Mesopotamia, but reports of court cases and texts for training judges also exist.

In Mesopotamia, the earliest codes of law were the Sumerian codes of kings SHULGI (ruled ca. 2094–2047 B.C.) and Lipit-Ishtar (ruled ca. 1930 B.C.) and the laws of ESHNUNNA (ca. 1800 B.C.). One of the most famous legal codes of the ancient world was the Code of Hammurabi. This code, set by Babylonian king HAMMURABI (ruled ca. 1792–1750 B.C.), was by far the most extensive of the preserved Mesopotamian codes. It was also more severe in its punishments than earlier codes, stating that for some crimes, the perpetrators should be punished by having the same crimes inflicted on themselves.

Other Mesopotamian law documents include records of court cases that summarized the events during the case, the final decision, and sometimes a statement quoting an important participant in the trial. In Babylonia during the first millennium B.C.*, trial records also included quotes of dialogues between the parties agreeing to the terms of the deal. Initially, only one copy of a case was written. In a lawsuit, it was given to the winning party for safekeeping. A contract or sale document was given to the party who was paying the money. In Neo-Babylonian times (612–539 B.C.), a copy was often made for each party.

In the most serious court cases in Mesopotamia, the oaths of those on trial were often combined with a test called an ordeal. One form of ordeal involved swearing an oath to the river god and then jumping into a river. If oath takers were telling the truth, they would survive; if they were not, they would die, because of the river god's knowledge of the truth.

Matters of inheritance in Mesopotamia were based on custom rather than a code. Usually, the majority of an estate went to the oldest son, and the rest of it was divided among younger sons. In Sumer, women were also able to inherit from their fathers if there were no sons.

Egypt. With the exception of some contracts and legal documents, very little evidence of the legal system in ancient Egypt exists. Historians believe that the law was based on local traditions and oral history, not on set legal codes. However, by the time of the New Kingdom (ca. 1539–1075 B.C.), there were certain national laws, particularly in areas where the state had a concern, such as in the runaway of a forced laborer.

Egyptian judicial cases were judged by members of the community, including members of the royal administration and ordinary people. Until the Late Period (664–332 B.C.), Egyptian courts were not permanent institutions, and unlike the situation in the rest of the Near East, the king almost never presided over a case himself. For state trials, there were two high courts, one for northern Egypt and one for southern Egypt, each led by a vizier*. The viziers presided over a tribunal (court of justice) made up of royal officials and possibly priests.

* **vizier** minister of state

National inheritance laws in Egypt probably developed because the elite members of society owned land in different areas and did not want to be subject to many laws that depended on different local traditions. The general law of the New Kingdom was that people could leave their goods and property to whomever they pleased. When a person died without a will, the child who took responsibility for the deceased's burial would inherit the deceased's property.

Hittites. Knowledge of the law the HITTITES comes mostly from their law codes, although there are a few scribal* records and some stories involving legal issues in Hittite literature. Even though no contracts from Hittite culture survive, scholars know that these documents were used because they are referred to in other texts.

The Hittite law codes were unusual in that when a new law was recorded, that law contained the old law it replaced. Moreover, unlike other ancient Near Eastern laws, Hittite laws tended to include statements of what is, as well as what is not, permitted. As a result, historians know that the Old Hittite Laws (ca. 1650 B.C.) had different penalties, depending on whether the victims and criminals were slaves or freemen. The most important difference between the Old Hittite Laws and the New Hittite Laws (ca. 1350–1200 B.C.) was that the later laws took into account a larger variety of legal situations.

The court system of the Old Hittite Kingdom (ca. 1650–1500 B.C.) consisted of the royal court, where the king was judge, and local courts run by magistrates*, who were the elite of the kingdom. These magistrates were chosen by the king and sent to the various districts of the realm. By around 1500 B.C., local elders also served as judges, along with representatives of the king and the district governor.

Hittite punishments were quite lenient compared with those of other societies of the time. Most punishments were in the form of fines. The amount of a fine was only intended to repay the victim, not punish the criminal. In fact, in many cases, the Old Hittite Laws replaced CAPITAL PUNISHMENT with fines or animal sacrifice. However, when the criminal was a slave, capital punishment or mutilation was still used.

Scholars do not know much about inheritance laws among the Hittites, but it appears that sons inherited the family property. Women could not inherit property directly from their fathers.

The Levant. Archaeologists* have found some letters and scribal records from the Levant, but the greatest source of knowledge of the law in the Levant is the Hebrew BIBLE. Most of the Israelite codes are recorded as divine revelations that were given to the people during the period the Israelites spent in the desert after leaving Egypt. Among these are the most famous laws in the Western world—the TEN COMMANDMENTS—which set basic boundaries for how people should behave. The oldest code in the Bible is the Covenant Code, from the Book of Exodus. It covers issues of slavery, theft, and crimes punishable by death.

According to the Bible, among the ancient Israelites, a father's land was divided among his sons, but the oldest son received a double portion. If a man had no male heirs, a daughter could receive an inheritance. However, she had to marry within her tribe so that property belonging to that tribe would not pass to others.

Apart from biblical law, no actual law codes from this region have been found. Nevertheless, letters, contracts, court declarations, and inscriptions have been discovered in both Phoenician and Canaanite ruins.

* **scribal** referring to people of a learned class who served as writers, editors, or teachers

To Catch a Thief

A sort of police force called the Medjay operated during the New Kingdom period in Egypt. After an offense was reported, the Medjay began pursuing suspects. Once a suspected criminal was in custody, the Medjay sometimes used such methods as torture to obtain a confession. One document from Egypt tells the story of a tomb robber who was being questioned under torture: "He was then examined again with the stick, the birch, and the screw. He would not confess anything beyond what he had said."

* **magistrate** person empowered by the state to administer and enforce the law

* **archaeologist** scientist who studies past human cultures, usually by excavating material remains of human activity

Persia. Most of the information about ancient Persia comes from Greek writers and historians. There is almost no direct knowledge of Persian law codes and court procedures. However, it is known that Persian law was based on faithfulness to the Persian god AHURA MAZDA and to the king.

In the court system of Persia, judges were appointed for life by the king. According to the Greek historian HERODOTUS, they judged all types of disputes. Another report says that judges traveled through the countryside judging cases. As in other societies, the king had the final word.

According to Persian law, women did not have the right to inherit. Persian men married more than one wife and also married relatives to ensure that they would have several descendants and that wealth remained within the family. (*See also* **Divorce; Mosaic Law; Property and Property Rights; Slaves and Slavery.**)

Lebanon

See *Phoenicia and the Phoenicians.*

Leprosy

See *Medicine.*

Levant, The

See *Canaan; Israel and Judah; Phoenicia and the Phoenicians; Syria.*

LIBRARIES
AND ARCHIVES

* **cuneiform** world's oldest form of writing, which takes its name from the distinctive wedge-shaped signs pressed into clay tablets

* **papyrus** writing material made by pressing together thin strips of the inner stem of the papyrus plant; *pl.* papyri

After writing was invented in about 3300 B.C., the people of the ancient Near East were able to keep records and accounts of business transactions. Over time, as the frequency and uses of writing increased, people needed to store their documents. This resulted in the creation of libraries where texts and documents were kept for reference and archives where records and historical documents were preserved.

In Mesopotamia and other places where the cuneiform* script was used, texts were written on clay tablets as well as on wooden boards covered with wax. Unfortunately, very few of these boards have survived. Consequently, our knowledge of Mesopotamian archives and libraries depends almost exclusively on the recovery of clay tablets. In Egypt, there are even fewer surviving records from both libraries and archives because papyrus*, the writing material the Egyptians used, was destroyed more easily than cuneiform tablets. Most of the surviving papyri were recovered from tombs.

Libraries. Libraries in the ancient Near East could be found in temples, palaces, and schools and at the homes of priests. Libraries began as places for storing texts, such as lists of words, samples of different scripts, and practice documents for students to copy. When ancient Near Eastern peoples began to write down and copy LITERATURE around 2500 B.C., libraries became places to store such texts as OMENS, medical knowledge, ASTROLOGY, MYTHOLOGY, magical spells, and wisdom literature, such as the teachings of a father to his son.

In Mesopotamia, temple libraries existed in the Assyrian capitals of Nineveh, Nimrud, and Dur-Sharrukin. All these temples housed important literature and were dedicated to Nabu, the god of scribes*. Palaces in Mesopotamia often did not have libraries at all. One major exception to this was King ASHURBANIPAL's library at Nineveh dating from the 600s B.C. The king personally oversaw the collection and sent scribes to Babylonia to confiscate or copy religious and scholarly texts. By the time Assurbanipal's library was complete, it had at least 1,500 tablets containing the most important literature of the day.

Although there is little archaeological* information available about libraries in ancient Egypt, literary evidence suggests that Egyptians had libraries dating back to the Old Kingdom period (ca. 2675–2130 B.C.) Later texts indicate that members of Egyptian royalty were interested in libraries, suggesting that palace libraries were perhaps more common in Egypt than in Mesopotamia. The most information about Egyptian libraries in Egypt comes from the Ptolemaic dynasty and the Roman era. The most famous library of the ancient world, that in Alexandria, was established in the 200s B.C. Although no trace of this library remains, it was reputed to hold a copy of every known scroll of ancient times in its collection. The library's holdings are believed to have exceeded 400,000 scrolls.

Archives. In ancient times, administrative and business records such as contracts, reports, letters, and ledgers were stored in archives. Today archives also contain old documents that are no longer used but are historically important. In the ancient Near East, archives contained documents that were still in use or that were needed for reference.

Administrative and institutional documents were stored at official archives. Temple archives in Mesopotamia were considered official even though a temple only stored those records that were directly related to its own business. Palaces, on the other hand, not only had archives relating to the business of the palace, such as lists of personnel and what they were paid, but also those relating to the business of the country, such as international treaties.

In Mesopotamia, even people of modest means had private archives that contained contracts, land use or sale documents, and records of lawsuits. The archives of merchants or traders probably contained business ledgers as well as lists of goods and their sale prices.

In ancient Egypt, more temple archives have survived than any other kind. However, historians believe that the state also kept extensive records, particularly with regard to military matters. Private household archives from ancient Egypt have been found as well. It is known that archival material was used in court cases throughout ancient Egyptian history. Documents could be binding over many generations, and the courts would refer back to documents created hundreds of years before.

* **scribe** person of a learned class who served as a writer, editor, or teacher

* **archaeological** referring to the study of past human cultures, usually by excavating material remains of human activity

One of the most impressive libraries of the ancient Near East was located in the palace of Assyrian king Ashurbanipal at Nineveh. Ashurbanipal's goal was to collect the most important scholarly and religious texts. Dating from the 600s B.C., this dictionary of synonyms, inscribed on a tablet made of baked clay, was part of Ashurbanipal's collection.

Library Rivalry

According to legend, parchment—writing material made from the skin of sheep or goats—became widely used because of a rivalry between libraries. In the 100s B.C., the library at the city of Pergamum in Anatolia was said to be almost as magnificent as the one in Alexandria in Egypt. The Egyptians wanted their library to be the best and refused to supply papyrus—the chief writing material of the time—to Pergamum. Because the scribes of Pergamum could no longer write on papyrus, they turned to using parchment instead. Parchment eventually replaced papyrus as a writing material.

Storage and Retrieval of Texts. Large libraries and archives had to organize all their documents for easy access. Labels were used to identify collections of tablets that were kept in baskets, boxes, or trays. Throughout the ancient Near East, both papyri and cuneiform tablets were stored in three main ways: in containers such as clay jars, wooden or reed boxes, or leather bags; on open shelves; and in niches built into walls.

Cuneiform tablets were organized by shape, size, and the layout of their text. Initially, library texts were not very long, and there was no great need to catalog the documents. Later when scribes began to write reference works as long as 100 tablets, the catalogs recorded their incipits—the first words or lines of each tablet. This system enabled people to find the tablet they needed. After 600 B.C., scribes used ink to write identifying information on the edge of a tablet in Aramaic, the common language of the time.

In ancient Egypt, different types of documents were written on papyrus rolls of various heights. This made it easy to catalog and identify them. In addition, papyri commonly began with a date, which could immediately be seen when one opened a scroll. Such papyri were organized by date. Libraries in Egypt from the Greco-Roman period (332 B.C.–A.D. 642) contained lists of texts on the walls. Some scholars believe that these were an inventory of the library's contents and that such lists were used in many Egyptian libraries from long before the Greco-Roman period. (*See also* **Books and Manuscripts; Clay Tablets; Cuneiform; Hieroglyphics; Record Keeping; Scribes; Writing.**)

LIBYANS

* **nomadic** referring to people who travel from place to place to find food and pasture

See map in Phoenicia and the Phoenicians (vol. 3).

In ancient times, the Libyans (LI•bee•uhnz) were a partially nomadic* people who lived in the desert lands west of Egypt. Although Egypt had seized control of other neighboring lands, such as NUBIA and KUSH to the south, it was not interested in controlling the Libyans' land. This was because Libya did not contain valuable raw materials or lie on any important trade routes.

However, the Egyptians wanted to prevent the Libyans from entering Egypt. Over the centuries, Libyans had migrated to Egypt in search of a better life. As the Libyan population increased in Egypt, especially as a result of several mass migrations, their power increased as well. Many of them lived like Egyptians and worshiped Egyptian gods, but they continued to honor their Libyan chiefs.

The Egyptians employed captured Libyans as professional soldiers, or mercenaries. As payment for their service, the Egyptians gave the Libyan soldiers land. This increased the Libyans' power and wealth. The Libyans also married into the Egyptian royal family, thus extending and cementing their influence.

Meanwhile, Libyans outside of Egypt had strong kings and armies. RAMSES II (ruled ca. 1279–1213 B.C.) recognized this potential threat and built forts along Egypt's western borders. However, this was not sufficient protection. The Libyan armies made repeated attacks. Egypt managed to repel these incursions, but the attacks left the Egyptian government in disarray. After a series of weakened kings and high priests, Egypt was ripe for infiltration and takeover.

The Libyan rule of Egypt began at the time of the Twenty-second Dynasty (ca. 945–712 B.C.), when Shoshenq I took the throne. Until that time, Thebes had been the royal residence, but Shoshenq ruled from Tanis, in the Nile Delta, which had long been a Libyan stronghold. Shoshenq gave the military considerable power to maintain order. Under his rule, the Egyptian economy prospered. Both Libyans and Egyptians received positions in government, which kept the kingdom unified. His son even married the daughter of his Egyptian predecessor. Shoshenq is best known for his invasion of the Levant*, which increased his kingdom's prestige and wealth. Many scholars identify Shoshenq with an Egyptian king in the Hebrew Bible named Shishaq, who plundered Jerusalem around 925 B.C.

However, this cohesiveness and prosperity did not last. Over the next 200 years, the kingdom was divided by civil wars fought among several rival dynasties. No single ruler was strong enough to unite the various parties into a cooperative group working toward a common goal.

By this time, the Libyan dynasties were ripe for takeover. Around 750 B.C., Nubians from the area of present-day Sudan and southern Egypt seized control of Egypt, initiating the kingdom's Twenty-fifth Dynasty.

* **Levant** lands bordering the eastern shores of the Mediterranean Sea (present-day Syria, Lebanon, and Israel), the West Bank, and Jordan

Life Expectancy

See *Health.*

LIONS

* **Levant** lands bordering the eastern shores of the Mediterranean Sea (present-day Syria, Lebanon, and Israel), the West Bank, and Jordan

* **relief** sculpture in which material is cut away to show figures raised from the background

* **sphinx** imaginary creature with a lion's body and a human head

* **griffin** imaginary creature with a lion's body and an eagle's head and wings

In ancient times, lions roamed wild throughout the Near East. These great beasts were eventually exterminated in most areas, but in parts of the Levant* and MESOPOTAMIA, they continued to live in remote areas until as late as the early A.D. 1900s.

As civilization developed in the ancient Near East, lions increasingly became a danger and nuisance to the people. In many regions, lion hunting became a necessity to prevent attacks on humans and their flocks and herds. Lion hunting was a popular activity of royalty, and the walls of Assyrian palaces contain many reliefs* of kings hunting the beasts from CHARIOTS or on foot. Although the earliest royal lion hunts took place in the wild, the Assyrians later kept lions in enclosures, where they were bred to be hunted by the king within a royal park.

The strength, power, and majestic appearance of lions made them a popular subject in Near Eastern art and literature. Images of lions appeared in many paintings, and lion sculptures were often placed in or near palaces and temples. Lions were also portrayed as protective guardian animals on city gates. In art, lions were often combined with parts of humans or other animals to produce a variety of demons and monsters, including sphinxes*, griffins*, and dragons. In literature, lions often symbolized strength and aggression. In Egypt, the lion was symbolic of the king.

Lions also served as powerful symbols in religion and mythology. A number of gods and goddesses who served as protectors—such as the Sumerian god Ningirsu, the Akkadian goddess Ishtar, the Syrian goddess Atargatis, and the Phrygian goddess Cybele—were associated with lions. The Egyptian goddess Hathor could take the form of Sekhmet, a lioness, when she was angry. (*See also* **Animals in Art; Cats; Hunting.**)

See color plate 2, vol. 3.

LISHT

See map in Pyramids (vol. 4).

L isht, also called al-Lisht, is the modern name of a site in northern Egypt where a field of PYRAMIDS is located. These pyramids were built around 1900 B.C., during the reigns of King Amenemhet I and his son and successor, King Senwosret I.

During his reign, Amenemhet moved Egypt's capital and royal residence from THEBES to a newly built city called Itjtawy, which was located between MEMPHIS and the Faiyum Depression, near the west bank of the Nile. The royal residence at Itjtawy became a model for later royal residences, and the city retained its importance as capital throughout the Middle Kingdom period (ca. 1980–1630 B.C.). Although Itjtawy has never been found, it is certain that its main cemetery was located at Lisht.

The tomb complexes of Amenemhet and Senwosret at Lisht each included a pyramid, a temple, and a number of monuments. Many smaller pyramids and mastabas* were also built at Lisht for high-ranking government officials and members of the royal family. In addition, there were numerous cemeteries containing the graves of common people.

Lisht was first explored in A.D. 1884 by an expedition of the French Institute of Oriental Archaeology. From 1906 through 1934, the site was explored by expeditions sponsored by the Metropolitan Museum of Art in New York. (*See also* **Burial Sites and Tombs; Egypt and the Egyptians.**)

* **mastaba** ancient Egyptian burial structure with long rectangular sides and a flat roof over a burial pit or chamber

Literacy

See Education; Writing.

LITERATURE

* **illiterate** unable to read or write

B efore WRITING was invented, people learned the history, MYTHOLOGY, religious rituals, and songs of their cultures through oral tradition; that is, they memorized what they heard from their elders. The invention of writing meant that information could be transcribed for future generations to read as literature. However, most of the population in the ancient Near East was illiterate*, so the oral tradition remained the most common way for stories and rituals to pass from one generation to the next. Consequently, most ancient literature was written with the understanding that it would be read aloud.

The literature of the ancient Near East can be divided into two main styles of writing: poetry and prose. Poetry includes HYMNS, songs, myths,

* **incantation** written or recited formula of words designed to produce a given effect

* **annals** record of events arranged chronologically by year

* **deity** god or goddess

Title and Author

Works of poetry and prose in the ancient Near East did not generally have titles. Instead, they were known by their incipits—the first few words of their first line. What modern historians call the *Epic of Gilgamesh* was known in the second millennium B.C. as "Surpassing Other Kings" and in the first millennium as "He Who Saw Everything." Moreover, the authors of these ancient literary works remain unknown. The *Epic of Gilgamesh* may be an exception, however. A tablet found in the library of Assyrian king Ashurbanipal attributes its composition to Sin-leqe-unninni, an exorcist.

* **Semitic** of or relating to a language family that includes Akkadian, Aramaic, Arabic, Hebrew, and Phoenician

* **exorcism** removal of evil spirits through specific rituals, incantations, and ceremonies

PSALMS, love poems, and magical incantations*. Prose writing includes stories, law codes, royal INSCRIPTIONS, histories, and annals*. Some types of literature were written in both poetry and prose. Occasionally, an elevated or lyrical prose bridged the two styles.

Poetry. Most literature in Mesopotamia until the end of the Old Babylonian empire (ca. 1900–1600 B.C.) was written in Sumerian, although the language was no longer spoken. Much of this literature was in the form of poetry, although its principles still largely escape modern researchers. Among the earliest pieces of poetry recorded were incantations and short hymns. Hymns were written to deities*, composed for kings to celebrate special occasions in their reigns, or written for specific rituals and ceremonies. In Sumerian literature, there are also narrative poems—poems that tell stories—that contain myths about various gods. For example, *Enki and the World Order* tells the story of the creation of the universe and how it is divided between the gods.

During the time of the Old Babylonian empire, new types of poems became popular. Poetic petitions were prayers addressed and written as letters to the gods. There were also debate poems, which presented arguments between characters representing opposites, such as summer and winter. In these poems, the characters praise themselves and insult each other.

Poetry written in the Sumerian language does not rhyme nor does it have a set rhythm. Various sections of poems are repeated, as are words or phrases. For example:

> King am I, warrior from the womb am I,
> Shulgi am I, mighty male from birth am I,
> Lion fierce of eye, born to be a dragon am I,
> King of the four corners of the universe am I.

Beginning around 2300 B.C., poems were written in Akkadian, a Semitic* language, but it was not until the 1700s B.C. that Akkadian poetry truly began to flower. Among the greatest poems written in Akkadian is the *Epic of Gilgamesh*, which was based on a series of earlier Sumerian poems. The Akkadians also wrote love songs and a great number of exorcism* rituals.

As with the Mesopotamians, hymns and poetry were by far the most common forms of Egyptian literature. Around the end of the Old Kingdom period, a type of protest literature developed. These texts, which criticized mainstream government, took several forms in poetry and could also be written in prose. Egyptians also excelled at love poetry:

> Of graceful step when she treads the earth,
> She has seized my heart in her embrace!
> She causes the neck of every male
> To turn about at the site of her;
> Happy the one whom she embraces!

The best-known literature from the ancient Near East is the Hebrew BIBLE, which contains a great deal of poetry and prose. The most famous

Literature

* **Levant** lands bordering the eastern shores of the Mediterranean Sea (present-day Syria, Lebanon, and Israel), the West Bank, and Jordan

* **secular** nonreligious; connected with everyday life

* **edict** pronouncement of the government that has the force of law

Autobiography was one of the most popular literary genres in ancient Egypt. Usually found inscribed on tombs, autobiographies recounted the deceased subject's deeds in life. The autobiographical inscription on this stela dates from Egypt's Twelfth Dynasty (ca. 1938–1759 B.C.) and recounts the life of Montuwosre, a steward.

Israelite poems are in the Bible, among them the "Song of Solomon" and the Psalms. From elsewhere in the Levant*, at Ugarit, comes a great deal of narrative poetry. The most famous Ugaritic poetry is the BAAL CYCLE, which is a series of stories about the god BAAL. Despite the differences between Hebrew and Ugaritic poetry, they used many of the same phrases, and both used repetition within and between phrases.

In Anatolia, the Hittites wrote songs with a straightforward, strong rhythmic structure and a refrain, a line that is repeated throughout. Most Hittite mythology texts were used for rituals and probably were not told as stories.

Prose. Among the earliest prose pieces in Mesopotamia were the Sumerian KING LISTS. These were part historical and part fictional lists of the leaders in Sumer's history. Other types of early Sumerian prose included stories and riddles, law codes, and royal inscriptions.

The Akkadians contributed to prose by composing works on religious issues written as essays, or as discussions. These could sometimes be written in the form of dialogues or monologues, such as *Dialogue of a Man with His God.* Comic stories, such as *The Poor Man from Nippur* were also preserved in prose. The Assyrians developed royal inscriptions, which detailed a king's accomplishments, into annals and CHRONICLES—accounts of past events.

Like Egyptian poetry, Egyptian prose paid attention to the secular* world. Tomb inscriptions, especially biographies, influenced all types of Egyptian literature. Ultimately, these texts developed into fictional narrative stories. One of the most popular was *The Story of Sinuhe,* which is about a man's escape from Egypt and his struggle to come to terms with his past and learn the advantages of returning home. Other types of Egyptian prose included myths and rules of conduct, or "teaching" texts in which a superior figure, such as a king, shares his views. Egyptians also excelled in writing short stories.

Hittite prose concentrated more on historical writing, which included edicts*, narratives, and annals. Among the earliest Hittite edicts is the *Edict of Khattushili [I],* from around 1620 B.C. In it, King Khattushili I presents his chosen heir to the dignitaries of his realm. The *Edict of Telipinu,* written around 1500 B.C., is a more general discussion of how an effective state should be organized. A remarkable text is the *Apology of Khattushili III,* from around 1250 B.C., in which a king justifies his move to take over the throne.

Perhaps the most interesting Hittite prose pieces are the historical narratives that tell the stories of a king's reign. These stories can be very descriptive and dramatic. For example, early Hittite prose frequently used similes such as "Then his mother bellowed like an ox." The Hittites also exaggerated the activities of their kings. In one story, the king describes his role in the universe:

> Who rules all the lands (with his hand)? Is it not I who hold fixed (in their places) the rivers, the mountains and the sea? I set the mountain in such a way that it does not move; I set the sea in such a way that it does not overflow!

The Canaanites and other peoples of the Levant also produced prose, including royal inscriptions and letters, but because they wrote on easily perishable materials, much less has survived there than in the rest of the Near East. (*See also* **Book of the Dead; Books and Manuscripts; Gilgamesh; Proverbs; Ten Commandments; Torah.**)

LOVE

* **deity** god or goddess
* **erotic** related to sexual excitement or pleasure

In the ancient Near East, people saw love as a force underlying the divine and social orders. Love linked not only men and women but also worshipers and deities*, parents and children, and rulers and subjects. People did not distinguish between the emotion of love and the sexual or physical expressions of love. Rather, both were seen as part of the same force, and even relationships that were not sexual, such as the union between gods and their worshipers, could be described in terms that in other contexts referred to physical or erotic* love.

In the Sumerian language, the verb for love could be used for a person, a thing, or an idea. The Akkadians also used their word for love, *râmu,* in various contexts. Gods could love other gods, people, animals, heaven, kingship, life, prayer, and sacrifice. People could love gods, other people, places, and ideas. Even animals were thought to be able to love their offspring and their owners.

The ancient Israelites used the same word to describe love for their god Yahweh, other people, objects, and ideas. Parents, however, were "honored" rather than "loved."

The Egyptian word for love, *mry,* was usually directed from the higher being to the lower. A god or a king might love people, but people held their gods and rulers in awe. The Egyptians used the same word for both the emotional and physical aspects of love. They also used it to mean wishing, wanting, or preferring.

Aspects of love appear in the poetry of the ancient Near East. Many Mesopotamian love poems are addressed not to human lovers but to gods and kings, although the language of attraction, sexual union, and marriage appears in them. Some poems, however, speak of passionate love between people. Topics include a woman advising her suitor how to win her parents' consent to their marriage and a description of the marriage ceremony.

Egyptian love poetry focuses on courtship and the world of happy young lovers. The poems praise romantic and erotic love, but historians do not know how such feelings ranked with social and financial considerations when people planned MARRIAGES. Romantic love was also a prominent feature in Egyptian tomb paintings. They often portrayed couples in tender poses—holding hands, in an embrace, or with one's arm resting on the other's neck or shoulder.

The best-known Hebrew love poetry appears in the Bible in "The Song of Songs," also called "The Song of Solomon." The poem is filled with themes such as the praise of love, the courting of the beloved, and the separation of lovers. Some scholars have interpreted the song as a symbolic account of the soul's relationship with Yahweh. (*See also* **Family and Social Life; Gender and Sex; Marriage.**)

LUNAR THEORY

People of the ancient Near East looked to the moon as a way to measure time. Astronomers watched the cycle of the moon's phases, the changes in its position in the sky, and how long it was visible on any given day. From their observations, ancient astronomers were able to develop lunar theory, a mathematical description of the moon's movements that attempted to predict its appearance, position, and phases.

One of the earliest known studies of the moon used to develop lunar theory is in a series of Babylonian tablets called *Enuma Anu Enlil*. The earliest surviving examples were written in the 1200s B.C. The fourteenth tablet in this series contains mathematical formulas that calculate the length of time the moon can be seen on any day of any month. Although very basic, these formulas are thought to be the first use of mathematics to understand and predict astronomical patterns.

The evolution of lunar theory was reflected by changes made to the Babylonian CALENDAR. The Babylonians' months, which were either 29 or 30 days long, were based on the phases of the moon. However, their year was based on the behavior of the sun. Since the 12 lunar months did not agree with the 365 solar days, the Babylonians added an extra month to the year periodically. By the 300s B.C., the addition of lunar months became standardized. This marked the high point of the development and use of lunar theory as a mathematical model of the behavior of the moon. (*See also* **Astrology and Astrologers; Astronomy and Astronomers.**)

LUWIANS

* **second millennium** B.C. years between 2000 and 1001 B.C.

* **cuneiform** world's oldest form of writing, which takes its name from the distinctive wedge-shaped signs pressed into clay tablets

* **hieroglyphic** referring to a system of writing that uses pictorial characters, or hieroglyphs, to represent words or ideas

* **assimilate** to adopt the customs of a society

The Luwians (LOO•ee•uhnz) were a group of peoples who settled throughout ANATOLIA (present-day Turkey) in the early second millennium B.C.* Their place of origin is unknown, but historians believe it may have been the area of southern Russia just north of the Black Sea. The Luwians probably moved into the Anatolian region sometime before 2000 B.C. Thereafter, they moved into northern SYRIA as well.

Throughout the second millennium B.C.*, part of southern and western Anatolia was referred to as Luwiya. However, this name probably did not refer to a specific state or kingdom. Instead, it referred to the common language spoken by the peoples of the region. The Luwian language, which has been preserved in cuneiform* and hieroglyphic* INSCRIPTIONS in Anatolia and Syria, later became the language of the Neo-Hittite states.

The Luwians assimilated* many aspects of Hittite culture, which they preserved for centuries after the Hittite empire collapsed around 1200 B.C. The Luwians formed Neo-Hittite states in southern Anatolia and northern Syria that survived until the Assyrians conquered them around 700 B.C.

Traces of the Luwians remained after the Assyrian conquest. For instance, the languages of the Lycians, another Anatolian people, may have descended from the Luwian language, and Luwian personal names survived to the time of the Roman Empire. (*See also* **Languages; Lycia and the Lycians; Neo-Hittites.**)

See map on inside covers.

L uxor (LUHK•sawr) is the name of the modern town nearest the ancient Egyptian city of THEBES. Located on the east bank of the Nile River in central Egypt, Luxor is best known for the ruins of the Great Temple of Amun.

Thebes was the capital of Egypt first during the Eleventh Dynasty (ca. 2081–1938 B.C.) and again during the New Kingdom period (ca. 1539–1075 B.C.). In about 1375 B.C., King Amenhotep III built the magnificent temple for AMUN, the king of the gods, on the city's southern edge. After the temple was built, the city developed around it and became famous. After Egypt's capital moved from Thebes to northern Egypt, Luxor remained an important religious center.

Luxor was the site of a long religious festival called Opet, which was celebrated when the Nile River flooded. Statues of Amun and his family were carried on sacred golden boats from their shrines at the Great Temple of Amun at KARNAK, a little more than one mile to the north of Luxor, to the Great Temple of Amun at Luxor. The statues were accompanied by a procession of Theban people. The route lay along an avenue lined with sphinxes*. The festival lasted about three weeks, at the end of which the statues were carried back to Karnak along the same route.

* **sphinx** imaginary creature with a lion's body and a human head

Amenhotep's original temple consisted of a large open court surrounded by columns. Beyond the court were many halls and chambers. One of the most striking features of the temple is a majestic row of 14 pillars, 52 feet high, and carved to look like the buds of papyrus plants.

Around 1250 B.C., King RAMSES II added an outer court surrounding the original temple. It was decorated with colossal statues of Ramses and 74 columns carved in the shape of papyrus buds. The court also had a pylon (gateway building) covered with scenes portraying a famous battle Ramses fought against the Hittites in Syria. In front of the pylon were huge images of Ramses and a pair of red granite obelisks*, each approximately 82 feet tall. One of the obelisks still stands in front of the ruins of the temple. The other was moved to Paris, France, in A.D. 1836. (*See also* **Egypt and the Egyptians; Feasts and Festivals; Palaces and Temples.**)

* **obelisk** four-sided pillar that tapers as it rises and ends in a pyramid

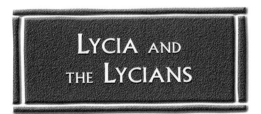

L ycia (LI•shee•uh) was an ancient region located in southwestern ANATOLIA (present-day Turkey). Because of its location, Lycia was greatly influenced by the peoples across the sea and to the east and west. Nevertheless, it was able to maintain its independence for many centuries.

History of Lycia. The Lycians, an Indo-European people, were descendants of the Lukka people, who were related to the HITTITES. Their origins are difficult to trace because the Lukka people were nomads* who left little evidence of their culture. Although Lycia is depicted at the time of the Trojan War (ca. 1100 B.C.) in Homer's *Iliad,* the earliest traces of Lycian culture are remains of buildings that date to the late 700s B.C. These remains were found in the Lycian city of Xanthus.

* **nomad** person who travels from place to place to find food and pasture

Lycia and the Lycians

At least 13 coin-minting centers existed in ancient Lycia, producing some of the most magnificent coinage in the Near East. The motif that characterizes these Lycian coins, that of a portrait head wearing a Persian tiara, was common during the 400s and 300s B.C. and reflects Lycia's political allegiance at that time.

* **satrapy** portion of Persian-controlled territory under the rule of a satrap, or provincial governor

* **dynasty** succession of rulers from the same family or group

See map in Anatolia (vol. 1).

* **diplomat** person who conducts negotiations or relations with foreign kingdoms, states, or nations

* **deity** god or goddess

Lycia remained independent until around 540 B.C., when it was conquered by the Persian king CYRUS THE GREAT. Around 516 B.C., Lycia was made a part of a satrapy* of the PERSIAN EMPIRE. During this time, a ruling dynasty*, supported by Persia, arose in Xanthus and controlled Lycia for about 100 years.

In the mid-400s B.C., Lycia became a member of the Delian League, a group of cities allied to the Greek city of Athens. Athenian influence in Lycia grew quite strong, but ended when the Peloponnesian Wars between the cities of Athens and Sparta began. By the 420s B.C., Lycia was again a satrapy of Persia. By the early 300s B.C., there was general unrest in Lycia, and a new Lycian leader, Perikles, emerged. Perikles' ambitions were in conflict with those of the Persian rulers, and in 367 B.C., the Lycians took part in a failed rebellion of the satrapies against Persia.

In 334 B.C., ALEXANDER THE GREAT of MACEDONIA invaded Lycia. Macedonia controlled Lycia until PTOLEMY I of Egypt invaded it in 309 B.C. Lycia was conquered by the Seleucid emperor Antiochus III in 197 B.C., but seven years later, the Romans defeated him and took Lycia.

During the late 100s B.C., several Lycian cities came together to form the Lycian League. This body made decisions about war, sent diplomats* to other lands, and elected judges to establish and oversee the laws of the land. After many diplomatic missions from the league, Rome granted Lycia independence in 168 B.C. However, shortly after 100 B.C., Lycia was invaded by Mithridates VI, the king of Pontus, in northern Anatolia. Rome retook Lycia in 42 B.C. and, in A.D. 43, combined it with the neighboring territory of Pamphylia to form a Roman province. Rome controlled Lycia for the next 300 years.

Language and Culture. The Lycian language was derived from the Luwian language, but much of it remains a mystery to scholars. Lycian religion also came from the LUWIANS and other earlier civilizations in Anatolia. However, by the 300s B.C., a strong Greek influence led to many local deities* being identified with Greek gods and goddesses. The main Lycian goddess, called *Eni mahanahi* (mother of the gods) became linked to the

priest or priestess through whom
a god is believed to speak; also, the
location (such as a shrine) where such
utterances are made

Greek goddess Leto, and she and her children Apollo and Artemis became Lycia's national gods. Lycia was known for its many oracles*. Among the ancient Greeks and Romans, Lycia was noted for its fine wine, perfumes, and timber from its famous groves of cyprus and cedar trees. The Lycians themselves had a reputation as people who appreciated order and respected the law.

Despite the strong influence of the Greeks and Romans, the Lycians preserved many of their traditional customs. This was particularly true in areas farther from the main cities and harbor towns that had the most contact with foreigners and foreign cultures. (*See also* **Religion; Satraps; Seleucid Empire.**)

LYDIA AND THE LYDIANS

years from 3000
to 2001 B.C.

succession of rulers from the
same family or group

independent state consisting
of a city and its surrounding territory

See map in Anatolia (vol. 1).

Lydia (LI•dee•uh) was a small kingdom in western ANATOLIA (present-day Turkey) that flourished between the early 600s and the mid-500s B.C. Although Lydia survived for only a brief time, it achieved fame throughout the ancient world for its legendary wealth. In fact, the name of its last ruler, King Croesus, came to symbolize fabulous riches.

History. During the third millennium B.C.*, Lydia was greatly influenced by TROY and other states bordering the AEGEAN SEA. In the second millennium B.C.* (years from 2000 to 1001 B.C.), the HITTITES of Anatolia and the Mycenaeans of Greece had a major impact on the region. With the collapse of the Hittite empire in the 1200s B.C., however, the Phrygians became the dominant influence over Lydia. According to tradition, two ruling dynasties* controlled Lydia before the 600s B.C. The second of these, the Herakleid dynasty, lasted about 500 years.

Lydia's rise to power began in about 680 B.C., when a ruler named Gyges came to the throne. Gyges allied with Egypt and Assyria and expanded his kingdom by warring with Greek cities on the Aegean coast of Anatolia. During his reign, Lydia faced attacks by the Cimmerians, warriors from eastern Anatolia. The Cimmerians captured the Lydian capital of SARDIS in 652 B.C., and for the next few decades, Lydia faced threats from these invaders. By 626 B.C., Gyges' successor Ardys, with the help of Assyria, defeated the Cimmerians and regained Sardis.

Lydia reached the height of its power under King Alyattes, who ruled from about 607 to 560 B.C. Alyattes brought many regions in western Anatolia—including a number of Greek city-states* in Ionia—under Lydian rule. He also countered threats from the MEDES, who had begun to push into the region from the east. The last and most famous Lydian king was Croesus, who succeeded Alyattes around 560 B.C. Croesus was known to the Greeks because of his wealth and the rich OFFERINGS he made at Greek temples. Despite his respect for Greek gods and religion, Croesus launched attacks on Greek cities in Ionia. By 547 B.C., he had brought much of coastal western Anatolia under his control.

Croesus planned to expand Lydian power to the Greek islands of the Aegean Sea. However, he had to abandon this goal because of growing threats from the Persians, who had replaced the Medes as the major

Lydia and the Lydians

* **siege** long and persistent effort to force a surrender by surrounding a fortress or city with armed troops, cutting it off from supplies and aid

threat in the east. Croesus formed alliances with Egypt, Babylonia, and the Greek city-state of Sparta, and set out to attack the PERSIAN EMPIRE.

In 547 B.C., Croesus and his army fought an indecisive battle with the Persian leader CYRUS THE GREAT. He then returned to Sardis to raise a larger army and wait for reinforcements from his allies. However, Cyrus surprised Croesus by pursuing him and attacking Sardis, which fell after a short siege*. This defeat marked the end of the Lydian kingdom. Lydia and the rest of Anatolia became part of the Persian empire. The Persians eventually made Sardis the western capital of their empire.

Economy and Culture. Lydia was famous in the ancient world for developing the first gold and silver coins for use as currency. It was also famed for establishing the earliest retail trade in which MERCHANTS sold small quantities of goods directly to consumers.

Lydia's wealth came from its fertile land and deposits of gold, silver, and other metals. Its supply of precious metals contributed to the development of coins as a medium of exchange. The widespread use of such currency in Lydia influenced the Persians and the Greeks. With the use of coins as currency, retail trade was easily established. This was a change from the traditional system in which goods reached a consumer only after they had passed through many middlemen. Among the products for which the Lydians were famed were carpets, golden cloth, red dye, and COSMETICS. Lydian healing ointments were sold in Anatolia, Greece, Italy, and North Africa in distinctively shaped vases called lydions.

Lydian culture was essentially Anatolian, with a strong blend of eastern Greek culture. There is little evidence of influence from other regions of the Near East. Lydian architecture, known primarily from the ruins of Sardis, included massive forts and large impressive burial mounds, many of which contained stone chambers and entrance halls. Little is known of the Lydian language or religion, except that the people spoke an INDO-EUROPEAN LANGUAGE related to such languages such as Hittite, Luwian, and Lycian. Few texts have survived, and there is no evidence that the Lydians had sophisticated literature such as epics* or drama.

* **epic** long poem about a legendary or historical hero, written in a grand style

Although the kingdom of Lydia flourished for only a little over 100 years, its remarkable wealth is legendary. Lydians are renowned for their distinctively shaped vessels, such as the boat-shaped vase shown here. They also boasted splendid textiles, dyes, and cosmetics.

66

* **cult** system of religious beliefs and rituals; group following these beliefs

Cybele was a major Lydian goddess, but little is known about other Lydian gods and cults*. Lydian religion borrowed heavily from the Greeks. This is evident from many carved images and INSCRIPTIONS that bear the names of Greek deities. At the same time, a number of Greek and Roman myths and legends may have a basis in Lydian MYTHOLOGY. (*See also* **Burial Sites and Tombs; Economy and Trade; Greece and the Greeks; Money; Mycenae and the Mycenaeans; Phrygia and the Phrygians.**)

MACEDONIA

* **dialect** regional form of a spoken language with distinct pronunciation, vocabulary, and grammar

Macedonia (ma•suh•DOH•nee•uh) was an ancient kingdom in northeastern Greece. The region contains fertile plains, swift rivers, and rugged mountains, which isolated Macedonia from its neighbors. Macedonia played an important role in the later history of the ancient Near East as the home of ALEXANDER THE GREAT, who created an empire that included much of the Near East as well as parts of India and CENTRAL ASIA. The Macedonians spoke a dialect* of the Greek language and adopted Greek religious beliefs. According to ancient Greek MYTHOLOGY, the Macedonians were descended from one of the sons of the god Zeus.

Around 650 B.C., King Perdikkas I began to expand Macedonia's territories. For the next 300 years, his descendants continued to strengthen and expand the kingdom, bringing Macedonia into periodic conflict with Athens, Sparta, Illyria, the PERSIAN EMPIRE, and other neighboring kingdoms and city-states*. In 338 B.C., King Philip II of Macedonia defeated an alliance of Greek city-states at the battle of Chaeronea. This victory left Macedonia in control of Greece. Philip's son Alexander the Great built on Philip's successes when he defeated the Persians and created the largest empire in the ancient world. By the time of Alexander's death in 323 B.C., the Macedonian empire stretched from Greece in the west to India in the east. Included in the empire were ANATOLIA (present-day Turkey), MESOPOTAMIA (present-day Iraq), IRAN, Egypt, SYRIA, and the Levant*.

* **city-state** independent state consisting of a city and its surrounding territory

* **Levant** lands bordering the eastern shores of the Mediterranean Sea (present-day Syria, Lebanon, and Israel), the West Bank, and Jordan

After Alexander's death, the empire was divided into provinces, each controlled by one of his generals. During the next 20 years, when the generals fought for control of the entire empire, Macedonia and Greece were ruled by General Antipater and his son Cassander. After Cassander's death in 297 B.C., Macedonia endured 20 years of civil war and attacks by the Galatians, invaders from the north. This period of strife ended in 276 B.C., when military leader Antigonus Gonatas drove back the Galatians and was proclaimed king by the Macedonian army. The Antigonid dynasty ruled Macedonia for about 100 years.

See map in Alexander the Great (vol. 1).

Between 215 and 148 B.C., Macedonia fought a series of conflicts known as the Macedonian Wars with the Roman Empire. Roman victories in the first two wars greatly reduced Macedonian territory and power. In 168 B.C., during the third war, the Romans defeated King Perseus and divided Macedonia into four separate republics*. Twenty years later, the Romans reunited these republics and made Macedonia a province of their empire. (*See also* **Greece and the Greeks; Seleucid Empire.**)

* **republic** government in which citizens elect officials to represent them and govern according to law

Magic

The people of the ancient Near East believed that the world was filled with supernatural beings and unseen powers that caused things to happen. Magic was the people's attempt to control or influence those beings and powers. Magical practices included ritual ceremonies, spells or incantations*, and everyday acts such as the wearing of protective charms called amulets*. All cultures, however, drew a clear distinction between white magic, the helpful or protective practices that were accepted in society, and black magic, which was considered destructive and was not tolerated.

Both magic and religion were expressions of humanity's relationship to the supernatural world of GODS, DEMONS, and spirits. Magic also had a practical aspect. The people who used it hoped to acquire some benefit—anything from quieting a crying baby to winning another's love to curing an illness.

Types and Uses of Magic. Magic is based on the idea that everything in the universe is somehow connected to everything else. A magician is a person who understands and can manipulate those connections. This concept of interconnection is clear in analogic magic, one of the most popular forms of magic. It drew on the analogies, or likenesses, among things and was used to drive evils, such as sickness or impurity, out of people. Among the HITTITES of ANATOLIA (present-day Turkey), for example, an object, such as a piece of wax, was shaped in a form representational of evil. A spoken incantation then established the magical connection between the evil and the object representing it. Destroying the object—for example, by melting the wax—then removed the evil. The Hittites also used contact magic, in which touching certain objects removed evil from a person and transferred it to an object. For example, people might pass between nets or thornbushes to rid themselves of evil.

Many magical practices in the ancient Near East were protective. People used spells and charms to keep themselves and their homes from harm. For example, in the Babylonian city-state* of NIPPUR, people buried bowls inscribed with incantations under the corners of their houses to drive away the demons that might harm the household. A stela* found in Egypt from the 300s B.C. contains magical spells seeking the protection of the god HORUS against dangerous demons and wild animals.

Some magic was directed at a specific demon, spirit, or ghost that was believed to be troubling the living. For instance, texts from ancient Mesopotamia give many examples of rituals against Lamashtu, a female demon who attacked pregnant women and babies. Other Mesopotamian magic rituals dealt with such problems as angry ghosts and the harmful WITCHCRAFT performed by human sorcerers.

Magic was closely associated with medicine. A healing treatment could include incantations, spells, rituals, and herbal potions. In Egypt, for example, the oldest known texts dealing with health care contain both medical and magical remedies. According to these texts, magic was the only treatment for the bites of snakes and scorpions.

Many surviving descriptions of Egyptian magic deal with funerary* rituals. Spells performed during the burial ceremony transformed a dead

A Purification Spell

A Mesopotamian text called *Shurpu*, which means burning, describes rituals to cleanse people of misdeeds and harmful influences. One spell requires the person to burn a clump of wool while reciting this text:

Just as this flock of wool is plucked apart and thrown into the fire, [and just as] the Firegod consumes it altogether, just as it will not return to its sheep, will not be used for the clothing of god or king: May . . . the sickness that is in my body, flesh, and veins, be plucked apart like this flock of wool, and may the Firegod on this very day consume it altogether. May the ban go away, and may I [again] see the light!

* **incantation** written or recited formula of words designed to produce a given effect

* **amulet** small object thought to have supernatural or magical powers

* **city-state** independent state consisting of a city and its surrounding territory

* **stela** stone slab or pillar that has been carved or engraved and serves as a monument; *pl.* stelae

* **funerary** having to do with funerals or with the handling of the dead

person into a spirit. Egyptians also relied on spells as their defense against demons and the roaming dead.

The Canaanites in the Levant* practiced therapeutic, or healing, magic. They recited incantations to the gods to prevent and heal snake-bites. A text from the Syrian city-state of UGARIT contains a spell that calls on the god BAAL to drive the illness out of a sick person.

Officially, the Israelites disapproved of magical practices, but in everyday life, people wore amulets and buried protective charms in tombs. Ugaritic, Canaanite, Phoenician, and Aramaic texts show that people throughout the Levant used magic to try to connect with the supernatural world. For instance, some Canaanite and Israelite texts refer to the practice of necromancy, a form of magic in which the spirits of the dead were evoked. The dead were thought to possess knowledge denied to the living, including knowledge of the future. Among the Israelites, necromancy was practiced only when other methods of divination* failed because their official religion disapproved of the practice of calling on the dead. If caught, the offender could receive harsh punishment.

Roles of Magicians. In all ancient Near Eastern cultures, the magician who worked within the public realm of religion and socially acceptable behavior was different from the wizard, sorcerer, or witch who performed magic for harmful purposes. Magicians often interacted with priests and healers. In Mesopotamia, magical experts called *ashipu* shared the responsibility for providing health care with physicians. A physician might use a magical spell to increase the effect of his medications, while an *ashipu* might own a library of handbooks on medicine and medical treatment. *Ashipu* also performed other acts of magic, such as casting spells or exorcising—driving away—demons, for private clients. In addition, some *ashipu* advised kings and served in temples. The profession of *ashipu* was generally handed down from generation to generation within a family.

The most important magician in the Hittite kingdom was often a "Wise Woman." She was an incantation priestess and performed rituals and spells. The Wise Woman worked alone or with other incantation specialists such as physicians and fortune-tellers. (*See also* **Amulets and Charms; Omens; Oracles and Prophecy.**)

This bronze statue dating from the Neo-Assyrian period (ca. 911–609 B.C.) depicts the Mesopotamian demon Pazuzu. Pazuzu was often invoked in spells and incantations to counteract the wicked acts of Lamashtu, a demon who wreaked havoc on pregnant women, young mothers, and babies. However, Pazuzu was also viewed on occasion as an evil force.

* **Levant** lands bordering the eastern shores of the Mediterranean Sea (present-day Syria, Lebanon, and Israel), the West Bank, and Jordan

* **divination** art or practice of foretelling the future

MAPS

* **Hellenistic** referring to the Greek-influenced culture of the Mediterranean world and western Asia during the three centuries after the death of Alexander the Great in 323 B.C.

Maps are used to show locations in all or part of an area. The people of the ancient Near East produced the oldest known maps, most of which covered fairly small areas and had practical uses. By the Hellenistic* period, however, mapmakers (cartographers) in the Near East were trying to envision the entire world and were laying the foundations of modern cartography, or mapmaking.

The First Maps. The first known maps come from MESOPOTAMIA. One of the oldest, dating from about 2300 B.C., is a CLAY TABLET from the ruins of the city of NUZI. The map shows several settlements as well as waterways

Maps

and hills. The writing on the map—the MEASUREMENTS of plots of land—offers a clue that the Nuzi map and others like it may have been records of land ownership. These records may have been used by tax collectors or other officials.

The Babylonians drew maps, or plans, of houses, temples, towns, and cities. One example, a clay tablet from about 1500 B.C., features a plan of the city of NIPPUR. The map shows the city wall, the GATES in the wall, and the moat protecting the wall, as well as a park, several canals, temples, and the nearby Euphrates River. Such plans may have had military or engineering uses. The Babylonians also drew maps of more distant regions, such as larger areas, districts, and towns.

Very few maps have survived from ancient Egypt. One example is a drawing on papyrus* from about 1300 B.C., which shows the central area of the Wadi Hammamat. It contains a sketch of some stone quarries and gold mines east of the Nile River and shows a road leading to the mines, a temple, and a small number of houses. Some fragments of the map also contain topographical details. The Egyptians also created maps to mark the locations and boundaries of the fields along the Nile after the yearly floods.

Ancient mapmakers were mostly concerned with fairly small areas—properties and cities. A district map might cover no more than half a dozen or so small towns, with roads and canals. One exception is a small Babylonian clay tablet, from around 500 B.C., which presents an image of the world. However, this map probably reflects the cartographer's vision of the universe more than geographical knowledge.

This Babylonian map, believed to have been drawn around 500 B.C., is the oldest surviving map of the world. The earth is depicted as a flat disk surrounded by an ocean (portrayed as a double ring) containing mythical islands. Babylon lies at the world's center, with the Euphrates River flowing through the city.

The Dawn of Scientific Cartography. Beginning around 600 B.C., the Greeks speculated about the shape of the world. At first, Greek philosophers, like the Babylonians, pictured the earth as a floating disk. Later, during the 500s B.C., the philosophers Anaximander and Hecataeus from the Greek city of Miletus in Anatolia (present-day Turkey) produced geographic writings and world maps based on this image. However, HERODOTUS, a well-traveled Greek historian who knew something of geography, claimed that their ideas were wrong. By around 350 B.C., the correct view of the earth as a sphere had been established, and by 300 B.C., geography and mapmaking had become more scientific.

During the 200s B.C., the mathematician and philosopher Eratosthenes of Cyrene (present-day Libya), working in the Egyptian city of Alexandria, calculated the size of the earth and drew a world map. In the A.D. 100s, another mapmaker who worked in Alexandria was Claudius Ptolemaius, better known as Ptolemy. Ptolemy was the most important figure in the later era of ancient mapmaking. His eight-volume *Guide to Geography* was the most complete and learned work of its sort in the ancient Near Eastern and Mediterranean worlds. However, Ptolemy was wrong about many details. For example, he thought that the Indian Ocean was enclosed by land like a vast lake. Notwithstanding his mistakes, he set down some of the basic principles of scientific mapmaking, such as methods for portraying the curved surface of the earth on flat maps. Later mapmakers in Europe and the Near East based their work on Ptolemy's. (*See also* **Astronomy and Astronomers; Geography; Science and Technology.**)

MARDUK

* **deity** god or goddess

* **pantheon** all the gods of a particular culture

* **ziggurat** in ancient Mesopotamia, a multistory tower with steps leading to a temple on the top

* **patron** special guardian, protector, or supporter

* **city-state** independent state consisting of a city and its surrounding territory

* **cult** formal religious worship

Known as the lord of the gods and father of mankind, Marduk became the national deity* of Babylonia after the 1200s B.C. As the chief god of the Babylonian pantheon*, his power and prestige were unrivaled. His main temples in BABYLON—the Esagila, meaning "House with Lifted Head," and a ziggurat* called the Etemenanki, meaning "House of Foundation of Heaven and Earth"—were considered the center of the universe. Their splendor was known throughout the ancient Near East.

According to Babylonian MYTHOLOGY, Marduk was the son of the god EA (or Enki) and brother of the goddess ISHTAR. Considered a god of wisdom, healing, and magic, Marduk also was associated with fertility. Over time, Marduk took over the traits and functions of other gods, making his nature and character increasingly complex. In art, he was depicted carrying a triangular spade or hoe, suggesting that he may have originally been an agricultural deity.

In the 2100s B.C., Marduk became the patron* god of Babylon. Thereafter, his rise to prominence was linked to the rising political power of Babylon, especially under King HAMMURABI, and to its transformation from a city-state* into the capital of an empire. The main story of Marduk and his rise is found in the Babylonian CREATION MYTH, *Enuma Elish*. The myth describes how Marduk saves the gods from a monster named Tiamat, creates the heavens and earth, brings order to the universe, and proposes the creation of humans. As a reward for his efforts, the gods give Marduk many of their powers and promote him to supreme deity, displacing the god ENLIL. The myth also lists Marduk's many names, essentially investing in him the power of other gods.

The cult* of Marduk gradually spread beyond Babylonia, especially during the Kassite period (ca. 1595–1158 B.C.). Marduk was adopted by the Assyrians, who honored him as a great god. However, during the reign of the Assyrian king SENNACHERIB (ruled 704–681 B.C.), some of Marduk's functions, traits, and rituals were transferred to the Assyrian national god, ASHUR. During the time of the Chaldean empire (626–539 B.C.) of NEBUCHADNEZZAR II, Marduk was referred to as Bel, meaning "lord." Following the Macedonian conquest, Marduk (Bel) became equated with the Greek deity Zeus. (*See also* **Babylonia and the Babylonians; Gods and Goddesses; Religion.**)

MARI

* **entrepôt** intermediary center of trade, usually on a caravan or sea route

* **artifact** ornament, tool, weapon, or other object made by humans

* **diplomatic** relating to the practice of conducting peaceful negotiations between kingdoms, states, or nations

At the height of its power, Mari was one of the wealthiest cities in MESOPOTAMIA. Located on the banks of the EUPHRATES RIVER near important caravan routes, the city gained its wealth and importance as an entrepôt*. The ruins of the city, a site known as Tell Hariri, have yielded remarkable artifacts*, including a magnificent palace and thousands of CLAY TABLETS, which contain records of the economic, administrative, and diplomatic* affairs of the city.

Founded in the beginning of the third millennium B.C.*, Mari quickly rose to prominence as a trading center. The city gained immense wealth from taxes on the trade goods that passed through it. One of its most important trading partners was the city-state* of EBLA in northern SYRIA. In the latter part of the third millennium B.C.*, Mari was ruled by Akkadian governors, who launched enormous building projects, including the

* **third millennium** B.C. years from 3000 to 2001 B.C.

* **city-state** independent state consisting of a city and its surrounding territory

* **dynasty** succession of rulers from the same family or group

* **archaeological** referring to the study of past human cultures, usually by excavating material remains of human activity

construction of a magnificent new royal palace and an expansion of the city's sacred temple area.

Around 1800 B.C., Mari and its surrounding territory came under the control of a succession of dynasties* of AMORITES. Around 1760 B.C., King HAMMURABI of BABYLON conquered and destroyed the city. By this time, Mari was no longer a great trading center, so the city was left deserted and used only as a cemetery.

The archaeological* discoveries at the site of ancient Mari are some of the most significant in the Near East. The Great Palace is one of the best-preserved and richest palaces of the period before 1000 B.C. The thousands of tablets found there have provided invaluable information about Mari and revealed much about culture and society in Mesopotamia during the third and second millennia B.C. (*See also* **Cities and City-States; Economy and Trade; Palaces and Temples; Trade Routes.**)

MARKETS

The term *market* has two distinct meanings. In one sense, a market is the physical location where goods are bought and sold and commercial transactions take place. This is more commonly known as a marketplace. The second meaning of the term is the mechanism by which goods or services are made available and by which the values of those goods or services are determined. For example, the term *labor market* refers to the overall demand for labor and the price at which that labor will be hired.

Historians have debated whether marketplaces in the modern sense of the word existed in the ancient Near East. However, there is little doubt that market forces of demand and supply did operate, especially to determine the value of goods and, in many instances, services.

Marketplaces. There is almost no evidence that ancient Near Eastern civilizations earmarked specific physical locations to serve as marketplaces. The physical remains of ancient cities offer little help, because marketplaces would probably have been open spaces with no special features to distinguish them from ordinary squares or courtyards. Although the Sumerian and Akkadian languages contained words for "open space" or "square," there is no indication that such places were centers of commercial activity.

The Greek historian HERODOTUS tells a story in which a Persian king says that towns in Persia did not set aside special places where people could cheat each other as did the Greeks in their agoras, or marketplaces. Some economists and historians believe that this remark implied that the Persians did not have markets. However, others believe that it implied that they did not cheat as much as did the Greeks.

In Egypt, some tomb paintings depict market scenes. For instance in the Deir el-Medineh tomb of Ipuy, women on the banks of the Nile River are shown selling goods to a man in a boat in exchange for grain. These traders, however, were not independent MERCHANTS, but were employed by other citizens or temples to sell surplus goods. Egypt never developed a prominent merchant class, and the existence of marketplaces is no more strongly attested in Egyptian sources than it is in Mesopotamian sources.

The Laws of Eshnunna, dating from around 1800 B.C., listed the prices of various household goods in ancient Mesopotamia, each of which could be bought for one shekel (0.3 oz) of silver. Although silver was often used as a standard of exchange, the prices of goods were also set in amounts of barley, small cattle, and sesame oil. The people of ancient Mesopotamia and other parts of the ancient Near East probably also used barter (trading one good for another) to meet their needs.

PRICE OF GOODS DURING THE OLD BABYLONIAN EMPIRE

1 *gur* barley	2 minas worked copper	3 minas copper
1.2 liters vegetable oil	**1 shekel silver buys**	2 *gur* salt
1.5 liters pig's fat	40 liters bitumen	6 minas wool

Note: 1 shekel = .3 oz.; 1 *gur* = 78 gallons; 1 liter = .264 gallons; 1 mina = 1.1 lbs.

* **city-state** independent state consisting of a city and its surrounding territory

* **commodity** article of trade

* **cuneiform** world's oldest form of writing, which takes its name from the distinctive wedge-shaped signs pressed into clay tablets

Market Forces. The lack of evidence of marketplaces does not mean that market forces did not operate in the ancient Near East. Perhaps the most obvious indication that markets existed is the fact that prices for different goods varied over time. Documents from the Sumerian city-state* of UMMA list the prices of various goods, most of which did change. This suggests that some market forces, such as supply and demand, did operate to alter the values of goods and that these values changed according to changing market conditions.

The forces existed and operated especially because households needed markets to obtain what they could not themselves produce. Virtually no household is totally self-sufficient, so it must go outside itself to obtain those things it lacks. When it does so, it must have some idea of the availability and cost of those things it needs. The market is the mechanism by which it obtains this information.

Unfortunately, it is difficult to trace the market value for many commodities* in the ancient Near East because the written records are incomplete. For example, no information about labor markets in the Near East before about 2100 B.C. has survived. The market value for land presents similar difficulties. There is no mention of land sales or prices in Mesopotamia before 2000 B.C. Beginning around 1800 B.C., wealthy households began to acquire large tracts of land, but there is no evidence that the people were motivated by economic concerns.

Kings occasionally listed the prices of certain staple goods, such as barley, dates, oil, wine, wool, and copper, in their royal inscriptions as a way of boasting about their prosperous reigns. Sometimes prices for such staples were set in Babylonian and Hittite law codes. A most unusual source of information about market prices, the Babylonian astronomical diaries, were written monthly in cuneiform* on clay tablets between the sixth and first centuries B.C. The tablets list not only the daily positions of the moon, planets, and stars, but they also contain information about the weather, the water level of the Euphrates River, historical events of the period, and the market prices of the same six staple commodities—barley, dates, wool, and three spices. Consequently, scholars studying these diaries are able to see how historical events such as the death of a king or a foreign conquest affected the market. (*See also* **Economy and Trade; Money.**)

Marriage

MARRIAGE

The basic unit of most ancient Near Eastern societies was the family. The foundation of the family was marriage, the formally recognized union of a man and a woman for producing CHILDREN. Although the institution of marriage was shared by most Near Eastern societies, the laws and customs surrounding marriage took various forms.

Making Marriages. Many modern societies view marriage as a choice made by two individuals and based on love and companionship. In the ancient Near East, marriages were not always a matter of personal choice, nor were they always based on love. Royal and noble families, for example, often arranged marriages as matters of state, to seal alliances or maintain the balance of power. For example, Nabopolassar of Assyria gave his son in marriage to the granddaughter of Median king Cyaxares to seal an alliance between the two kingdoms.

Marriage was the business of two families. In MESOPOTAMIA, fathers arranged the marriages of their children. Girls were married as teenagers to men about ten years older. After selecting a bride for his son, a father paid the girl's family a bride price—a certain amount of money, goods, or property. She was then considered the chosen bride of the groom's family. From her father, the bride received an equal amount of money or goods as a dowry, which she took as her contribution to the marriage. Marriage contracts between families described these arrangements in detail. A man whose wife did not bear children could take a second wife.

Among the Canaanites and Israelites of the Levant*, fathers arranged some marriages. Others were arranged by individuals in the community who acted as matchmakers. Some men, however, chose wives without

* **Levant** lands bordering the eastern shores of the Mediterranean Sea (present-day Syria, Lebanon, and Israel), the West Bank, and Jordan

As in Mesopotamia, Hittite brides wore veils until the moment the wedding was complete. In this endearing fragment from a relief vase, a Hittite groom lifts his bride's veil following the wedding ceremony—a scene repeated at many weddings today, thousands of years later.

the consent of their parents or even in defiance of their wishes. Just as in Mesopotamia, marriage agreements included a bride price from the family of the groom and a dowry from the bride's family. Such payments could consist of money, livestock, slaves, land, or goods. Marriage was generally monogamous, or limited to one spouse, although royal and noble men often had more than one wife.

Polygamy, or the practice of taking multiple wives, was common among the Persians. Men took multiple wives to have many children, and the Persian king encouraged a high birthrate by giving prizes to the heads of the largest families. The Hittites of ANATOLIA (present-day Turkey) also practiced polygamy, although it was less common there than in Persia and may have occurred mostly within the royal family. Hittite marriage contracts were usually arranged by the parents of the couple to be wed and required a bride price and a dowry.

Historians know little about the marriage practices of the ancient Egyptians. Men might have married in their 20s or 30s, while women were usually somewhat younger. Although parents might have arranged many marriages, Egyptian women had considerable freedom, and historians doubt they were forced to marry against their wishes. Poems and artworks show that ancient Egyptians hoped for marriages that included affection, harmony, and physical attraction. The Egyptians did not require marriage contracts, but parents negotiated settlements to ensure the financial well-being of married daughters, who usually brought various goods to their new households. Sometimes the husband or his family paid the bride a "sum for becoming a wife."

> **Remember:** Words in small capital letters have separate entries, and the index at the end of this volume will guide you to more information on many topics.

Wedding Ceremonies. The Egyptians may not have had any requirement for registering a marriage or conducting a standard ceremony. Families may have held a feast when a couple set up house together.

Records from Mesopotamia suggest that wedding ceremonies often lasted five to seven days. During the ceremony, the groom removed the bride's veil. According to some ancient texts, the bride had "best men" responsible for protecting and guarding her until the wedding night.

In Israel, marriages began with an engagement that could last several months. The second stage of marriage was marked by seven days of celebration, with singing, dancing, and wine drinking. The couple, adorned in special clothing and jewelry, stood under a canopy and declared, "You shall be my wife" and "You shall be my husband."

Several ancient texts hint that the Persians celebrated marriages in group ceremonies. One account says, "Seats were placed in several rows for a number of bridegrooms. After they toasted each other's health, the brides came in and seated themselves, each one near her future husband. The bridegrooms took them by the hand and kissed them."

Hittite weddings could be elaborate and costly. Sometimes men who had promised to pay for religious festivals had to ask priests or other temple authorities to delay the festivals until they had recovered from the expense of a wedding. As in Mesopotamia, Hittite brides wore veils until the moment the wedding was complete. This act is repeated at many weddings today, thousands of years later. (*See also* **Divorce; Family and Social Life; Gender and Sex; Love; Women, Role of.**)

Mathematics

MATHEMATICS

M athematics is the science of numbers and the relationships among them. The people of the ancient Near East were familiar with arithmetic, which includes counting, adding, subtracting, multiplying, and dividing. The operations of arithmetic later developed into algebra and geometry—more specifically, formulas. Ancient mathematicians also studied and practiced metrology, the science of measurement, to determine the relationships between the various units of length, area, volume, and weight. Modern scholars know about Mesopotamian and Egyptian mathematics from surviving CLAY TABLETS and papyri* as well as from ancient Hebrew documents that were written by rabbis.

* **papyrus** writing material made by pressing together thin strips of the inner stem of the papyrus plant; *pl.* papyri

Mesopotamia. More than 1,000 mathematical tablets dating from the Old Babylonian and the Seleucid periods have been recovered in Mesopotamia. According to these tablets, Babylonian mathematicians used the sexagesimal system (counting by sixties) more often than they did the decimal system (counting by tens). This was probably because the base-sixty system included a large number of factors—1, 2, 3, 4, 5, 6, 10, 12, 15, 20, and 30. Remnants of the base-sixty system are preserved today, especially in the way we tell time—60 seconds to a minute, 60 minutes to an hour—and in measuring a circle—360° is 6 times 60.

Dating from the mid-1500s B.C., the Rhind Mathematical Papyrus, shown here, is one of the most valuable sources of information about Egyptian mathematics. This section of the papyrus deals primarily with the area of triangles and the area of a circle inscribed in a square.

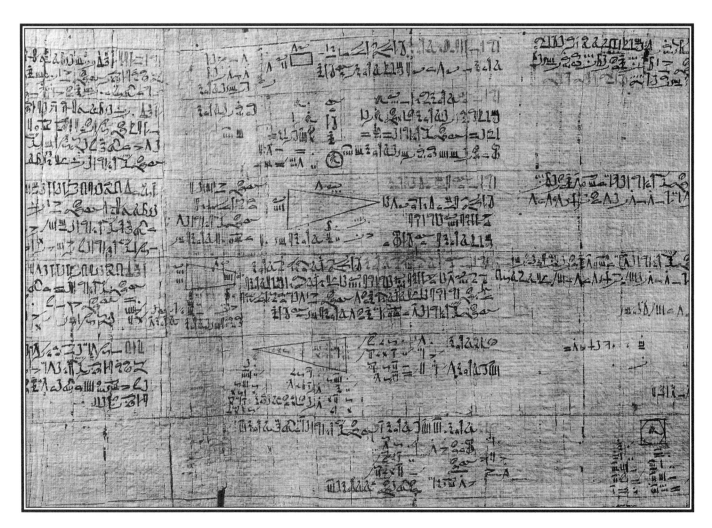

Babylonian mathematics also used a place-value system, that is, a limited number of symbols whose value is determined by its position within the number. The higher values were placed on the left and the lower values on the right. For each place a number moved to the left, its value was multiplied by 60, and for each place it moved to the right, the value was divided by 60.

Addition, subtraction, and multiplication were performed in the sexagesimal system. However, there was no division. Instead, numbers were multiplied by their reciprocal. A reciprocal of a number, n, is 1 divided by n or $1/n$, except when n equals zero. There was no special sign for the number zero until the first millennium B.C.* Before then, some mathematicians left blank spaces or used signs that indicated spaces between words to represent zero.

Mathematical texts written in the cuneiform* script can be divided into three main categories—table texts, coefficient lists, and problem texts. The table texts dealt mostly with multiplication and reciprocals (for division). They also contained information on squares and cubes, square roots and cube roots, exponential tables, logarithms, and meteorological lists and tables. The coefficient lists contained fixed values for categories of items, such as geometric shapes, to help solve mathematical problems.

Problem texts contained anywhere between one and several hundred problems, some of which were accompanied by drawings. The algebraic and geometric problem texts generally contained problems relating to areas, not volumes. These problems were solved using linear and quadratic equations. The solution to most problems in geometry was algebraic because the purpose was to find length, width, and volume. For instance, a problem might contain references to brick works, the excavations of canals, and the construction of walls, dams, and ramps.

Babylonian mathematicians also possessed considerable knowledge of geometric shapes and formulas. For instance, to solve problems on right-angled triangles, they used a concept similar to the Pythagorean theorem ($a^2 + b^2 = c^2$) more than 1,000 years before the Greek mathematician Pythagoras was born. They used $\pi = 3$ in measurements dealing with circles, although a coefficient list from Susa in southwestern Iran suggested a more precise value of $\pi = 3\frac{1}{8}$. Mathematicians now know that π is approximately 3.14159. Babylonian texts did not include proofs or detail the steps in the formulation of theorems. Consequently, scribes* performed the steps leading to the solution without explaining them.

Egypt. Because Egyptian mathematicians recorded their work on papyrus, fewer documents have survived there than in Mesopotamia. These texts, unlike their Mesopotamian counterparts, show the method of instruction and even prove that the correct answer was reached.

One of the most important Egyptian texts is the Rhind Mathematical Papyrus, which contains calculations with fractions and applies this knowledge to practical problems. This document provided a value of $\pi = 3.16$, which was calculated by drawing a circle within a square. Another well-known text is the Papyrus Anastasi I, a document that contains the calculations required for digging a lake, building a ramp, and transporting an obelisk—information that a scribe was required to know.

---

* **first millennium B.C.** years from 1000 to 1 B.C.

* **cuneiform** world's oldest form of writing, which takes its name from the distinctive wedge-shaped signs pressed into clay tablets

Mathematical Text

A Babylonian text contained the following problem:

I found a stone but did not weigh it; I added one-seventh and added one-eleventh. I weighed it: 1 mina. What was the original (weight) of the stone?

The answer: The original (weight) of the stone was $\frac{2}{3}$ mina, 8 sheqels, $22\frac{1}{2}$ barleycorns.

The student places the stone on a scale against one mina. Then he balances the scale by adding two known weights to the side of the stone. He then determines the weight of the stone by adding the two known weights and subtracting that amount from one mina.

* **scribe** person of a learned class who served as a writer, editor, or teacher

Using the decimal system, Egyptian mathematicians manipulated whole numbers and fractions. They performed operations in multiplication by repeatedly doubling a number and adding the results and they performed division using reciprocals. As in Mesopotamia, geometry consisted of formulas—but no proofs—that were calculated using arithmetic operations. Egyptian trigonometry (study of the properties of triangles) was not very developed—the measurement of slope was assumed to be 45°, and right angles, 90°. The Egyptians also used fractions, usually written with a numerator of one, to solve problems.

Ancient Israel. Knowledge about mathematics of ancient Israel is confined to one biblical reference describing the diameter of King Solomon's pool as 10 cubits wide and the circumference, 30 cubits, yielding $\pi = 3$. In A.D. 150, Rabbi Nehemiah gave the value $\pi = 3\frac{1}{7}$, but the Talmud* later restored the value of π to 3. Around the 200s, the Jews began to apply the Pythagorean Theorem to determine the length of the diagonal of a square or rectangle. This is apparent from the Mishnah (a code of oral law, religious laments, and teachings), which describes a variety of geometric patterns that a gardener or farmer might or might not use when planting different types of seeds. (*See also* **Astronomy and Astronomers; Education; Measurement; Numbers and Numerals; Record Keeping; Science and Technology.**)

* **Talmud** collection of recorded interpretations and teachings of hundreds of rabbis who lived before A.D. 500

MEASUREMENT

As governments and temple administrations became more centralized and domestic and international trade relations became more complex, the peoples of the ancient Near East began to develop standardized measures and notation systems. These developments enabled them to maintain a record of goods produced, distributed, and traded.

Early Development of Numbers and Units of Measurement.
Beginning around 8000 B.C., clay tokens came into use in the ancient Near East as a form of RECORD KEEPING. The tokens were geometrically shaped objects that represented items and their quantities. This method of record keeping remained in use for more than 5,000 years and became the main accounting system in palaces, temples, and markets. Tokens gave rise to the earliest known system of WRITING and the invention of MATHEMATICS. Once the ancient Near Eastern people became familiar with arithmetic, they began to practice metrology, which is the science of measurement. This enabled them to determine and evaluate the relationships between the various units of length, area, volume, and weight.

In Mesopotamia, scribes* learned metrology from lists or tables. During their training, scribes were often required to memorize these tables, which contained the ratios between the different units of measurement. Sometimes, they consulted the tables to perform simple calculations involving ratios.

* **scribe** person of a learned class who served as a writer, editor, or teacher

Length. In Mesopotamia, the basic unit of length was the cubit, which means forearm, or the distance from the elbow to the end of the middle finger. Other units of length included reeds, rods, ropes, stages, the distance marched between two rest stops that were two hours apart, and the fingerbreadth, or the width of the thumb. In Egypt, length was measured in palms (of a hand), royal cubits, fingerbreadths, and the *skd,* which was the measure of the slope of a pyramid. The few wooden, stone, and metal measuring devices that have survived in Mesopotamia and Egypt measure cubits or parts of cubits. From these devices, it is apparent that the length of a cubit varied greatly.

In ancient Israel, there were two basic measures—the "sad measure," which was a little less than a full measure, and the "smiling measure," which was larger than a full measure. The basic unit of length was the fingerbreadth, which ranged from about 3/4 to 1 inch. Other units of measure were the handbreadth—the width of a clenched fist—and the reed, which is mentioned in the Hebrew BIBLE.

Area. In Mesopotamia, area was most often measured by the *sar,* or garden plot. Other measures included dikes (of land), holes, and barleycorns, which referred to seeds of barley and were the smallest measure of area. In both Mesopotamia and ancient Egypt, land areas were measured as irregular quadrilaterals, their area being the product of the average of opposite sides.

In Israel, area measures were based on two systems. One was based on squaring standard units of length, such as square fingerbreadth, square handbreadth, and square cubit. The other was used for larger measures, such as large surface units or to measure a space needed to plant certain quantities of produce. The two systems were compatible, and scribes could easily convert the measures from one to the other.

Volume. In Mesopotamia, the units that measured volume were the same as those that measured area, including *sar,* dike, hole, and barleycorn. Bricks were counted in units of *sar,* where 1 *sar* was equal to 720 bricks. The Jewish Talmud* refers to several systems of volume that used different terms for the same measure.

* **Talmud** collection of recorded interpretations and teachings of hundreds of rabbis who lived before A.D. 500

Weight. The basic units of weight in ancient Mesopotamia were the mina (1.1 lbs.) and the sheqel (0.3 oz.). The smallest unit was the barleycorn. The Egyptian system of weights was based on a unit called the *kite,* which ranged from 4.5 to 29.9 grams. During Hellenistic* and Roman times, the common units of weight throughout the Near East were the sheqel, mina, and talent. They came to be used as units of currency because they sometimes described the weights of gold and silver.

* **Hellenistic** referring to the Greek-influenced culture of the Mediterranean world and western Asia during the three centuries after the death of Alexander the Great in 323 B.C.

Measures of Capacity. Mesopotamians measured the volume of barley and oil in units called *sila,* which was the basic small capacity unit equal to about 1 liter. Other units of measurement included *ninda,* the amount of grain (or flour) used to make 1 flatcake; *gur* (78 gallons); granary, which was sometimes called king's measure, normal, or correct measure; and greater measures. Throughout ancient times, the Mesopotamians devised measures relevant to their needs, such as sacks, standard pots, and ass-loads.

See color plate 3, vol. 2.

Meat

* **fourth millennium B.C.** years from 4000 to 3001 B.C.

In both Mesopotamia and Egypt, wooden and metal baskets were used for capacity measures. No wooden measures have survived, however. By the end of the fourth millennium B.C.*, bevel-rimmed bowls and conical cups were used as measures in Mesopotamia. The bevel-rimmed bowls, which constitute up to 80 percent of the pottery excavated in that region, all measured the same approximate volume. They were probably used to measure corn or flour for daily rations.

In ancient Israel, the Bible and the Talmud list units to measure large amounts of liquids or dry goods. Rabbis devised many smaller measures based on the bulk of an egg. Most units were based on the capacity of utensils, human measurements, and objects in nature.

Problems with Ancient Measurements. Historians face many challenges in analyzing the values and systems of ancient measures. One of the main problems is the lack of evidence. Archaeologists have excavated many ancient weights, but few measures of length have survived. Reliable measures of volume are scarcer still. Another difficulty is that most ancient weights and measures do not contain inscriptions or markings to indicate what unit of measure they represent.

Determining the measures of volume in the ancient Near East is particularly difficult because the only vessels that have survived are jars or pots marked with their intended capacities. However, these were simple storage jars and not the original vessels used to set standards of volume. They contain no markings to indicate how full the vessel should be when it contained the amount of liquid marked on the jar.

Documents that discuss various units of measurement have provided historians with some clues that have helped them better understand ancient measures. However, even knowing how ancient measures related to each other has been of little help in determining their modern equivalents. Some ancient documents relate Near Eastern measures with units from Greek and Roman cultures, but these too are of limited value since the values of many Greek and Roman measures are themselves not well known. In addition, the accuracy of the measurements found in these ancient documents are often quite doubtful. (*See also* **Money; Pyramids; Calendars.**)

Meat

See *Food and Drink.*

MEDES

The Medes were a people of northwestern IRAN who spoke an INDO-EUROPEAN LANGUAGE and inhabited a plateau region that became known as Media. Together with the Persians, their neighbors and rivals, they left a lasting heritage that greatly influenced the culture of Iran.

Because no written documents of the Medes have been excavated, knowledge of these people is based on other archaeological* evidence and the writings of people who came in contact with them. Several Median sites in Iran have been excavated by archaeologists, including the religious center of Tepe Nush-i Jan and Godin Tepe, which contained a large

* **archaeological** referring to the study of past human cultures, usually by excavating material remains of human activity

For hundreds of years, the Medes were engaged in struggles for freedom and the acquisition of territory. Beginning in the 600s B.C., the Medes gained their independence from the Scythians and then, along with the Babylonians, took over the Assyrian empire. They also fought against the Persians and Seleucids. This relief depicts a Median warrior leading his horse.

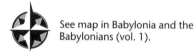 See map in Babylonia and the Babylonians (vol. 1).

* **first millennium** B.C. years from 1000 to 1 B.C.

* **indigenous** referring to the original inhabitants of a region

* **vassal** individual or state that swears loyalty and obedience to a greater power

fortified palace. The Medes first appear in written sources in the mid-800s B.C. in the records of the Assyrian king SHALMANESER III. The Greek historian HERODOTUS also wrote about the Medes in the 400s B.C.

Migration into Iran. The Medes migrated into northwestern Iran as early as the 1600s B.C. They probably came from the area north of the Black Sea and Caspian Sea, crossing the mountains of the CAUCASUS region and settling in the Zagros Mountains of northwestern Iran. Most of these early Median settlers were farmers who lived in small villages and sheepherders who tended their flocks on mountain slopes. A related group of Indo-European speakers, the Persians, entered Iran around the same time as the Medes and settled in southern Iran.

By the first millennium B.C.*, the Medes had gained control of most of the eastern Zagros Mountain region and had begun to push westward through the mountains and toward the borders of Mesopotamia. As they moved west, they mixed with indigenous* groups but also met with resistance from some local populations, who looked to URARTU, Assyria, and ELAM AND THE ELAMITES for help in holding back the invaders.

Until the 700s B.C., the Medes consisted of many independent tribes, each led by a chieftain and characterized by great diversity in culture and social and political organization. By the time they first appear in written records in the 700s B.C., the Medes had become Assyrian vassals*. At the time, the Assyrians were the dominant force in Iran and one of the major powers in the ancient Near East. Soon, however, the Medes began to grow more powerful and started to build towns and fortresses. In the mid-700s B.C. Assyrian king TIGLATH-PILESER III reported his conquest of Zakruti, the "city of the mighty Medes," which may indicate growing Median power in the region.

Kingdom of the Medes. Sometime in the 700s B.C., the various independent tribes of Medes united to form a single Median kingdom, which

Medes

See
color plate 7,
vol. 2.

* **nomadic** referring to people who travel
  from place to place to find food and
  pasture

* **satrapy** portion of a Persian-controlled
  territory under the rule of a satrap, or
  provincial governor

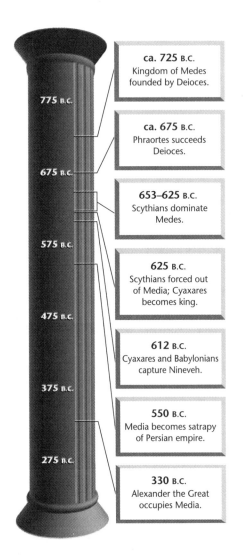

775 B.C.

ca. 725 B.C.
Kingdom of Medes
founded by Deioces.

ca. 675 B.C.
Phraortes succeeds
Deioces.

675 B.C.

653–625 B.C.
Scythians dominate
Medes.

575 B.C.

625 B.C.
Scythians forced out
of Media; Cyaxares
becomes king.

475 B.C.

612 B.C.
Cyaxares and Babylonians
capture Nineveh.

375 B.C.

550 B.C.
Media becomes satrapy
of Persian empire.

275 B.C.

330 B.C.
Alexander the Great
occupies Media.

became the first Iranian state. The early history of this kingdom is reported by the Greek historian Herodotus. Some scholars think that Herodotus's version of the founding of the Median kingdom may be based more on myth than fact, and they argue that there is no written or archaeological evidence of such a state at that time.

According to Herodotus, the kingdom of the Medes was founded as early as 725 B.C. by a king named Deioces, who established the Median capital at Ecbatana (present-day Hamadan) and ruled the Medes for several decades until about 675 B.C. Deioces was succeeded by his son Phraortes, who ruled for 22 years. Phraortes conquered the Persians and led the Medes in an unsuccessful revolt against their Assyrian overlords. He was killed while fighting the Assyrians in 653 B.C.

After Phraortes died, the kingdom was overrun by the Scythians, nomadic* warriors who had entered western Iran from the Caucasus region. The Scythians dominated the Medes until 625 B.C., when Phraortes' son Cyaxares took the throne and forced them out of Media. Cyaxares greatly expanded Median power and strengthened his army by creating separate units of spearmen, archers, and CAVALRY.

Faced with a continued threat from Assyria, Cyaxares formed an alliance with the Babylonians by marrying his granddaughter to the son of King NABOPOLASSAR, who later ruled Babylonia as NEBUCHADNEZZAR II. In 612 B.C., Cyaxares and his Babylonian allies attacked and captured the Assyrian capital of NINEVEH. This victory ended Assyrian rule and left the Medes and Babylonians as the two dominant powers in Mesopotamia.

Thereafter, the Medes and Babylonians divided the Assyrian empire between them. The Medes took the northern and eastern parts of the empire, including most of Iran, northern Mesopotamia, and parts of ANATOLIA. They extended their power westward in Anatolia until they encountered the Lydians. A battle between the Medes and Lydians in 585 B.C. ended in a draw, after which the two groups formed an alliance. Around the same time, Cyaxares' son Astyages took over the Median throne. He ruled for 35 years, but little is known about his reign.

The Medes and Persians. After the Assyrian conquest, relations between the Medes and Babylonians remained friendly for awhile. Soon, however, hostilities arose as both groups claimed the same lands. As their relations with the Medes soured, the Babylonians encouraged and supported uprisings by the Persians, who were vassals of the Medes.

In 550 B.C., the Persian king CYRUS THE GREAT led a successful revolt against Astyages, who was taken prisoner. Cyrus marched to Ecbatana, which he took with no resistance when the Median nobility accepted him as their king. Cyrus quickly took control of the rest of the Median kingdom, and Media became a satrapy* of the growing PERSIAN EMPIRE.

On several occasions, the Medes tried unsuccessfully to revolt against their Persian overlords. Still, relations between the two groups were good, and the Medes enjoyed a privileged position under the Persians. After the Persians, the Medes were the most important people in the Persian empire, and they exerted a strong cultural influence. For example, the Persians adopted Median court ceremonies and moved the Persian royal court to Ecbatana each summer. Other elements of Median culture, including religious practices, were blended with Persian traditions and became the foundation of the later culture of Iran.

Later History. In 330 B.C., ALEXANDER THE GREAT of MACEDONIA conquered the Persian empire and occupied Media. After Alexander's death in 323 B.C., northern Media was ruled by a Persian general named Atropates, who founded an independent kingdom called Atropatene. Southern Media became a province of the SELEUCID EMPIRE. This area remained a Seleucid province for about 150 years, during which time it was greatly influenced by Hellenistic* culture. In the centuries that followed, the Medes gradually lost their distinctive character, though various Median traditions blended with those of other groups to form a single Iranian culture. (*See also* **Babylonia and the Babylonians; Lydia and the Lydians; Migration and Deportation; Scythia and the Scythians.**)

* **Hellenistic** referring to the Greek-influenced culture of the Mediterranean world and western Asia during the three centuries after the death of Alexander the Great in 323 B.C.

MEDICINE

Medicine in the ancient Near East was a blend of religious rituals, folk remedies, and customs, all based on observation and results. Basic ideas of health and medical practice were different from those of modern medicine because Near Eastern cultures did not differentiate between medicine and RELIGION. Illness, disease, accidents, and other misfortunes were considered the work of the gods. Near Eastern peoples believed that such ailments were usually a punishment from the gods, who had been offended. Consequently, medical treatment consisted of pleading with gods to restore the patient's health and attempting to expel the evil from the body. Physicians mixed their treatments with religion and MAGIC and made determined efforts to cure their patients.

Life in the ancient Near East was challenging for physicians. Limited knowledge, uncertain food supplies, lack of food preservation, unsafe water supplies, and poor sanitation contributed greatly to human suffering. Common infectious diseases included tuberculosis (which attacks the lungs and is spread by coughing), pneumonic and bubonic plague (which are spread by fleas and rodents), typhus (a disease carried by parasites, such as lice), and smallpox. Leprosy, which affects the skin, nerves, and mucous membranes, was another disease that afflicted Near Eastern peoples.

Mesopotamia. In the 400s B.C., the Greek historian HERODOTUS erroneously claimed that Mesopotamians had "no regular doctors." In fact, medical workers were known in the region as early as the third millennium B.C.*, and they recorded their treatments. The most important Mesopotamian sources are medical texts describing treatments and remedies for different problems. The earliest of these from the city-state* of UR date from about 2000 B.C. and are written in Sumerian. Other texts date from later periods, such as those from the Neo-Assyrian library of ASHURBANIPAL (ruled 668–627 B.C.). These and other texts show that although their practices included magic and OMENS, Mesopotamian doctors recognized natural causes of such ills as overexposure to heat or cold, eating too much, drinking alcohol, and eating spoiled food.

* **third millennium B.C.** years from 3000 to 2001 B.C.

* **city-state** independent state consisting of a city and its surrounding territory

Medicine

* **incantation** written or recited formula of words designed to produce a given effect

Two kinds of physicians, *asû* and *ashipu,* treated the sick. Although both used incantations* to heal their patients, it is generally believed that the *asû* worked more with medicines and may have been the more practical in his methods, and the *ashipu* with spirits. However, both relied on magic. Little is known about their training or whether they worked in organized groups.

An *asû* treated such ailments as broken bones, wounds, boils, and infections. He might use herbs for both internal and external illnesses. Women were allowed to train to become an *asû.*

An *ashipu,* a type of exorcist, diagnosed supernatural causes of problems and prescribed ritual treatments. He had other religious roles, such as cleansing temples, but his chief role was to interpret symptoms. Sometimes an *ashipu* might work with an *asû* on a problematic case. Women were not permitted to become an *ashipu,* and the profession passed from father to son.

Because Mesopotamians believed that sins caused illnesses, they first tried to find out what a patient might have done to offend the gods. Physicians examined a patient and asked for a description of the symptoms. They took the person's temperature and pulse, noted skin conditions, swellings, and even the colors of bodily fluids. All these findings were recorded, and over time, the records became the basis of treatments and prescriptions. Many of the medical texts excavated in the Near East are descriptions of symptoms and catalogs of remedies, most of which begin with omens. For instance, what a physician saw on the way to a patient's house was considered an omen—a white pig meant the patient would live; a black pig meant death.

In this Egyptian relief, female druggists squeeze an animal skin filled with herbs to make herbal medicine. Because the Egyptians believed that supernatural forces caused illnesses, treatments such as these were administered to repel the evil force that was believed to have entered the body and caused the illness. Sometimes a magical incantation was spoken while treatment was administered.

Mesopotamian healers also experimented with medicinal treatments. For instance, prescriptions included herbal treatments with instructions for the best time to collect the herbs and the method of preparation. Other medicines included salt, potassium nitrate, milk, snake skins, thyme, fir, figs, dates, and turtle shells. These materials were used as ointments for external use or as powders for dissolving in drinks. One Assyrian document lists more than 400 plants, fruits, and other substances, about half of which have medicinal value.

Mesopotamian physicians treated a variety of ills. Eye problems were common, perhaps because of vitamin deficiencies, but no treatments for blindness existed. Ear problems are also recorded in medical texts, but they contain no word for deafness. There is little evidence for dentistry, but texts show that toothaches were common, and various medicines were prescribed for the pain. Skin problems were treated with ointments and lotions. Midwives took care of women's health and CHILDBIRTH, but physicians treated children. Some surgery may have existed, but there is little mention of it. Diseases of the stomach and intestines were serious and common. Contaminated water, spoiled food, and parasites led to many digestive ailments. However, because Mesopotamians did not dissect human bodies, they knew little of the workings of internal organs. Some scientists regard early attempts to deal with digestive illnesses as the basis of human medical efforts.

Medical knowledge did not advance much because illnesses were mainly thought to be caused by supernatural elements. Moreover, medical texts gradually became sacred documents, and physicians tended to follow old treatments and not experiment with new methods and procedures.

Egypt. Like the Mesopotamians, the Egyptians also believed in the supernatural cause of illness. Nonetheless, their approach to medicine was systematic. More than a dozen important documents have been found describing Egyptian medical practices. These medical papyri* date from the Middle Kingdom period (ca. 2100–1600 B.C.) but may have been copied from earlier sources. They include descriptions of illnesses, treatments, case studies, and magical chants. Although magical treatments were part of medicine, Egyptian physicians developed orderly approaches to treating injuries.

Most Egyptian healers came from highly educated groups of scribes* and priests and were palace or temple officials. Some were affiliated with the army, civil service, or local villages. From the earliest times, physicians seem to have divided into specialties, but it is not clear how well these titles relate to modern ideas of specialization. Physicians trained as apprentices*. Women may have been healers, though rarely.

Egyptians learned about the body from studying slaughtered animals and from treatment of wounds at battlefields and work sites. The practice of embalming* seems not to have added much knowledge. Egyptians knew about pulse, for example, but not that blood circulates. Arteries, veins, tendons, and nerves were considered to be tubes connecting the heart, limbs, and lower digestive system.

Most ancient Egyptian medical texts focus on the treatments offered to members of the elite classes, and there is little evidence of any health

* **papyrus** writing material made by pressing together thin strips of the inner stem of the papyrus plant; *pl.* papyri

* **scribe** person of a learned class who served as a writer, editor, or teacher

* **apprentice** individual who learns skills or a profession from an experienced person in that field

* **embalming** treating a corpse with oils or chemicals to preserve it or slow down the process of decay, usually after body fluids have been removed

Medicine

* **parasitic** referring to a disease caused by a parasite, an organism that lives inside another organism and is often harmful to the host organism

* **epidemic** spread of a particular disease within a population

A Life Saved

Although many ancient medical practices and rituals seem simplistic by modern standards, the ancients often accurately diagnosed and treated medical problems. In the biblical Book of 2 Kings, a child collapsed in the field, perhaps of sunstroke, apparently dead. The prophet Elisha arrived

and he went up, and lay upon the child, put his mouth upon his mouth, and his eyes upon his eyes, and his hands upon his hands; and as he stretched himself upon him, the flesh of the child became warm. Then he got up again, and walked once to and fro in the house, and went up, and stretched himself upon him; the child sneezed seven times, and the child opened his eyes.

This vivid account of artificial resuscitation was recorded in the 800s B.C.

care of peasants. Conditions were probably miserable, with many forms of parasitic* disease, pest-borne illness, and epidemics* caused by poor nutrition and sanitation. Even the homes of the elite had open garbage dumps nearby. Bread was the main food, and the sand in it wore down teeth, causing frequent dental problems.

Egyptian medicine contributed significantly to the treatment of physical injuries. Doctors closely followed an established procedure. First, they examined the patient and described the wounds. Next, they decided whether to treat the patient. The recognition that some problems were beyond their knowledge demonstrates a rational approach to medical problems. If a physician decided to treat the patient, he recorded his proposed treatment in logical steps. Medical records also show other comments, including definitions of words and explanations of unusual procedures. One of the most noted papyri describes 69 cases, including treatments for wounds to the skull, broken jaws, injuries to the throat and neck, and broken shoulders, vertebrae, breastbone, and ribs.

Egyptians made many compounds for medicinal purposes. One written source records 600 such compounds made from substances native to the Nile River valley. Most medicines came from plants, but animals, including insects, and mineral substances were used as well. These drugs helped expel illness from the body. Some medicines had no use other than their magical or religious association—yellow drugs for jaundice, or turquoise, the color of the god HATHOR, for charms for protection.

Although simple by modern standards, Egyptian medical practice was the best in the ancient Near East. Such treatments as applying honey as a salve, using stitches and tapes to close wounds, and cauterizing (burning or searing the skin with a hot needle to seal and prevent infection) probably originated in Egypt. Egypt's greatest medical gift to the ages was the procedure followed by physicians. Examining carefully before deciding whether to treat, using simple treatments first before moving to complex ones, proceeding with care and caution, and recording results carefully were great achievements. These careful procedures indicate a thoughtful and systematic approach to medicine.

Iran. Few ancient medical texts have survived in Iran; therefore, the Iranians' health care practices are difficult to determine. However, evidence unearthed at excavations suggests that the same conditions prevailed in Iran as elsewhere in the ancient Near East. A Zoroastrian sacred text mentions three types of healing specialists: herbalists, surgeons, and incantation priests. Historians believe that Persian rulers favored early Greek and Egyptian methods. For instance, his interest in public health may have caused DARIUS I to support medical efforts in Egypt and elsewhere.

Anatolia. Just as in Mesopotamia and Egypt, the people of ANATOLIA (present-day Turkey) believed that illnesses were a punishment from the gods. The best-known residents of Anatolia, the HITTITES, borrowed ideas and texts from Mesopotamia. Many Hittite physicians were likely trained by Assyrians, while unorganized folk healers probably treated most common people. Anatolian physicians treated disorders of the eyes, throat, mouth, and digestive system with medicines made from plants and minerals. Accounts of plagues and illnesses affecting kings are recorded in Hittite texts. For instance, the *Plague Prayers of Murshili II* mention an epidemic that lasted 20 years, causing great damage to the kingdom and its economy.

* **Levant** lands bordering the eastern shores of the Mediterranean Sea (present-day Syria, Lebanon, and Israel), the West Bank, and Jordan

The Levant. Many gods in Syria and the Levant* were divinities of disease and healing. Early texts from UGARIT identify EL, the supreme god, with healing. The Phoenician god Eshmun was also a god of healing (and perhaps the same as the Greek healing god Asclepius). Temples may have provided health care. Texts from the 1300s B.C. mention epidemics and physicians in the ancient Canaanite royal court. Israelites also viewed disease as divine punishment for sins.

Poor sanitation, ineffectual waste removal, and contaminated water caused most diseases. Insect-borne diseases were probably a significant problem as well, although incense and other aromatic substances may have helped repel insects. Other ailments included intestinal diseases caused by tapeworms and whipworms.

Although most treatment was left to the gods, physicians frequently isolated their patients. In the Hebrew BIBLE, the Book of Numbers directs physicians to "put out both male and female, putting them outside the camp, that they may not defile the camp." The Book of Leviticus discusses snakebites.

Summary. In most of the ancient Near East, illness was a part of divine will and beyond human control. Omens and rituals played an important role in medicine. Despite poor sanitation and a lack of thorough medical knowledge, ancient Near Eastern physicians made medicines of local materials and recognized that some diseases were contagious and infectious. (*See also* **Amulets and Charms; Famine; Health; Priests and Priestesses.**)

Mediterranean Islands

See *Crete; Cyprus; Rhodes; Sardinia; Thera.*

MEDITERRANEAN SEA, TRADE ON

In ancient times, the Mediterranean Sea became a natural marine highway for the expanding civilizations of the Near East. Trade encouraged growth, advanced technology, spread and shared cultures, developed economic systems, and furthered relations between empires.

* **fourth millennium** B.C. years from 4000 to 3001 B.C.

Equipment and Techniques. Because most Near Eastern civilizations developed along rivers, SHIPS AND BOATS were early features of life. Excavations on the island of CRETE show that seacraft were built there as early as 5000 B.C. During the fourth millennium B.C.*, both the Mesopotamians and the Egyptians were sailing large river boats. By 2600 B.C., sea trade was well established in the region, and early sailors navigated lengthy routes.

In the earliest times, navigation probably consisted of hugging the shore and memorizing landmarks along the way. Nevertheless, voyages well out of sight of land took place as well, sometimes without navigational instruments. Sailors then depended on the sun and stars and on journals from earlier voyages. Although the oldest preserved journal dates only from the 400s B.C., such journals were probably in use long before that time.

The Mediterranean Sea offered some advantages to shipping. Its wind patterns were consistent, making it easy for sailors to tell the difference between a cold north wind and a warmer southerly one. Sailors identified eight distinct winds and plotted them on a device called a wind rose, which was in common use in the region in the 600s B.C. Ancient sailors also detected ocean currents in the sea, which they learned to use to their advantage. These currents generally run from the Nile Delta northward to Crete, making possible much Egyptian shipping on the Mediterranean.

Trade. The region surrounding the Mediterranean Sea and its islands was well settled by the fourth millennium B.C. As cultures expanded, they came in contact with each other, leading to trade and the exchange of cultural ideas. For instance, artworks found in Crete and Egypt show ships from both countries, and Cretan textile patterns appear in Egyptian cloth.

Trade on the Mediterranean developed rapidly because of the desire for materials not available locally. To this end, Egyptian ships pushed northward to Crete and eastward to SYRIA and CYPRUS to obtain such goods as timber, aromatic spices, wine, olive oil, tin, and copper. This type of exchange was typical of trade on the Mediterranean, with states exchanging what they had much of for things they wanted or needed.

Syria was a center of trade because it was midway between Mesopotamia and Egypt. Although much of the trade there was controlled by the state, private enterprise developed as well. Small-scale trade in textiles, foodstuffs, and personal goods such as sandals occurred. Many of the merchants acted on behalf of their governments as well, and these contacts furthered political communication.

Cyprus was another center of Mediterranean trade. Archaeological* records show that Cyprus had more contact with the ancient Near East than any other island. Moreover, because Cyprus remained neutral in international power struggles, the island was able to preserve its trading fortune. Many nations sought copper from Cyprus, and the island augmented its wealth from that trade.

The HARBORS at SIDON and TYRE were established by the Phoenicians, who also built the greatest trading empire in the region during the first millennium B.C. (years from 1000 to 1 B.C.). In fact, their empire was almost entirely built on commerce. Phoenician sailors and their "round boats" carried metal, glass, textiles, and dyes to customers throughout the region. In order to expand their trading activities and find sources for raw materials, the Phoenicians established many colonies throughout the Mediterranean region from the Red Sea to Spain. The most famous of these was Carthage, which was founded in 814 B.C. in North Africa. Carthage itself became the center of a great commercial empire until its defeat by Rome in the Punic Wars (264–146 B.C.).

* **archaeological** referring to the study of past human cultures, usually by excavating material remains of human activity

The Greeks followed the example set by the Phoenicians and also established trading colonies on the Mediterranean. Between 750 and 550 B.C., Greek settlers established colonies in Italy, Sicily, southern France, and Libya. These colonies brought great wealth to the Greeks. (*See also* **Aegean Sea; Clothing; Economy and Trade; Maps; Naval Power; Phoenicia and the Phoenicians; Shipping Routes; Textiles.**)

MEGIDDO

* **Levant** lands bordering the eastern shores of the Mediterranean Sea (present-day Syria, Lebanon, and Israel), the West Bank, and Jordan

See map in Israel and Judah (vol. 3).

* **siege** long and persistent effort to force a surrender by surrounding a fortress or city with armed troops, cutting it off from supplies and aid

An important town in the Levant*, Megiddo (mi•GI•doh) occupied a strategic location where two main military and trade routes crossed. One of these was a widely used transportation route between Egypt and Mesopotamia. The other connected Phoenician cities on the Mediterranean coast to Jerusalem and other towns in the Jordan River valley. Because of its location, Megiddo was a target of numerous conflicts between kingdoms and groups struggling for control of the Levant.

Megiddo was first settled around 7000 B.C., and the first town appeared about 3,000 years later. By 2000 B.C., Megiddo had become a walled city containing a palace and several temples. The original inhabitants of this city were Canaanites. In about 1479 B.C., the Egyptian king THUTMOSE III captured Megiddo and made it a major trading center. The Canaanites later recaptured the city, but the Israelites gained control of it sometime around 925 B.C. King SOLOMON of Israel began building Megiddo into a major political and military center, and King AHAB completed the work begun by Solomon. By the 800s B.C., the Israelite city had massive walls and an impressive water supply with underground wells that could withstand a lengthy siege*.

The Assyrians conquered Megiddo in 732 B.C. and built a new city there. When the Persians captured Megiddo, the city was in decline. It was finally abandoned after ALEXANDER THE GREAT conquered the region in 332 B.C. Because the Hebrew BIBLE mentions that several significant battles were fought near Megiddo, many people believe that the final battle of

A king receives prisoners and tribute in a victory procession in this ivory plaque dating from between 1300 and 1100 B.C., which is reproduced in a modern sketch below it. Many such ivory fragments were found scattered in a Canaanite palace at Megiddo. Archaeologists believe that the ivory pieces were the remains of pieces of furniture that had been disassembled and stored with other valuable items, such as jewelry and alabaster vessels.

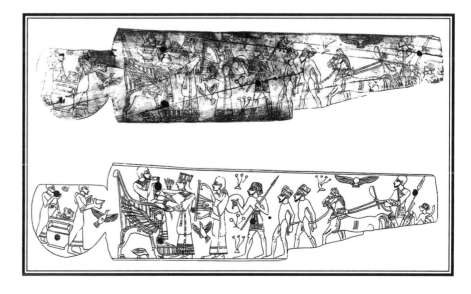

earth's history (as described in the Christian New Testament Book of Revelation), known as Armageddon (meaning "hill of Megiddo"), would be fought there too. (*See also* **Hebrews and Israelites.**)

* **maritime** related to the sea or shipping
* **city-state** independent state consisting of a city and its surrounding territory
* **decipher** to decode and interpret the meaning of

* **assimilate** to adopt the customs of a society

Melukkha (me•LUK•ka) was a maritime* state that engaged in trade with Mesopotamian kingdoms and city-states*, including Akkad, Sumer, Ur, and Babylon, from about 2300 to 2000 B.C. Although it is clear from ancient texts that Melukkha was a coastal state and that trade between it and the Near East was by sea, its exact location is unknown. Most scholars believe that it was located in the Indus River valley region of India and Pakistan and that it was probably part of the Harappan civilization.

The Harappan civilization flourished in the Indus River valley between about 2500 and 1600 B.C. It is noted mainly for its town planning, building technology, and writing system, which remains to be deciphered*. The Harappan economy was based on agriculture and trade, and it is likely that the Harappans were the first to grow rice. The civilization collapsed after 1600 B.C., perhaps due to environmental change and invasions by tribes of ARYANS.

Melukkha was known in the Near East as the source of exotic items, including gold, tin, ivory, and a black wood thought to be ebony. It was also a source of lapis lazuli and carnelian—semi-precious stones used in JEWELRY—and peacocks. Though ancient sources list these products as trade items from Melukkha, it is not known whether they were native to that region or obtained by Melukkhan traders from other places.

Melukkha never came under the rule of any of the ancient Near Eastern kingdoms. However, it appears that some people from Melukkha, most likely traders, settled in Sumer and were assimilated* into that society. (*See also* **Economy and Trade; Metals and Metalworking; Shipping Routes; Trade Routes.**)

* **deity** god or goddess

One of the most important and longest-occupied cities in ancient Egypt, Memphis was located on the west bank of the NILE RIVER near the head of the Nile Delta. The city was first settled around 3000 B.C., when King Menes united the kingdoms of Upper and Lower Egypt and chose Memphis as his capital, probably because of its strategic location.

Known originally as White Fortress—because of its whitewashed walls—Memphis became an important religious and ceremonial site. Its principal god, Ptah, was a major creator deity*, and the great temple of Ptah became a focal point of the city. Memphis was also the center of court ceremonies, including the crowning of the king. The city had many palaces, temples, markets, and manufacturing zones, as well as large private estates and other residential areas.

Memphis was the capital of Egypt until about 2100 B.C., when the capital moved to THEBES in Upper Egypt. Nevertheless, Memphis remained an

BY∃◁1∃KＺＴＹＴW◁ΦΤΟ∫WↃＹＢＢY∃◁1∃KＺＴＹ

important political, economic, and religious center. It served as the administrative center of Lower Egypt until about 1075 B.C. In the 700s B.C., Memphis was taken during a siege* by the Assyrians. In about 690 B.C., Egyptian king TAHARQA regained control of Memphis but was ousted around 667 B.C. Shortly thereafter, the Persians gained control of Memphis. In the late 300s B.C., ALEXANDER THE GREAT conquered Egypt, and Memphis remained a major city with a large Greek population. When Memphis came under Roman rule in 30 B.C., it was still considered a strategic and important city.

Today all that remains of ancient Memphis is a vast complex of cemeteries, tombs, and monuments stretching for miles along the west bank of the Nile River. These include the famous PYRAMIDS at Saqqara and GIZA. (*See also* **Cities and City-States; Egypt and the Egyptians.**)

* **siege** long and persistent effort to force a surrender by surrounding a fortress or city with armed troops, cutting it off from supplies and aid

MERCHANTS

One of the most important consequences of the establishment of cities in the ancient Near East was the development of large-scale trade and commerce. Although the royal courts and temples organized most economic activities in ancient times, merchants were still needed to handle business transactions. As time passed, the role of the merchant expanded as private individuals and families gradually assumed more responsibility for long-distance trade.

The Earliest Merchants. It is clear that regular long-distance trade existed between MESOPOTAMIA and other parts of the Near East as early as 2700 B.C. Texts from Mesopotamia mention individuals called *tamkaru,* an Akkadian word meaning "merchant." Historians are unsure whether early *tamkaru* worked exclusively for the state or whether they engaged in private business as well. They also do not know whether the *tamkaru* traveled themselves or if they traded with travelers.

Business records from the Sumerian city-state* of UMMA detail the nature of transactions made on behalf of the state and temple. The state produced surplus goods, particularly wool and grain, and traded these with other city-states for goods not available locally. Merchants were given a certain amount of these surplus goods as well as silver to trade. After acquiring goods either in other lands or in Mesopotamian markets, the merchants returned to Umma. There they distributed the goods as directed by the state officials for whom they undertook the trade missions. How merchants were paid is not entirely clear. They may have earned a fixed amount of income in foodstuffs such as barley.

During and after the third millennium B.C.*, merchants in the ancient Near East traveled to foreign lands. Dilmun, present-day Bahrain in the Persian Gulf, was one of the most important Mesopotamian trading partners, even though it was not a source of goods. Rather, merchants in Dilmun acted as brokers for goods that were sent there on their way to other places as far away as India. Egyptian merchants traveled to the land of Punt, which may have been in the present-day Sudan or Ethiopia or in Southern Arabia. Punt was a source of exotic animals, spices, gold, and slaves.

* **city-state** independent state consisting of a city and its surrounding territory

* **third millennium B.C.** years between 3000 and 2001 B.C.

91

Merchants

The excavated ruins of a merchant's house in the ancient Assyrian colony of Kanesh, as well as a ground plan of the house (see inset), are shown here. The strong room (second from top) is where merchants kept their valuables under lock and seal. Some of the items kept in this room included trade goods, silver and gold, precious objects, business documents and letters, promissory notes, loan contracts, and judicial records.

Assyrian Merchant Communities. By the late 1900s B.C., the Assyrians, who ruled from the northern Mesopotamian city of ASHUR, rose to prominence and assumed a central role in Near Eastern trade. Scholars have gained their most detailed knowledge of merchant activities in the ancient Near East from the extensive economic records of the Assyrians. Beginning in the early 1800s B.C., the Assyrians established merchant communities called *karu* in southeastern ANATOLIA (present-day Turkey). The most important *karum* was located at the city of Kanesh, and records suggest that smaller *karu* were attached to settlements throughout Anatolia. The *karu* answered to the Assyrian rulers in Ashur, who determined what goods they could bring into Anatolia and what they would receive in return. Since the *karu* were many hundreds of miles away from Ashur, the merchants handled many of their own affairs. In this sense, they were independent settlements, headed by the most important Assyrian merchants operating in the region and dealing with matters of local politics and law. Each *karum* negotiated its own trade treaties with local Anatolian city-states. These treaties spelled out the types of goods they were allowed to deal in, the amount of taxes to be paid to local officials, and the rights of the merchants who lived in the communities.

The trading houses located in the *karu* were run by members of prominent Assyrian merchant families. The heads of the families remained in Ashur, where they organized the trading missions between Assyria and Anatolia. The goods involved were primarily tin, obtained from regions in present-day northwestern Iran and Afghanistan, and fine woolen textiles from southern Mesopotamia. Merchants collected these goods in Ashur and, two times a year, loaded them on donkey CARAVANS for the six- to eight-week trip north to Anatolia. They hired agents to manage the caravans and to ensure that they arrived safely at their destination. The tin and textiles were traded for gold and silver or for local products such as copper that were then traded elsewhere for precious metals.

Your Money for My Life

Merchants who traveled abroad faced so many dangers that local kings felt compelled to sign treaties guaranteeing their protection. In the 1200s B.C., the Hittite city-state of Karkamish and the Syrian city of Ugarit signed such an agreement. According to the treaty, if a merchant from one city was killed in the other, the latter city would pay three times the value of the merchant and three times the value of any goods that were taken from him. However, this only applied if the killers were caught. If they were not caught, the city had to pay three times the value of the merchant and the normal value of the stolen goods.

* **domestication** adaptation for human use

To finance their trading missions, merchants often organized groups of investors who contributed sums of silver. In return, investors were guaranteed a 100 percent return on their investment. They also received one-third of the profits earned from the trip. The merchant kept one-third for himself, and the remaining one-third may have been set aside to finance future trips. The merchants assumed all the risks involved with the trip, including payment of taxes to states through which their caravans passed and the loss of goods or human life due to accidents, bandits, or wild animals. The men who were hired to lead the caravans bore the brunt of these hazards, but such a position could be the stepping-stone to greater wealth. A caravan leader with a solid record and a good relationship with a trading firm might be entrusted with more responsibilities. These added responsibilities would enable him to earn the capital needed to become an independent merchant.

Later Merchant Activities. Internal political problems in Anatolia led to the collapse of the *karu* system by about 1750 B.C. However, Assyrian and Babylonian merchants continued to trade with city-states throughout the Near East. Beginning in about 1000 B.C., Phoenician merchants, who specialized in dyes and other goods, conducted much of the sea trade between Egypt and other civilizations along the Mediterranean coast. References from Hebrew sources also suggest that foreign merchants were common in CANAAN after about 1000 B.C. The domestication* of CAMELS around this same time led to an increase in the number of Arab merchants, who established trade routes through the desert between Egypt and Mesopotamia.

After the rise of the PERSIAN EMPIRE in the 500s B.C., more of the Near East was united under one rule than ever before, widening the scope of trading and merchant activity. By this time, Near Eastern merchants were making more contacts with cultures in the West such as Greece. These contacts increased after ALEXANDER THE GREAT conquered Persia in the 320s B.C. Near Eastern merchants maintained a busy trade with the West until the fall of Rome shortly before A.D. 500. (*See also* **Economy and Trade; Mediterranean Sea, Trade on; Money; Phoenicia and the Phoenicians; Shipping Routes; Taxation; Trade Routes.**)

Meroë

See *Kush and Meroë.*

MESOPOTAMIA

The term *Mesopotamia* was derived from a Greek word meaning "between the rivers," an apt description for a land that lay mainly between the TIGRIS RIVER and EUPHRATES RIVER in present-day Iraq. Mesopotamia was a cradle of early civilizations in the Near East—the home of the Sumerians, Babylonians, Assyrians, and others. Because these groups spread beyond the land "between the rivers," the term often includes

Mesopotamia

* **Levant** lands bordering the eastern shores of the Mediterranean Sea (present-day Syria, Lebanon, and Israel), the West Bank, and Jordan

* **assimilate** to adopt the customs of a society

Mesopotamia was a cradle of civilization, the home of many cultures, and a place important for the growth of urban settlements, city-states, and empires. Throughout ancient times, however, the landscape of Mesopotamia changed greatly, affecting the region's settlement patterns.

Around 4000 B.C., the Persian Gulf coastline began to advance as the gulf's waters rose. Modern archaeologists have uncovered evidence indicating that the gulf coastline was not far from the ancient cities of Ur and Eridu. However, by about 1500 B.C., the waters began to recede, and the coastline retreated to its present position. The Tigris and Euphrates Rivers also changed course several times during this period, affecting settlements along their banks.

areas surrounding the rivers in nearby SYRIA, ANATOLIA (present-day Turkey), and IRAN. The influence of Mesopotamian civilizations spread throughout the ancient Near East, reaching as far as Egypt in the west and the Indus River valley of present-day India in the east.

LAND AND PEOPLE

The landscape of what was once Mesopotamia ranges from high mountains to rolling countryside to broad level plains. Much of the region receives relatively little rainfall or only seasonal rains, with the more mountainous regions in the northeast receiving more rain than the areas in the south. However, the region is watered by a number of rivers and streams, and many areas are well suited to AGRICULTURE, especially the floodplains of the Tigris and Euphrates Rivers. Mesopotamia lay at the eastern end of a broad arc of fertile land known as the FERTILE CRESCENT, which curves to the west through the Levant* into Egypt.

An important geographic feature of Mesopotamia was its openness. There were few natural boundaries or defenses to isolate and protect it from surrounding areas and peoples. Throughout history, Mesopotamia experienced periodic waves of invasions and migrations of people, most of whom settled in the region and became assimilated* to the populations already living there.

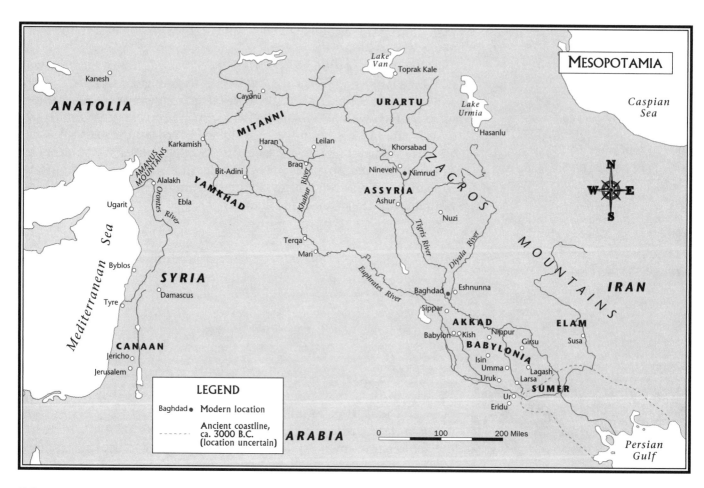

The first civilizations in Mesopotamia arose in the fertile areas of the region when people developed IRRIGATION to harness the waters of the rivers and to increase the productivity of the land. An abundance of food led to increased populations and urbanization*, and the need to manage farmlands and urban populations led to the formation of GOVERNMENTS and bureaucracies*. These included organized states with boundaries and political institutions, religious and political leaders to direct society, a hierarchy* of social classes, a specialization of labor, and the development of arts and intellectual ideas.

Ancient Mesopotamia contained many ETHNIC AND LANGUAGE GROUPS. Besides the Sumerians, Babylonians, and Assyrians, there were Akkadians, AMORITES, ARAMAEANS, KASSITES, and HURRIANS. The Sumerians—among the earliest of these groups—spoke a unique language and developed a distinct and highly influential culture. Many of the other peoples of Mesopotamia spoke Semitic* languages, but some also spoke INDO-EUROPEAN LANGUAGES. Mesopotamians ranged from nomads* to settled farmers and city dwellers. The various groups in Mesopotamia often intermingled and adopted certain aspects of other cultures, including religious beliefs.

OVERVIEW OF MESOPOTAMIAN HISTORY

The history of ancient Mesopotamia included remarkable achievements, from the development of agriculture and the domestication* of animals by about 9000 B.C. to the rise of empires that began around 2300 B.C. Mesopotamia's history was marked by conflicts between states, invasions, conquests, and the rise and fall of governments and societies.

Origins of Mesopotamian Cities. By the early fourth millennium B.C.*, large agricultural settlements in Mesopotamia had begun to act as religious, administrative, and economic centers for the people of surrounding areas. Among the earliest of these emerging centers was URUK in southern Mesopotamia, an area known first as Sumer, and later as southern Babylonia. The main institution at Uruk and similar centers was the temple, which regulated all aspects of society and economy. It was through the temples that writing, government, judicial and economic systems, official art, and other elements of civilization first developed.

The economy of these centers was based primarily on agriculture, herding, and trade. Through trade and the contacts it created with other areas, the urban culture of southern Mesopotamia gradually spread to other parts of the region. By about 2800 B.C., disputes began to occur among urban centers, especially over water rights and territorial boundaries. The resulting unrest transformed these centers into fully developed cities, as people in rural areas migrated to them.

Many rivalries existed between the cities of southern Mesopotamia as each sought to gain an advantage over its neighbors or to expand its territory. Before long, many of these cities had gained control of large areas of surrounding territory, forming city-states*, such as KISH, LAGASH, UMMA, and UR, that were ruled by kings. Despite political differences, these Sumerian city-states shared the same language, religious beliefs, and customs.

The More Things Change, the More They Stay the Same

Despite the conquests, invasions, and political changes that Mesopotamia experienced during its thousands of years of history, Mesopotamian civilization remained remarkably uniform. It also had a great capacity to restore itself after major disasters. One of the reasons for this stability in the face of change may have been the unchanging nature of the small agricultural communities that remained the basic unit of Mesopotamian society. These communities provided a framework within which most people worked and lived. They remained stable and unchanged over generations and centuries despite disruption by flood, war, and famine.

---

* **urbanization** formation and growth of cities

* **bureaucracy** system consisting of officials and clerks who perform government functions

* **hierarchy** division of society or an institution into groups with higher and lower ranks

* **Semitic** of or relating to a language family that includes Akkadian, Aramaic, Arabic, Hebrew, and Phoenician

* **nomad** person who travels from place to place to find food and pasture

* **domestication** adaptation for human use

* **fourth millennium B.C.** years from 4000 to 3001 B.C.

* **city-state** independent state consisting of a city and its surrounding territory

Mesopotamia

Rise of Early Empires. Around 2350 B.C., the king of Umma seized several city-states and became ruler of all of Sumer. Soon after, he was defeated and replaced by Sᴀʀɢᴏɴ I, a ruler from Akkad (a region north of Sumer in northern Babylonia), who established the first centralized state in Mesopotamia. Sargon and his successors, including his grandson Nᴀʀᴀᴍ-Sɪɴ, launched programs of territorial expansion, spreading their control as far as parts of Syria, Iran, and Anatolia. Their conquests transformed the "land of Sumer and Akkad" into a true empire.

The Akkadian empire lasted nearly 200 years. The period was dominated by rivalry between southern Babylonia, which was peopled with non-Semitic Sumerians, and northern Babylonia, which was inhabited by Semitic-speaking Akkadians. At the same time, however, the culture of the two groups began to merge.

After a period of decline and invasion by the Gutians, a people from the northeast, Babylonia was reunited by about 2112 B.C. under Uʀ-Nᴀᴍᴍᴜ, who founded a new dynasty* known as the Third Dynasty of Ur. Sʜᴜʟɢɪ, perhaps the most important ruler of this dynasty, expanded the territory of the kingdom and launched a series of political, administrative, and economic reforms that transformed it into a highly centralized state with a governing bureaucracy. The period of the Third Dynasty of Ur is known as the Neo-Sumerian period.

The Age of the Amorites. Weakened by internal rebellions, raids by the Elamites, and migrations of nomadic peoples called Amorites, the Third Dynasty of Ur collapsed around 2004 B.C. This resulted in the reemergence of independent states, many of which gradually fell under the control of two rival powers: the city-states of Isin and Larsa. For nearly 250 years, Larsa and Isin vied for supremacy of Babylonia.

In the 1760s B.C., an Amorite ruler of the city of Bᴀʙʏʟᴏɴ named Hᴀᴍ-ᴍᴜʀᴀʙɪ united southern Mesopotamia and established a powerful new empire that dominated the region. One of Hammurabi's best-known achievements was his system of laws known as the Code of Hammurabi. Meanwhile, in northern Mesopotamia, a new kingdom had arisen. It was centered on the city of Asʜᴜʀ and ruled by an Amorite leader named Sʜᴀᴍsʜɪ-Aᴅᴀᴅ I. This kingdom became the foundation of the state of Assyria, which played a major role in later Mesopotamian history.

The Dark Age and the Kingdom of Mitanni. Following a series of raids by the Hittite king Murshili I in about 1595 B.C., Babylonia was overrun by the Kassites, who established various small independent kingdoms there. Little is known about the Kassites and their culture and of the first 200 years of their rule in Babylonia, a period referred to as the Dark Age. More is known about the Kassites from their contacts, shortly after 1400 B.C., with the later kings of Egypt's Eighteenth Dynasty. The Kassite period was relatively peaceful, except for periodic conflicts with Ashur. Kassite rule came to an end around 1158 B.C., when the Elamites raided and looted Babylon, taking many of its monuments to their capital of Susa in southwestern Iran. In the years that followed, Babylon and other cities in the region regained much of their independence under local rulers.

* **dynasty** succession of rulers from the same family or group

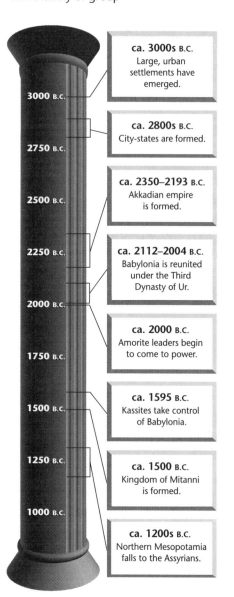

ca. 3000s B.C.
Large, urban settlements have emerged.

ca. 2800s B.C.
City-states are formed.

ca. 2350–2193 B.C.
Akkadian empire is formed.

ca. 2112–2004 B.C.
Babylonia is reunited under the Third Dynasty of Ur.

ca. 2000 B.C.
Amorite leaders begin to come to power.

ca. 1595 B.C.
Kassites take control of Babylonia.

ca. 1500 B.C.
Kingdom of Mitanni is formed.

ca. 1200s B.C.
Northern Mesopotamia falls to the Assyrians.

3000 B.C.
2750 B.C.
2500 B.C.
2250 B.C.
2000 B.C.
1750 B.C.
1500 B.C.
1250 B.C.
1000 B.C.

The king seated atop the throne in this cylinder seal impression dating from around 2100 B.C. is believed to be Ur-Nammu, founder of the Third Dynasty of Ur. During his reign, Ur-Nammu extended his kingdom's influence throughout southern and central Mesopotamia. He also launched several building campaigns in Ur and constructed the first ziggurats in the ancient Near East.

The Many Faces of Mesopotamian Religion

Different regions in ancient Mesopotamia shared the same religious beliefs. However, because of variations in their history, they developed independent religious practices and ideas as well as different ways to represent divine powers. This was most evident in the names of deities, or gods and goddesses. A complete list of Mesopotamian deities would include more than 3,000 different names. They were not all different deities, however. Many of the gods and goddesses were actually the same, but they were known by different names. Even in neighboring cities, for example, the same deity might be worshiped under different names. Although there were many faces to Mesopotamian religion, religious belief was much more similar than it would seem.

* **diplomacy** practice of conducting negotiations among or between kingdoms, states, or nations

* **cult** formal religious worship

As centralized rule in Mesopotamia declined after 1500 B.C., a group of people known as the Hurrians from northwestern Iran established a number of small states in northern Mesopotamia as well as in Syria and Anatolia. Around this time, a powerful Hurrian state called Mitanni arose in the north. Mitanni extended its authority over many neighboring kingdoms, eventually controlling a region that extended from the Mediterranean Sea in the west to Iran in the east.

The Rise of Assyria. While the Kassites controlled Babylonia, the region of Assyria in northern Mesopotamia emerged on the international scene. In the 1300s B.C., the city-state of Ashur expanded its borders and became a territorial state. The Assyrians conquered parts of Mitanni and divided up other areas in the north between themselves and the Hittites in Anatolia, with whom conflicts frequently arose. During the 1200s B.C., northern Mesopotamia fell entirely under Assyrian rule.

Beginning in the early 1100s B.C., Aramaean nomads began migrating into Mesopotamia from north Syria. They raided many cities in Assyria and Babylonia but were unable to gain a foothold in the cities and thus settled primarily in rural areas. One of the main contributions of the Aramaeans was their language, Aramaic, which eventually became the official language of diplomacy* and trade throughout Mesopotamia.

Assyria entered a period of decline in the 1000s B.C. that lasted until the 900s B.C., when Assyrian power was again on the rise. Over the next 300 years, the Neo-Assyrian empire reached its greatest extent under such rulers as SARGON II, ESARHADDON, and ASHURBANIPAL. The Assyrians created a large, centralized state, and their aggressive military might made them the undisputed masters of the ancient Near East.

The Fall of Assyria and Babylonia. For many years, the Assyrians let Babylonia keep its independence. The region had many cult* centers dedicated to gods also worshiped in Assyria. Babylonia was also revered

Mesopotamia

for its ancient culture. However, beginning in the 700s B.C., Assyria faced periodic problems with Babylonia and had to put down several rebellions there.

Assyrian power began to decline in the 600s B.C., while the power of Babylonia began to increase under the leadership of the Chaldeans, a people from the coastal areas near the Persian Gulf. The Babylonians rebelled in 626 B.C. and forced the Assyrians out of Babylonia. Later the Babylonians joined forces with the Medes of Iran and began attacking Assyrian provinces. In the late 600s B.C., the Assyrian empire collapsed as a result of repeated attacks by these invaders. Although some army units continued to fight, the Assyrian empire had effectively ended, and its lands were divided among the victors.

Babylonia then experienced a brief period of peace and prosperity. Babylonian rulers, especially NEBUCHADNEZZAR II, launched spectacular building programs and restored cultural and religious institutions long forgotten. Trade and commerce flourished, and Babylon became the largest and most magnificent city in the ancient world. This period was short-lived, however. In 539 B.C., Babylonia was conquered by the Persians, who made the region a province of the PERSIAN EMPIRE.

Mesopotamia Under the Persians, Greeks, and Parthians. At the height of their power, the Persians ruled all of Mesopotamia as well as other parts of the Near East. Babylonia, known as the breadbasket of the Persian empire, remained a prosperous land, but Assyria sank into poverty and obscurity. Although controlled by Persia through satraps, or provincial governors, Babylonia and other parts of Mesopotamia remained relatively unchanged in their culture, society, and religion.

The Persians controlled Mesopotamia until 330 B.C., when ALEXANDER THE GREAT conquered the Persian empire. Under Alexander and the SELEUCID EMPIRE that was created after his death, Mesopotamia experienced great changes. Although Mesopotamian cities generally kept their old systems of local government, the Hellenistic* culture introduced by the Seleucids brought Greek ideas, language, customs, and religious beliefs to the region. Mesopotamia also prospered greatly under the Seleucids.

In the mid-100s B.C., Mesopotamia was conquered by the Parthians, an originally nomadic people who had conquered neighboring Iran in the mid-200s B.C. Little changed in the region under the Parthians, who generally allowed local governments to remain autonomous*. Hellenistic culture continued to flourish, blending Greek and Iranian ideas. After the 30s B.C., Parthia had to compete with the Romans for dominance in Mesopotamia. Soon the Romans gained increasing advantage in the region, and in the A.D. 100s, Mesopotamia was conquered by the Romans and made a province of the Roman Empire. (*See also* **Akkad and the Akkadians; Animals, Domestication of; Archaeology and Archaeologists; Architecture; Art, Artisans, and Artists; Assyria and the Assyrians; Babylonia and the Babylonians; Chaldea and the Chaldeans; Cities and City-States; Economy and Trade; Elam and the Elamites; Geography; Hellenistic World; Parthia; Sumer and the Sumerians.**)

* **Hellenistic** referring to the Greek-influenced culture of the Mediterranean world and western Asia during the three centuries after the death of Alexander the Great in 323 B.C.

* **autonomous** self-governing

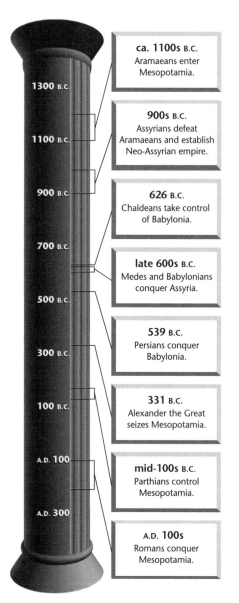

ca. 1100s B.C.
Aramaeans enter Mesopotamia.

900s B.C.
Assyrians defeat Aramaeans and establish Neo-Assyrian empire.

626 B.C.
Chaldeans take control of Babylonia.

late 600s B.C.
Medes and Babylonians conquer Assyria.

539 B.C.
Persians conquer Babylonia.

331 B.C.
Alexander the Great seizes Mesopotamia.

mid-100s B.C.
Parthians control Mesopotamia.

A.D. 100s
Romans conquer Mesopotamia.

MESSENGERS

* **diplomat** person who conducts negotiations or relations with foreign kingdoms, states, or nations

* **vassal** individual or state that swears loyalty and obedience to a greater power

Messengers provided an important means of COMMUNICATION in the ancient Near East, particularly over long distances. By carrying written or oral messages from one place to another, they served a basic function within every society. They became the principal means by which states conducted international business. According to the Greek historian HERODOTUS, "neither snow, nor rain, nor heat, nor gloom of night" could stop royal messengers as they carried messages between places.

There were three classes of messengers in the ancient Near East. The first was simply an individual—a servant, slave, or even a child—who traveled within a city carrying messages between households or businesses. The second class of messengers was composed of individuals who traveled long distances but only delivered a message and received the reply. The third, and most important class of messengers, was made up of individuals who delivered messages and had the authority to negotiate with the recipient, usually the ruler of another kingdom or state. Such messengers could negotiate treaties, trade relations, and other political, economic, or social matters. This last group of messengers served as ambassadors and diplomats* between states.

Only trustworthy, loyal, and fast individuals were chosen as messengers. They came from all classes in society, from slaves to royalty. Women served as messengers, too, most often carrying messages for other women. A royal messenger serving as an ambassador might be a trusted servant, a soldier or military officer, a member of the royal family, or a vassal* king traveling on behalf of another ruler. When communications involved personal matters or sensitive negotiations, a ruler might choose a member of the royal family to carry the message.

Royal messengers were skilled and intelligent individuals. They needed to know their own rulers and to understand the nature and terms of the negotiations taking place. They also had to know the culture and customs of the country where a message was to be delivered, as well as the personality of the ruler receiving the message. In learning the customs, politics, and news of the places they visited, messengers became the state's main link to its neighbors and the world. Royal messengers and their staff generally stayed at the palaces of the recipient rulers or in the homes of local individuals responsible for foreign relations. The messengers received normal rations of food and drink. In special instances, they might dine with the king or receive special gifts.

Long-distance messengers might travel by boat, by horse-drawn wagon, or on horseback. However, most traveled by foot, either walking or running, depending on distance and the urgency involved. As kingdoms expanded, systems of roads were constructed to make travel and communication easier. Many roads had rest stops for messengers set up at certain intervals. During the 2000s B.C., King SHULGI of UR described how he "enlarged the footpaths, straightened the highways [and] established rest houses." Later, the Persians and Romans both became famous for their extensive and well-organized systems of roads and messengers.

Although being a messenger was an important job, it was also difficult and dangerous work. Messengers generally had to travel on bad roads in all kinds of weather and faced threats from robbers as well as enemies in hostile states. (*See also* **Transportation and Travel.**)

Metals and Metalworking

METALS AND METALWORKING

* **artisan** skilled craftsperson

* **ore** mineral or rock containing a high concentration of one or more metals

Metals have fascinated humans for thousands of years. Early artisans* fashioned the first objects out of metal more than 9,000 years ago. However, it was not until some 7,500 years ago, with the invention of metallurgy—the science of extracting metal from ore* and creating useful objects from it—that metal came to be widely used for TOOLS, weapons, decorations, and currency. The art and science of metalworking probably began in the ancient Near East, and the civilizations there were at the forefront of metallurgy for thousands of years.

METALLURGY

To produce useful metal objects, one must learn how to separate metals from ore, melt metal, work with it in a liquid form, and change its properties through heating and other processes. These skills are known as metallurgy, and their discovery was a turning point for humanity.

Native Metals and Ores. Most metals are embedded in rocky minerals called ores, from which they must be extracted before they can be used. However, small quantities of some metals occur naturally as pure nuggets already separated from ore. These so-called "native" metals—such as gold, silver, and copper—result from the action of water passing over and through the ore-bearing rock formations. Such metals can be easily collected with a minimum of effort. The oldest metal objects found in the Near East—a pin and a needle of native copper dating from between 7500 and 7000 B.C.—were found in ANATOLIA.

Native metals can be worked in their natural state by hammering them into the desired shape. Because such metals make up only a small fraction of the metals contained in the earth, however, only a limited number of objects can be made from them. Moreover, hammering makes metals brittle and the shapes and uses of objects produced in this manner are limited. To produce a larger variety of metal items, it is necessary to apply the basic techniques of metallurgy.

Melting and Smelting. The most basic metallurgical technique is heating metal until it becomes soft or melts into a liquid. By pouring the liquid into a mold and letting the molten metal cool, early peoples discovered that they could create metal objects of any desired shape. Working copper in this way also made it less brittle. Evidence suggests that by about 7000 B.C. early metalworkers in the Near East learned how to change the nature of metals by heating them. The first metal to be worked in this way was copper.

Another basic metallurgical technique is smelting, a process by which an ore is heated together with another substance that combines chemically with the nonmetal in the ore and separates it from the metal. The earliest evidence of copper smelting in the ancient Near East—a lump of slag, a waste product of the smelting process, dating from about 5500 B.C.—comes from Anatolia. However, lumps of copper ore have been found at various sites in MESOPOTAMIA dating from about the same period, suggesting that the smelting process may have been known there as well. By 3000 B.C., copper smelting technology had become widely known throughout the Near East. The process was essential to the growth and further development of metalworking in the region.

Alloying. As early artisans in the Near East worked with various types of metals, they eventually discovered that some metals could be combined by melting them together, a process known as alloying. Alloying enabled metalworkers to change the properties of metals and produce metals that were stronger and more durable. One of the first alloys used in the Near East, and the most important, was bronze, a mixture of copper and tin. The production of bronze and its use in making weapons, tools, and other objects was so important that historians call the period from about 3000 to 1200 B.C. the Bronze Age.

METALS OF THE ANCIENT NEAR EAST

The people of the ancient Near East used precious metals—gold and silver—as well as common metals—copper, tin, and iron. In addition, they produced alloys, such as bronze, that were used extensively. A later invention was steel, an alloy of iron and carbon.

Copper. The first metal to be used throughout the ancient world was copper. This was largely because native copper and copper ores are abundant throughout the Near East. Large copper deposits existed in Anatolia, in northern IRAN and Mesopotamia, on the island of CYPRUS, in parts of the Levant* and SYRIA, in the deserts of eastern Egypt, and on the OMAN PENINSULA of Arabia.

Archaeologists* have discovered evidence of copper metallurgy in Anatolia, Iran, and the Levant dating from between 5500 and 3500 B.C. This technology appeared later in Mesopotamia. The earliest copper objects there were made from metal mined in Iran and brought to Mesopotamia by traders. After about 3000 B.C., the Sumerians began to import copper from the land of Magan (present-day Oman) because it was cheaper to import copper from Magan by ship through the Persian Gulf than through overland trade from Iran.

Bronze and Tin. The earliest bronze objects appeared around 3000 B.C. By about 1900 B.C., tin bronze (copper and tin) had replaced arsenical bronze (copper and arsenic) in much of the Near East. The Egyptians, however, continued the use of arsenical bronze because arsenic forms a silvery surface on copper that can be polished to a mirrorlike finish. Bronze was used to make domestic utensils, furniture, lamps, sculpture, arms, armor, coins, tools, and implements.

Scholars are uncertain about the origins of the tin that was used to make the earliest tin-bronze alloys. Native tin may have been used for some early bronze work, but deposits of the metal were much too small to have supported a widespread bronze industry. Anatolia contains some tin ores, but there is little evidence to suggest that ancient peoples either knew about or mined them. The best current evidence of ancient sources of tin points to eastern Iran and areas in present-day Afghanistan, which contain large quantities of native tin and tin ores.

* **Levant** lands bordering the eastern shores of the Mediterranean Sea (present-day Syria, Lebanon, and Israel), the West Bank, and Jordan

* **archaeologist** scientist who studies past human cultures, usually by excavating material remains of human activity

The Copper-Silver Dispute

An ancient Sumerian text called *The Dispute Between Copper and Silver* contains an interesting "dialogue" between copper and silver. Copper mocks silver for its uselessness, saying that it has a place only in the palace: "If there were no palace, you would have no station; gone would be your dwelling place." Even in the home silver is "buried away in its darkest spots," while copper is widely used every day. The "dispute" goes on to mention the use of copper tools for planting crops, harvesting grain, and cutting wood. Because of copper's great usefulness, the text concludes of silver: "That's why nobody pays any attention to you!"

Metals and Metalworking

See
color plate 3,
vol. 4.

Gold and Silver. The major sources of gold in the region were eastern Anatolia, eastern Iran, Afghanistan, and Egypt. Because gold could be easily bent or drawn out, it was impractical for tools or weapons. It was almost exclusively used for JEWELRY and luxury items, as well as for decorations in temples, palaces, and other official buildings. Although gold was being worked in Egypt, Anatolia, and Mesopotamia before 3000 B.C., its use did not become widespread until later.

Silver was used widely throughout the ancient Near East prior to 3000 B.C. Among the most important sources of silver were Iran, Afghanistan, and Anatolia. This precious metal, like gold, was used mainly for jewelry and luxury items. Silver was also accepted in Mesopotamia as a medium of exchange, or type of currency, and some societies in the Near East used a natural alloy of silver and gold, known as electrum, for making coins.

Iron. Although iron was found everywhere in the ancient world, it was the last metal to be widely used in the ancient Near East. The oldest piece of ironwork found in the Near East comes from Mesopotamia and dates from about 5000 B.C. Fewer than 25 iron objects have been discovered that date from between 3000 and 2000 B.C. Almost all of these came from the graves of wealthy individuals, temples, or collections of treasure, suggesting that they were rare and valuable items.

Increasing numbers of iron objects were produced in the Near East between about 2000 and 1200 B.C., but these were probably by-products of copper smelting. It was not until after 1500 B.C. that iron was produced in any quantity, and it was not used for tools and weapons until the 1200s B.C. The HITTITES are considered the earliest ironworkers of the ancient Near East, and some historians credit their rise as a military power to the early use of iron weapons.

The helmet shown here belonged to King Meskalamdug of Ur. It was made from a hammered sheet of electrum (an alloy of gold and silver) and was decorated by hammering the metal from both sides. Originally, the interior was lined with cloth or leather attached by the holes along the helmet's outer edges. The helmet was excavated at the Royal Cemetery of Ur and dates from about 2600 B.C.

By about 1100 B.C., metalworkers in the Near East had mastered the techniques for producing steel from iron, and by 900 B.C., ironworking had spread throughout the region. Although bronze continued to be used widely for hundreds of years after that time, the period after about 1200 B.C. and until 500 B.C. is known as the Iron Age.

METALWORKING

The term *metalworking* refers to the ability to make useful objects out of metal. This ability dramatically transformed ancient society, and because of the advantages of metal items, ancient metalworkers became important members of ancient Near Eastern societies.

Metalworkers. Those who mastered the arts of melting, smelting, and casting metals such as copper or tin were called smiths. Although highly valued for their skills, they had the lowest social status among metalworkers. For example, an ancient Egyptian text described coppersmiths in unflattering terms, saying that their "fingers are like crocodile scales" and their flesh "stinks more than fish eggs."

Those who worked metal and created metal objects, considered metalworkers, were more highly respected. The most highly esteemed members of the metalworking profession were jewelers and goldsmiths. These artisans typically worked in royal workshops making personal items for the wealthy and powerful. They also created cult* objects and official items such as metal SEALS.

Metalworking Techniques. Near Eastern metalworkers used two basic techniques: casting and hammering. Casting involved pouring molten metal into molds of various shapes and allowing the metal to cool and harden. Ancient Near Eastern artisans used a complex type of casting called the lost-wax method. Here an artisan made a wax model of the desired object and covered it with clay. When the clay hardened into a mold, it was heated until the wax ran out through a hole on the bottom. Molten metal was then poured into the mold through the same hole. When the metal cooled the mold was broken, leaving a metal reproduction of the original wax model. This method was used for making small objects as well as larger works such as statues.

Hammering, which involved pounding metal into a desired shape, produced one-of-a-kind objects. Artisans used one of five methods of hammering: raising, sinking, repoussé, chasing, and punching. In raising, the metal was hammered into shape from the outside, while in sinking it was hammered into a depression cut into wood or another material. In repoussé, the design was hammered into sheet metal from the back to form a raised pattern. In chasing, a reverse of repoussé, the metal was hammered from the front to produce a sunken design. Punching involved hammering holes into a piece of metal. It was often used for artistic decoration and to cut INSCRIPTIONS into metal objects. Another more specialized type of metalworking skill was gilding, in which an artisan applied a thin layer of gold to the surface of an object. Gilding was used for only the most valuable or sacred objects.

The Lame Smith

One of the common characters in myths and folktales around the world is the blacksmith. In stories from the Near East and the Mediterranean world, the smith is typically lame. For example, the Greek smith god Hephaestus and his Roman counterpart Vulcan were always depicted as lame. This may reflect a reality of life for early metalsmiths, who often worked with bronze ores that contained arsenic. While working with arsenic over a period of time, ancient smiths absorbed the dangerous substance into their skin. This could easily have led to chronic arsenic poisoning, which causes decay of the muscles, loss of reflexes, and eventually lameness.

* **cult** formal religious worship

Local Metalworking Traditions. Archaeologists have uncovered metal artifacts that demonstrate the great skill of ancient metalworkers and the differences in metalworking traditions. For example, copper axes and weapons from Iran feature elaborate decorations, often including animal forms. The wide distribution of such objects indicates that they were traded throughout the region.

Some of the most interesting and impressive metalwork of the ancient Near East was produced in the kingdom of URARTU from about 650 to 600 B.C. Urartu had especially gifted bronze workers who created highly decorated bronze objects such as belts, plates, bells, plaques, and statues. Other Urartian treasures include bronze statuettes covered in gold leaf and inlaid with precious stones. While the Urartian culture was particularly gifted in the arts of metalworking, they were not unique. Metalworking played a key role in the advancement of Near Eastern civilization, and metalworking skills were essential to every society that made its mark on the region. (*See also* **Art, Artisans, and Artists; Economy and Trade; Jewelry; Mining; Money; Science and Technology; Weapons and Armor.**)

Midas

See *Phrygia and the Phrygians.*

MIGRATION AND DEPORTATION

* **famine** severe lack of food due to failed crops

* **drought** long period of dry weather during which crop yields are lower than usual

In the ancient Near East, people often migrated for economic reasons: to search for better agricultural or grazing land or to escape famine* or drought*. They also migrated for political reasons: to escape oppression or to flee from invaders. Sometimes they were forcibly removed from their homelands and taken elsewhere. This occurred when one state conquered another. Such involuntary movement from one place to another, known as deportation, was much less common than other types of migration.

MIGRATION

Most migration in the ancient Near East occurred as people wandered in search of better land for farming or grazing livestock. Some of this migration was seasonal and generally involved small numbers of people and had only a minor impact on settled communities or societies. More permanent migrations involving thousands of people also occurred. These great migratory movements caused profound political, economic, and social changes throughout the ancient Near East.

Pastoral Nomadism. From as early as 8000 B.C., ancient Near Eastern societies contained both farmers and herders. Over time, the herders developed a lifestyle known as pastoral nomadism, which was quite different from that of farmers. They had no fixed residence and wandered from place to place. They were also pastoralists, which means that their lifestyle was based on the breeding and herding of animals. Some scholars believe that pastoral nomadism arose in the Near East as human populations increased and fertile lands became increasingly scarce. To conserve land for crops, herders had to move away from communities to graze their herds, leading to the nomadic lifestyle.

Drought, famine, and other problems sometimes forced even farmers to take up a nomadic pastoral lifestyle because they could no longer support themselves by raising crops. They often returned to farming when agricultural conditions improved. Similarly, pastoral nomads often settled in communities, perhaps to farm or because they needed a home from which to manage their herds over a large area. Such changes back and forth between nomadism and farming occurred in ancient times, contributing to the migrations of people throughout the Near East.

Large-Scale Migrations. ENVIRONMENTAL CHANGE, political instability, war, and other factors also caused large-scale migrations. However, these were very different from pastoral nomadism because they involved larger numbers of people. Often these people were from different ethnic backgrounds, worshiped different gods, and spoke different languages than those of the inhabitants of the lands to which they migrated.

The people in these types of migrations were usually seen as invaders, even if their purpose was not to conquer but to escape some problem or disaster in their homelands. The movement of such groups often caused great upheaval, leading to changes in government, the rise of new states, the disappearance of old traditions, and the emergence of new cultural and religious ideas.

One of the earliest large-scale migrations known from ancient sources involved the Gutians. This pastoral nomadic group from the Zagros Mountains region of western IRAN migrated to MESOPOTAMIA sometime before the 2100s B.C. and possibly contributed to the collapse of the Akkadian empire.

The best-documented series of migrations in the ancient Near East were probably those of the AMORITES, a nomadic people who migrated from northern Mesopotamia and SYRIA to central and southern Mesopotamia beginning in about 2000 B.C. Although the Amorites attacked some areas, their migration was largely peaceful. Records from the city-state* of MARI indicate that it tried unsuccessfully to control the Amorites and their migration. Other city-states probably attempted to do the same. Eventually, however, the Amorites took over many areas and established small, independent kingdoms. They were absorbed into the local populations and assimilated* many local customs, beliefs, and institutions. Among the most famous Amorite rulers were HAMMURABI and SHAMSHI-ADAD I.

By about 1600 B.C., the Amorites were being forced westward by migrations of KASSITES, a pastoral nomadic group that probably originated in the Zagros Mountains. Around 1595 B.C., the Kassites seized power in Babylonia and established various small kingdoms. Another group of people known as the HURRIANS, who had moved from northwestern Iran, settled in northern Mesopotamia and founded a number of states there, including the powerful Mitanni.

Opposing Lifestyles

In ancient times, many nomads mistrusted farmers and the city life, while farmers and city dwellers distrusted the nomads. A letter written in Syria by one Yaminite leader to another around 1770 B.C. expresses perhaps a common view about the opposing viewpoints of city life and the nomadic existence:

You look forward to eating, drinking and sleeping, but not to accompanying me? Sitting or sleeping will not redden you [from the sun]. As for me, if I keep myself inside just one day, until I leave the city walls behind to renew my vigor, my vitality ebbs away.

* **city-state** independent state consisting of a city and its surrounding territory

* **assimilate** to adopt the customs of a society

Migration and Deportation

* **Levant** lands bordering the eastern
  shores of the Mediterranean Sea
  (present-day Syria, Lebanon, and Israel),
  the West Bank, and Jordan

In about 1200 B.C., Egypt was invaded both by land and by sea by groups historians call the SEA PEOPLES. These peoples were not one group but various tribes, including the PHILISTINES. After Egyptian king RAMSES III drove the Sea Peoples out of Egypt, they appear to have settled in the Levant* and in Syria. During the following century, many cities including KARKAMISH and UGARIT in Syria, and KHATTUSHA, the capital of the HITTITES in Anatolia were violently destroyed. Many scholars believe that these widespread destructions resulted from the migrations of Sea Peoples into these regions.

Around 1100 B.C., another nomadic group known as the ARAMAEANS began migrating into the settled areas of Syria, Assyria, and Babylonia. Scholars believe that the Aramaeans came from the desert fringes of Syria, although there is no evidence of them before about 1300 B.C. The Aramaeans captured various city-states in Syria, and their growing power eventually brought them into conflict with the Assyrians. Assyrian king Tiglath-pileser I spoke of crossing the EUPHRATES RIVER many times to chase them away. Around 926 B.C., the Aramaeans had established a large state called Bit-Adini. Aramaean culture gradually spread throughout Syria and Mesopotamia, and the Aramaic language became the common language of government and business in many parts of the Near East.

Another series of migrations had a great impact on the later history of the Near East. Around 1500 B.C., a nomadic people called the ARYANS began migrating from CENTRAL ASIA to Iran. The two most important Aryan tribes were the MEDES and the Persians. The Medes settled in northwestern Iran, established a kingdom in the 700s B.C., and played an important role in the collapse of the Assyrian empire in the following century. The Persians settled in southern Iran, and by the late 500s B.C., the PERSIAN EMPIRE had become the mightiest empire in the Near East.

DEPORTATION

At various times in the ancient Near East, rulers forcibly moved groups of people from one place to another. Such forced migration, or deportation, generally was done for political purposes. Rulers deported people from a conquered territory to limit the possibility of rebellion, to improve their ability to control the area, and to punish rebellion or refusal to pay tribute*. Deportation not only broke up any unified opposition but also created forced labor that could be used to build monuments or work in farm colonies.

* **tribute** payment made by a smaller or
  weaker party to a more powerful one,
  often under the threat of force

Most deportations in the Near East were carried out by the Assyrians. Around 1235 B.C., King Tukulti-Ninurta I deported several Babylonians into Assyria as retaliation for an attack by the Kassites. In the 800s B.C., King ASHURNASIRPAL II began a military conquest in the Levant to gain control of various trade routes. He ordered the deportation of Phoenicians and Aramaeans from their homelands.

In the 700s B.C., after conquering Syria, King TIGLATH-PILESER III launched mass deportations that removed at least 80,000 people from the area. He then brought people from other parts of his empire to replace them. SARGON II forced an even larger number of people to move in 707 B.C. After conquering Babylon, he deported more than 100,000 Aramaeans and Chaldeans to SAMARIA, the former capital of Israel, and other distant regions and moved in others to replace those deported. Earlier, in 722 B.C., the Assyrians had moved large numbers of people from Israel to northern Mesopotamia.

The Assyrians were not the only ones to use deportation, however. The Babylonians used the tactic against the Jews around 587 B.C., when the kingdom of Judah rebelled against Babylonian control. After destroying the city of JERUSALEM, the Babylonians deported a large part of the Jewish population to Babylonia, where they were enslaved. When the Persian king CYRUS THE GREAT conquered Babylonia in 538 B.C., he freed the Jews and permitted them to return to their homeland. However, many chose to stay in their new home.

The Hittites also deported people from conquered territory and resettled them in Hittite lands. These people became slaves and provided labor for the state. (*See also* **Drought; Famine; Labor and Laborers; Nomads and Nomadism; Slaves and Slavery; Wars and Warfare.**)

* **archaeologist** scientist who studies past human cultures, usually by excavating material remains of human activity

* **artifact** ornament, tool, weapon, or other object made by humans

Mining is the recovery of metal or metal-bearing minerals called ores from deposits in the earth. Archaeologists* have uncovered evidence of metal use in the ancient Near East from at least 7000 B.C. However, the earliest metal artifacts* were probably made from metals found above ground, such as gold, silver, or copper taken from streambeds. The actual mining of metals and metallic ores probably did not develop until around 5000 B.C. Because of the usefulness of metal for making tools, weapons, and other objects, mining became an important economic activity in the ancient Near East.

THE MINING PROCESS

Most metals are embedded in ores that contain varying amounts of metal. Ore deposits are typically located in mountains or beneath the earth's surface, and recovery of the ores often requires a great deal of effort. To reach ore deposits, workers usually must cut shafts or tunnels into the rock and then dig out the ore. The earliest miners did this with picks and hammers made of stone. The ore is then transported to workshops where the metal is removed through various techniques.

Mining and the recovery of metal from ore involve complex processes. They require the technical expertise to locate and recognize ore deposits, the organizational ability to assemble a large workforce to extract ores from the earth, and the technology to separate metal from ore so that it can be worked to produce useful items.

MINING IN THE ANCIENT NEAR EAST

Very little is known about early mining in the ancient Near East. Many regions, including MESOPOTAMIA, SYRIA, and Egypt, have few mineral deposits. Extensive mineral deposits were found in ANATOLIA (present-day

Mining

* **fifth millennium** B.C. years from 5000 to 4001 B.C.

* **artisan** skilled craftsperson

* **Levant** lands bordering the eastern shores of the Mediterranean Sea (present-day Syria, Lebanon, and Israel), the West Bank, and Jordan

Turkey), and studies in that region have produced significant information about ancient mining activities. That information, combined with knowledge about trade and metalworking in the Near East, has provided an overview of mining and the metals recovered.

Copper. The first metal mined extensively in the ancient Near East was copper. Large deposits of copper were found in a belt that extended across Anatolia into northern Assyria and IRAN. The earliest evidence of copper mining in these regions dates to the early fifth millennium B.C.*

At a site called Tepe Ghabristan in northern Iran, archaeologists discovered the remains of a copper workshop from about 4500 B.C. Equipment found at the site included a deep bowl containing pieces of copper ore and a furnace for smelting, a process by which an ore is heated together with another substance that combines chemically with the nonmetal in the ore and separates it from the metal. The fact that artisans* were smelting copper at this site suggests that copper probably was mined in the area at the time.

Archaeologists have also discovered evidence of copper metalworking in the Levant*, dating from as early as 3500 B.C. The copper ore for this industry probably came from deposits in present-day Jordan, although some may have also come from sites in southern Israel.

The Egyptians were mining copper in the SINAI PENINSULA as early as 3000 B.C. In Mesopotamia, there is little evidence of copper metalworking before about 2000 B.C., probably because the area had few deposits of ore. The copper used in the region in early times probably came from mines in Iran. CYPRUS and parts of the OMAN PENINSULA contained significant deposits of copper. After 3000 B.C., the Mesopotamians began to import copper from the mines of Oman instead of from Iran.

Tin. The metal tin is often contained in a mineral ore called cassiterite, which can be found in streambeds or on plains where it has been deposited by running water. When tin is combined with copper by melting the two metals together—a process known as alloying—the result is bronze, a much harder and more useful metal than either copper or tin.

The appearance of bronze items in Anatolia indicates that people in that region were using tin by the early third millennium B.C. (years from 3000 to 2001 B.C.) Bronze items dating from about 2500 B.C. have been found in cities as far apart as TROY and UR. Although tin is currently mined in southeastern Turkey, there is little evidence that tin mining occurred there in ancient times. The most likely source of ancient tin was present-day Afghanistan. Tin from mines there was traded over much of the Near East. MERCHANTS brought much of this tin to such cities as ASHUR and MARI, where it was shipped to various places in Anatolia and the Levant.

Iron. Bronze was the most important metal in the ancient Near East from about 3500 B.C. to 1200 B.C., when it was replaced by iron. Although remains of iron objects dating from as early as about 5000 B.C. have been found in the Near East, these were probably by-products of copper smelting, because some copper ores contain small amounts of iron. Iron was not produced in significant quantities until after 1500 B.C., and it was not used for tools or weapons for another 300 years.

Life in the Mines

Ancient texts and other evidence provide a glimpse of the difficult conditions that ancient miners often had to endure. Remains of mining sites in eastern Egypt reveal that miners not only had to travel across the harsh desert to the mines, but they also had to carry their own food with them from home. Egyptian records show that mining for turquoise in the desert of the Sinai peninsula took place in winter at altitudes where the cold was intense and water was scarce. Copper and gold mining took place in the same region during the blistering heat of the summer. According to Greek sources, water was rationed, and many Egyptian miners died under such harsh conditions.

The most abundant metal on earth, iron makes up nearly 6 percent of the earth's crust. Deposits of iron ore as well as meteoric iron existed in almost every part of the ancient world. Yet iron mining and metalworking were slow to develop. The primary reason is that ironworking requires more advanced techniques than were available in the earlier periods of ancient Near Eastern history. Once these techniques were developed, however, iron became very important because it provided a stronger, cheaper, and more practical alternative to bronze. Because of the importance and abundance of iron, evidence of iron mining and metalworking have been found in many areas of the ancient Near East.

Other Metals. The people of the ancient Near East also mined lead, silver, and gold. Evidence indicates that lead ores were being smelted to produce metallic lead as early 3500 B.C. and perhaps earlier. This suggests that lead mining existed at that time as well. The Egyptians were mining gold by about 2700 B.C., with most mining activity taking place in the desert east of the NILE RIVER and in the region of Nubia south of Egypt. Silver mines were located in many places in the ancient Near East. Most of the silver in ancient Egyptian jewelry came from mines in Anatolia, Cyprus, and CRETE. (*See also* **Art, Artisans, and Artists; Economy and Trade; Metals and Metalworking; Science and Technology; Tools; Weapons and Armor.**)

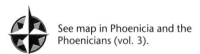

MINOAN CIVILIZATION

* **archaeologist** scientist who studies past human cultures, usually by excavating material remains of human activity

See map in Phoenicia and the Phoenicians (vol. 3).

* **domesticated** adapted or tamed for human use

In A.D. 1900, English archaeologist* Sir Arthur Evans made an amazing discovery on the island of CRETE in the Mediterranean Sea. He uncovered the ruins of a unique and distinctive culture dating from about 3000 to 1000 B.C. He called this culture the Minoan civilization, named after King Minos, a legendary king of Crete in Greek MYTHOLOGY.

Despite many discoveries since Evans, the Minoan civilization remains a mystery and a matter of disagreement among modern historians. Experts generally agree, however, that the Minoans were a mostly peaceful and sophisticated people who developed extensive trading networks and created beautiful POTTERY, JEWELRY, WALL PAINTINGS, and SCULPTURE.

Geography and Early Settlements. Crete is located south of Greece at the edge of the AEGEAN SEA. Apart from CYPRUS, it is the largest island in the eastern Mediterranean. With a mild climate, abundant resources, and an excellent location for sea trade, it is not surprising that a great civilization arose on the island in ancient times.

The earliest inhabitants of Crete probably arrived on the island around 6000 B.C., but their exact origins are unknown. Continuous migration over the next 3,000 years led to the introduction of domesticated* plants and animals from the ancient Near East, and this contributed to the development of a flourishing agricultural economy.

By about 3000 B.C., the people of Crete had become successful farmers, herders, and traders, and their settlements were scattered throughout the island. They exported wine, wool, textiles, timber, and olive oil and

Minoan Civilization

* **Levant** lands bordering the eastern shores of the Mediterranean Sea (present-day Syria, Lebanon, and Israel), the West Bank, and Jordan

* **fresco** method of painting in which color is applied to moist plaster so that it becomes chemically bonded to the plaster as it dries; also, a painting done in this manner

* **city-state** independent state consisting of a city and its surrounding territory

* **hieroglyphic** referring to a system of writing that uses pictorial characters, or hieroglyphs, to represent words or ideas

imported metals and jewels. Long-distance trade was strong with ANATOLIA (present-day Turkey) and the Levant*. Cretan society at this time consisted of various social classes, and political power began to centralize in several of the largest settlements.

The Rise of Minoan Power. By about 2000 B.C., the Minoans began to construct palaces at a number of major towns. Among the most important of these were at KNOSSOS, Phaistos, and Mallia. Built around an open central courtyard, Minoan palaces were multistory buildings with a maze of rooms and beautiful frescoes*, baths, and running water.

Each palace was centrally located in a town. The palaces became important focal points of Minoan society and served as the seats of government, administration, and centers of trade and as sites where food products, raw materials, and manufactured goods were collected and redistributed. It is possible that the palaces became the centers of small city-states*, which competed with each other for trade.

Because of extensive trade and an abundance of resources, Minoans of all social classes were well off. Many scholars believe that wealth was spread more evenly throughout Minoan society than in any other culture of the Near East. Peace and prosperity allowed the Minoans to devote more time to enjoying life, which explains their remarkable achievements in the arts. During this period, the Cretans used a hieroglyphic* writing system that has not been decoded and interpreted.

In the early 1700s B.C., EARTHQUAKES damaged some Minoan palaces, but they were rebuilt. By about 1600 B.C., the Minoan civilization had reached its peak, and its influence extended beyond Crete. The Minoans

The Minoan civilization, which flourished from about 3000 to 1000 B.C., was renowned for its extensive trading networks throughout the Aegean and beyond. Among the commodities the Minoans traded were splendid works of pottery and metal. This fresco from the nearby island of Thera shows an Aegean boat similar to those that the Minoans used for their maritime trade.

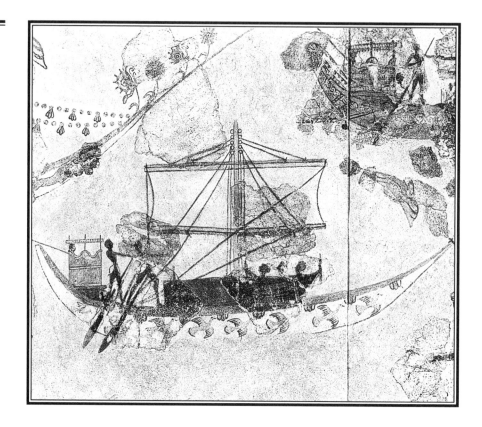

possibly colonized—and certainly influenced—many islands in the Aegean Sea, including THERA. It is also likely that, through trade, the Minoans and other Near Eastern peoples influenced each other. Minoan goods have been found as far away as Egypt and MESOPOTAMIA, and there are wall paintings in Egypt depicting Minoan traders. The Minoans of this period used a simple script that modern scholars call Linear A, which has not been deciphered*.

The Collapse of Minoan Power. Around 1500 B.C., many Minoan palaces on Crete were again destroyed, probably because of a volcanic explosion on Thera. Although they were rebuilt and were as beautiful and elaborate as before, the size and number of settlements outside the palaces declined. Within the next 100 years, all the palaces—with the exception of the one at Knossos—ceased to be important political or trading centers.

At the same time, Crete was being increasingly dominated by MYCENAE AND THE MYCENAEANS, who brought a warrior-based culture from mainland Greece. Certain Cretan burial practices and artistic themes from this period reflect Mycenaean influence, as does the adoption of a new writing system—Linear B—used to write the Mycenaean Greek dialect*.

Around 1400 B.C., the palace of Knossos was destroyed by fire, perhaps a result of a Mycenaean invasion or natural catastrophe. The destruction of Knossos marked the collapse of Minoan power, although regional Minoan cultures continued to flourish for some time on various parts of Crete. When Minoan power collapsed, the center of culture in the Aegean region passed to the mainland of Greece and the Mycenaeans.

Religion, Politics, and the Arts. A unique feature of Minoan civilization was the absence of great temples such as those found elsewhere throughout the ancient Near East. Minoan religious rites took place in the palaces, in sacred caves, and on mountaintops. Minoan religious beliefs focused on nature worship, female goddesses, and fertility cults*, and sacred symbols included doves, trees, bulls, and snakes.

Strangely, no individual leader is named on any artifact* created by the Minoans, and archeologists have found no evidence of any type of warrior class before Mycenaean influence took hold. This has led many scholars to believe that the Minoans were ruled by their religious leaders. Scholars cannot agree whether these rulers were priest-kings, priestess-queens, or both. It is certain from studying Minoan art, however, that women played prominent roles in religious ceremonies.

Minoan civilization is probably most famous for its artwork. Delicately shaped pottery pieces were decorated with scenes of animals and plants and used a beautiful style of light on dark. Frescoes were brightly painted and depicted both religious and secular* scenes. Some showed magical gardens full of animals. In later periods, art became increasingly realistic, and by the 1400s B.C., artists were creating a sense of depth in wall murals through the use of relief*.

One of the most interesting features of Minoan art is the pictures of "bull leaping." Painted on vases and frescoes, these pictures show young men and women leaping over the horns of bulls. Scholars are uncertain

King Minos and the Minotaur

In Greek mythology, King Minos of Crete was the son of Zeus. Minos once angered Poseidon by not sacrificing a white bull to the god. To punish Minos, Poseidon made his wife, Pasiphaë, fall in love with the bull, and she bore a creature with a bull's head and a man's body called the Minotaur. Minos kept the Minotaur in an enormous labyrinth, or maze, beneath his palace. To avenge the death of his son at the hand of the king of Athens, Minos made the Athenians give him seven young men and seven young women each year. He locked these youths in the labyrinth, where they died of starvation or were killed and eaten by the Minotaur. One of these youths, the Greek hero Theseus, later killed the Minotaur. Although the story of the Minotaur is only a myth, there may once have been a real king of Crete named Minos.

* **decipher** to decode and interpret the meaning

* **dialect** regional form of a spoken language with distinct pronunciation, vocabulary, and grammar

* **cult** system of religious beliefs and rituals; group following these beliefs

* **artifact** ornament, tool, weapon, or other object made by humans

* **secular** nonreligious; connected with everyday life

* **relief** sculpture in which material is cut away to show figures raised from the background

whether "bull leaping" was a sport or a religious ceremony, although most believe it was connected to fertility rituals. (*See also* **Animals in Art; Architecture; Mediterranean Sea, Trade on.**)

* **mint** to make coins; place where coins are made

Coins and paper currency have been used for so long that most people today consider them the only acceptable forms of money. However, the first coins were not minted* until after 700 B.C., and paper money has only been in existence for a few hundred years. This does not mean, however, that money did not exist in ancient times. Different items served Near Eastern societies as money, including precious metals, such as silver and gold, and grain.

Defining Money. To understand how grain and other items served as money, it is important to consider the technical definition of money. Most economists consider money to be anything that can be used as a means of exchange, a form of payment, and a standard for accounting.

The first definition is probably the broadest. Money is anything used to obtain an item one desires. Even items traded in barter can function as a form of money, because each party gives the other some item in exchange for another item. Although the second definition seems at first glance the same as the first, there is a difference. As a form of payment, money is anything used to settle a debt or obligation that does not necessarily involve receiving something in return, such as taxes. Farmers in ancient Egypt gave the state a portion of their harvest as tax. The third definition considers money to be any commodity* used as a measure of value against other commodities. The value of items in ancient MESOPOTAMIA was expressed as a fixed amount of silver or grain. Thus, a particular piece of cloth might be valued at so many shekels of silver or a certain number of bushels of grain. Goods could be and were purchased with things other than silver or grain. However, the value of the goods acquired and the value of the goods given were both calculated in terms of either silver or grain. This ensured that both parties received items of equal worth regardless of the items they exchanged.

* **commodity** article of trade

* **city-state** independent state consisting of a city and its surrounding territory

The oldest known coin, shown here, was minted in Lydia around 650 B.C. However, it took time before coins replaced more traditional forms of money, such as barley and sesame oil, in the ancient Near East. Only after the Greeks began minting coins around 575 B.C. did the use of coins become widespread. The earliest coins were made of locally available electrum, a natural alloy of gold and silver.

Early Money. Before the rise of cities and city-states*, barter was the basis for economic activity. People acquired goods from one another by trading items that they judged to be of roughly similar value. However, barter was too cumbersome, especially in complex urban economies. To regulate economic activity, ancient peoples fixed standards of value, and the commodities used to set such standards functioned as money. Records from the ancient Near East indicate that silver and grain were used as money in nearly every society. Both shared qualities that made them ideal for this use. They had value, could be stored for long periods without losing their value, and were interchangeable for similar items. That is, one shekel of silver was the same as any other, as was one bushel of grain.

The choice of silver and grain as money stemmed from their abundance. Because ancient Near Eastern societies were based on AGRICULTURE,

They Were Coins, but Were They Money?

By about 400 B.C., many Near Eastern societies were minting coins, but not all of them were used as currency in the states that produced them. For example, King Nectanebo I minted the first Egyptian coins shortly after 400 B.C., but these were used to pay Greek mercenary soldiers, not circulated as local currency. The relative lack of small coins in ancient Greece suggests that they were not used in everyday transactions. Most coins found in hoards, even as late as the Roman era, are also of high denominations, indicating that coins were not widely used for simple transactions.

* **archaeologist** scientist who studies past human cultures, usually by excavating material remains of human activity

grain was not only essential for life but also easily available. Silver was also quite abundant, which explains why it was used as money more often than gold. Around 1600 B.C., an increase in Egyptian gold production led to a temporary increase in its use as money. When gold production decreased after about 1200 B.C., so did its popularity as a form of money. Other metals occasionally served as money as well. Copper, for example, was the most common form of money in Mesopotamia in the 700s B.C.. Silver money often took the form of rings or coils. To pay for an item, one broke off a piece of silver whose value was equal to that of the item acquired. Archaeologists* have found hoards of silver, including ingots (bars) in Near Eastern sites, but these are too large to have been used in everyday transactions. The absence of smaller pieces of silver suggests that ingots were used as a store of value or a standard against which smaller pieces of silver were measured.

Coinage. The earliest coins were minted around 650 B.C. in the kingdom of Lydia in present-day Turkey. The Lydians invented coins to guarantee that a certain amount of precious metal had a fixed value. Pieces broken from a ring or coil had to be weighed to determine their value, but coins of the same type supposedly contained the same amount of silver, making weighing unnecessary. However, because people often shaved off bits of coins, they reduced the coins' true worth, making the promise of standard value worthless; when such coins were used for payment, they were always weighed.

Despite their convenience, coins only slowly replaced other forms of money. This was partly because many people believed that the system used for thousands of years was still quite useful and that coins offered little advantage over traditional forms of money. Moreover, they believed that a shortage of precious metals could be disastrous for a society that relied solely on coinage. However, in flexible monetary systems, grains or other forms of money could be used when silver or gold ran short. The use of coins only became widespread after the PERSIAN EMPIRE conquered much of the Near East in the 500s B.C. (*See also* **Economy and Trade; Merchants; Taxation.**)

MONOTHEISM

* **doctrine** principle, theory, or belief presented for acceptance
* **pantheon** all the gods of a particular culture

Monotheism is the belief in only one god. This doctrine* is most closely associated with the three great modern religions that originally developed in the Near East: Judaism, Christianity, and Islam. Most of the cultures in the ancient Near East practiced polytheism, the belief in many gods. However, a number of Near Eastern religious traditions in ancient times also developed monotheistic tendencies.

Early Monotheism. One of the earliest examples of monotheistic beliefs appeared in Egypt during the reign of Amenhotep IV in the mid-1300s B.C. The Egyptian pantheon* at that time contained many gods, including the sun god ATEN. Amenhotep singled out Aten for worship and proclaimed that he was the only true god. Amenhotep renamed himself AKHENATEN, which means "he who is effective for Aten," and forbade the

* **cult** system of religious beliefs and rituals; group following these beliefs

* **first millennium B.C.** years from 1000 to 1 B.C.

* **prophet** one who claims to have received divine messages or insights

worship of other gods. This displeased the priests of other cults* and many Egyptians, and after his death, the cult of Aten disappeared.

Other tendencies toward monotheism occurred in MESOPOTAMIA during the first millennium B.C.* In Babylonia, the ancient god MARDUK rose to great prominence and became head of that region's pantheon. He also took over the characteristics and functions of many other gods, making him far superior to them. A similar tendency toward unifying many gods into one deity occurred in Assyria with the god ASHUR. Though not truly monotheistic, these religious beliefs were moving in that direction.

A more authentic type of monotheism developed in Persia in the 600s B.C. with the rise of a new religion called Zoroastrianism. This religion was founded by Zoroaster, a prophet* who taught that there was only one true god—AHURA MAZDA, the Wise Lord, who represents all that is good. Opposing him are the evil spirits led by AHRIMAN, the spirit of darkness and lies. Zoroastrianism shares many aspects with Judaism and Christianity, including the belief that at the end of time, all souls will be judged and those only found worthy will enter paradise.

Israelite Monotheism. The ancient Israelites did not originally practice a pure form of monotheism. According to the Hebrew BIBLE, they worshiped their god YAHWEH in various manifestations of the Canaanite god EL. After MOSES led the Israelites out of Egypt, they entered into a special covenant, or agreement, with the god Yahweh. Even then, however, Yahweh was not seen as the only god but rather as the supreme god.

When the Israelites settled in CANAAN, some of them began to worship other local gods, such as BAAL. Eventually, however, they came to see Yahweh as not only their supreme god but as the only true god and the creator of the universe. The Israelites saw themselves as the "chosen people" who were given the land of Canaan because they believed in and obeyed Yahweh. Later they hoped that this unique god would recall his covenant and bring them back from their exile in Babylon. Their belief in the "oneness" of Yahweh marked a dramatic break with the polytheism of other ancient Near Eastern religions. Israelite monotheism, Judaism, formed the basis of the monotheistic beliefs of both Christianity and Islam, which arose centuries later. (*See also* **Cults; Gods and Goddesses; Judaism and Jews; Religion; Theology.**)

Moon

See *Lunar Theory.*

MOSAIC LAW

The Mosaic Law is a set of legal provisions contained in Exodus, Leviticus, Numbers, and Deuteronomy—four of the five books of the TORAH, one of the three parts of the Hebrew BIBLE. At the core of the Mosaic Law are the TEN COMMANDMENTS, which according to tradition, were given to MOSES by YAHWEH during a meeting on Mount Sinai. Like earlier law codes, such as the Code of Hammurabi, the Mosaic Law includes legislation for criminal and civil punishments. The Mosaic Law also deals with personal matters (health, grooming, marriage, and sexual relations) as well as religious matters (construction of the ark and tabernacle*), which were rarely included in other Semitic* laws. The Mosaic Law became the basis of Jewish practices and remains so today.

Origin and Nature of Mosaic Law. According to the Bible, Moses freed the Israelites from slavery in Egypt and led them through the desert to the Promised Land*—CANAAN. During the journey, Moses received the Ten Commandments from Yahweh. The commandments were basic prohibitions on actions such as murder, theft, worship of other gods, and adultery.

As the Israelites continued their journey to Canaan, it became clear that the Ten Commandments did not address many issues. Through Moses, Yahweh then began to issue additional laws to cover the gaps in the commandments. Ultimately, the body of laws grew quite large and was set down in the Torah, or the Pentateuch.

In ancient times, the Mosaic Law served as a way to distinguish the Israelites from the pagans* who lived among them. After the exilic period, the laws were interpreted differently. They forbade Israelites from marrying or interacting with non-Israelites, emphasizing that the Israelites are a special people chosen by Yahweh. At its heart, the Mosaic Law is the formal expression of the covenant, or agreement, between the Israelites and their god Yahweh.

An important subset of the Mosaic Law concerns the Israelites' diet. These laws prescribe what types of animals Israelites can and cannot eat. For instance, they may not eat animals that do not ruminate (chew their cud) and do not have split hooves (such as pigs and horses) or consume the products of such animals. The laws also forbid Israelites to eat fish without fins and scales (such as shrimp, crabs, and lobster), animals that creep, carnivorous birds, or the blood of any animal. Certain portions of acceptable animals are also prohibited. During the Passover festival, Israelites may not eat bread containing yeast.

The laws warn Israelites to avoid wearing garments woven from different fibers (for example wool and linen), urge men and women not to dress in each other's clothing, tell them to have tassels on the four corners of their garments, and instruct them on grooming their hair.

Some laws instruct the Israelites on building their homes and holy constructions. When building homes, Israelites are required to build a wall around the roof to prevent people from falling to the ground and polluting the house with blood. The laws provide exact specifications for the construction of the tabernacle and the ark—two major components in the worship service. The tabernacle was to be constructed with offerings given by Israelites, such as gold, oil to feed lamps, and fine linen. The ark—a cabinet that, according to some passages, held the original Ten Commandments, which symbolized the covenant (agreement) between Yahweh and the Israelites—was to be constructed of acacia wood according to the specifications provided by the Mosaic Law.

When Was the Mosaic Law Written? Scholars disagree on whether the Mosaic Law was handed down during the time of Moses or written

* **tabernacle** portable place of worship that the Israelites carried with them during their journey through the wilderness and into the Promised Land

* **Semitic** of or relating to people of the Near East or northern Africa, including the Assyrians, Babylonians, Phoenicians, Jews, and Arabs

* **Promised Land** land promised to the Israelites by their god, Yahweh

* **pagan** one who believes in more than one god

later. Many of the individual laws mentioned in the Torah were not relevant to the Israelites' situation at the time of their journey from Egypt to the Promised Land. For example, laws about ownership of land or different types of crops are clearly meant for a settled agricultural society, and laws about kingship and temple rituals presume an urban society.

Many scholars feel that such laws were added much later, perhaps hundreds of years after the settlement of Canaan. A few even argue that none of the laws originated during the time of Moses. Historians have isolated what they believe are discrete compilations or codes within the Torah in addition to the Ten Commandments—which appear in Exodus, Chapter 20, and Deuteronomy, Chapter 5—such as the Holiness Code (Leviticus, Chapters 17–26), the Book of Covenants (Exodus, Chapters 20–23), and the Deuteronomic Code (Deuteronomy, Chapters 12–26). They believe that these codes may have come from separate periods of Israel's history. Regardless of its origin, the Mosaic Law remains the most important part of the Hebrew Bible for followers of Judaism. (*See also* **Hebrews and Israelites; Judaism and Jews; Law.**)

MOSES

ca. 1200s B.C.
Israelite leader

* **Promised Land** land promised to the Israelites by their god, Yahweh

* **pharaoh** king of ancient Egypt

* **nomad** referring to one who travels from place to place to find food and pasture

According to Jewish tradition, Moses freed the ancient Israelites from slavery in Egypt and led them to the Promised Land* of CANAAN. The Hebrew BIBLE says that it was Moses who received the TEN COMMANDMENTS from the god YAHWEH on Mount Sinai and brought them to the Israelites. Moses was also believed to be the author of the TORAH, or Pentateuch, the first five books of the Hebrew Bible.

The Book of Exodus claims that Moses was the child of Israelite slaves in Egypt (the Egyptians referred to the Israelites as Hebrews). When the pharaoh* ordered all newborn Israelite males to be killed to control the Israelite population, Moses' mother set her child adrift in a basket on the NILE RIVER. He was found by the pharaoh's daughter and raised in the royal court. One day when Moses was touring a region where the Israelites were working, he saw an overseer beat an Israelite slave. Moses killed the overseer, but his deed was discovered and he had to flee to the land of Midian (in the Sinai and northwestern Arabia). There he met and married Zipporah, the daughter of a nomad* chieftain. Later when he was tending his sheep, he came to a burning bush, from which the voice of Yahweh told him to return to Egypt and free his people.

Moses returned to Egypt and demanded that the pharaoh release the Israelites, but the pharaoh refused. Under Yahweh's instruction, Moses brought down a series of ten plagues (disastrous events) on Egypt, the last one resulting in the death of every firstborn Egyptian male. The pharaoh let the Israelites leave, but he soon tried to bring them back. His army followed the Israelites across the RED SEA, where Yahweh had miraculously parted the waters. After the Israelites had passed, the waters flooded the Egyptian army and destroyed it. For the next 40 years, Moses guided the Israelites on their journey from Egypt to Canaan. During this period, Moses received the Ten Commandments from Yahweh and assumed the role of lawgiver and judge for the Israelites. Once near the Promised Land,

Yahweh refused Moses entry because he had failed to follow precisely one of his directives. Moses died on Mount Nebo in Moab (in present-day Jordan), just outside Canaan, but his burial place has not been found.

Modern historians disagree about which parts of the story are based in fact and which are fictional. Some believe the story is historically accurate but combines the deeds of several people and presents them as the work of one man. Others accept it as a historical event, often setting Moses and the journey to Canaan (the Exodus) during the reign of Ramses II (ruled ca. 1279–1213 B.C.). Some claim that the story is entirely fictional because there is no certain evidence of the Exodus or Moses in the historical and archaeological* record. Nevertheless, Moses is considered a symbol of the covenant, or agreement, between the Israelites and their god, Yahweh. (*See also* **Ark of the Covenant; Egypt and the Egyptians; Hebrews and Israelites; Judaism and Jews; Mosaic Law.**)

* **archaeological** referring to the study of past human cultures, usually by excavating material remains of human activity

MUMMIES

* **embalm** to treat a corpse with oils or chemicals to preserve it or slow down the process of decay, usually after body fluids have been removed

* **Egyptologist** person who studies ancient Egypt

See
color plate 9,
vol. 3.

A mummy is a dead body that has been dried both inside and out, embalmed*, and wrapped in cloth for preservation. Preserving dead bodies in this way before burial was common in ancient Egypt because the ancient Egyptians believed in the AFTERLIFE, or life after death, including the continued existence of the physical body. Men, women, and children were mummified, as were certain animals that were considered sacred, such as CATS, bulls, and crocodiles. Thousands of mummies from ancient Egypt have been recovered from PYRAMIDS, tombs, and graves, and many are on display at museums throughout the world.

Development of Mummification. The first Egyptian mummies may have come about accidentally, when Egyptians buried the dead in the desert sands, which naturally dried out and preserved the bodies. In fact, some Egyptologists* believe that the natural preservation of dead bodies in this way spurred the Egyptian belief in the afterlife. In turn, this belief led to a search for ways to preserve the bodies of the dead.

As early as 3000 B.C., the Egyptians had developed many techniques to preserve dead bodies. The techniques reached their peak toward the end of the New Kingdom period, around 1080 B.C. By that time, they were so successful that today we can look at a mummy, such as the well-preserved mummy of TUTANKHAMEN, and get a good idea of what the person looked like several thousand years ago.

The process of mummification took several months to complete. The process was very expensive, and only royalty and other wealthy individuals could afford it. Bodies of the poor, in contrast, were simply wrapped in cloth and buried in the desert a few days or weeks after they died.

The Mummification Process. The mummification process began with the removal of the dead person's lungs, stomach, and intestines through an incision on the left side of the body. The organs were then covered with a natural drying agent—a salt called natron—until they dried out. Then the organs were wrapped in linen and stored in jars that

Mummies

* **amulet** small object thought to have supernatural or magical powers
* **scarab** representation of the dung beetle, held as sacred by Egyptians

---

Mummification—a process for preserving dead bodies for burial—was a common practice in ancient Egypt. Mummification was both time- and labor-intensive, taking several months to complete its several stages. The mummy shown here is that of an Egyptian named Ankhef and dates from Egypt's Twelfth Dynasty (ca. 1938–1759 B.C.).

Egyptologists call canopic jars. The lids on the jars were shaped like the heads of gods, which was believed to help protect the organs contained within. Later the jars were buried with the dead person.

Next, the heart was removed from the body, dried out, wrapped in linen, and replaced in the body. Sometimes the heart was sewn into place in the chest cavity. The Egyptians returned the heart to the body because they believed it was the seat of intelligence. The brain, on the other hand, was considered insignificant to the body. It was crudely removed with a long hooked rod inserted into the skull through the nostrils and discarded. Then resin was injected into the skull with a funnel to prevent the head from collapsing.

Once the internal organs and brain were removed, the blood and other fluids were drained from the body. Then the body was filled and

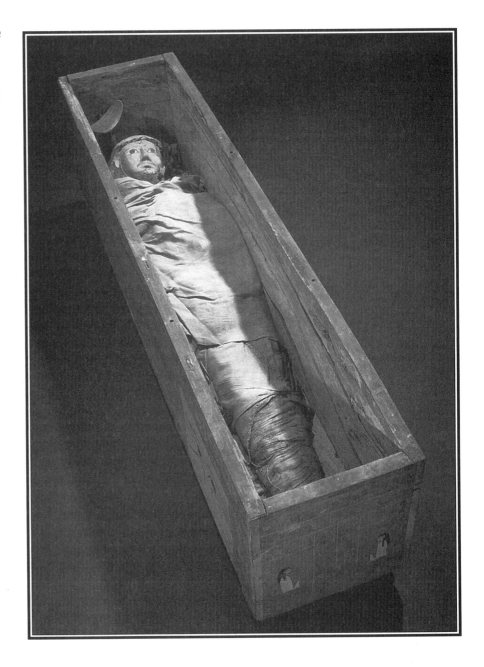

Learning from Mummies

Archaeologists, historians, and anthropologists have learned a great deal about ancient Egyptians by studying mummies. For example, by examining the body wrapped within the strips of cloth, these scientists have learned about the diseases that afflicted ancient Egyptians and how those diseases were treated. From X rays of mummy bones, they have been able to estimate the average height and life span of ancient Egyptians. They have even inferred ties of kinship in royal families from examining the similarities and dissimilarities in the appearance of kings who were mummified.

covered with natron until it dried out completely. After a few weeks, the natron was removed and the body was carefully cleaned and rubbed with scented oils. It was also packed with resin-soaked linen and bags of fragrant materials, such as myrrh and cinnamon. At this time, the eyes were replaced with artificial eyes made of glass.

The last step in the process was wrapping the body in about 400 yards of linen strips. First, the head was wrapped, followed by each individual finger and toe. This was followed by the hands, feet, legs, and arms. The arms were then crossed over the chest. Finally, the entire body was wrapped. A mask was placed over the head and shoulders before the last layer of wrappings.

The linen was soaked in fragrant resins before it was wrapped around the body. This helped mask the odor of decay. In addition, when the resin dried, it made the wrappings stiff so that the cloth held the body's shape even after the body started to decompose. Sometimes the body was padded with sawdust, sand, or clay to help preserve its shape.

The Egyptians often painted facial features on the outer layer of wrappings to make the mummy look more lifelike. In addition, up to 100 amulets* were placed among the wrappings, including a scarab* over the heart, to protect the mummy after burial. Sacred writings were also wrapped with the body to guide the deceased in the afterlife. (*See also* **Book of the Dead; Death and Burial; Egypt and the Egyptians.**)

MUSIC AND MUSICAL INSTRUMENTS

* **artifact** ornament, tool, weapon, or other object made by humans

* **secular** nonreligious; connected with everyday life

* **deity** god or goddess

Music was important to the cultures of the ancient Near East, particularly during temple rituals, funeral rites, and religious and royal festivals and ceremonies. Little is known about the role of music in the daily life of the people. However, ancient texts and artifacts* indicate that music provided a form of entertainment at important family events and gatherings, particularly among the upper classes of society. In both religious and secular* events, music was performed for its own sake as well as an accompaniment to DANCE.

Occasions for Music. Temple rituals throughout the ancient Near East often included music. The music served to honor and please the gods, some of whom were linked to music and specific musical instruments. In ancient Egypt, for example, several deities*, including HATHOR and OSIRIS, were closely associated with music. When HYMNS were sung in praise of the gods at temple rituals, the singers were usually accompanied by musical instruments. Music also accompanied daily rituals and other religious activities. Each culture, of course, had its own forms of religious music as well as instruments used to perform it.

Although little is known about secular music, it is certain that most Near Eastern peoples enjoyed music. Mothers no doubt sang lullabies to their young children, and men and women probably sang work songs while laboring in the fields. Musical entertainment was a part of royal feasts, processions, and other celebrations, while ordinary families enjoyed music at family gatherings and on special occasions. Sometimes music was performed on serious or dangerous occasions, such as during

There were two main types of harps in ancient Egypt, arched and angular. In the more popular arched harp, the neck and sound box (at the lower end) formed a continuous curve. The angular harp had a vertical sound box and a horizontal neck. This wooden statuette of a young girl playing an angular harp is from the 1200s B.C.

* **cult** system of religious beliefs and rituals; group following these beliefs

* **first millennium** B.C. years from 1000 to 1 B.C.

eclipses or childbirth. Music even played a part in military activities, with musicians accompanying armies while they marched. Ancient Hittite texts mention a number of military battle songs.

Musical Performers. Both men and women sang and played musical instruments in the ancient Near East. Temples employed professional musicians to perform in orchestras, choral groups, and as solo performers. These musicians sometimes functioned as priests. In ancient Egypt and MESOPOTAMIA, female musicians in religious cults* often were of high rank. Sometimes the wives of priests might serve as musicians in the same cults as their husbands.

Temple musicians occupied a high social rank. In ancient Egypt, individuals who held the title "great one of the musical troupe" were responsible for training performers, overseeing musical practice, and ensuring that performances in temple activities went well. Some temples in Mesopotamia established their own schools to train musicians.

Musical troupes, or groups, were sometimes attached to secular institutions, such as the palaces of kings. On special royal occasions, hundreds of musicians might sing and play instruments. As in temples, palace musicians and singers were organized by rank, with such titles as "master of singers" or "superintendent of performers." Secular troupes also consisted of both men and women. Some of the musicians who performed in secular events were professionals. Others, however, were amateurs who performed music only occasionally. Among the Hittites, singers were distinguished by the language in which they specialized.

Musical Instruments. Musicians played a variety of instruments. Although the specific design of these instruments might vary from one region to another, they fell under four basic categories: stringed instruments (chordophones), wind instruments (aerophones), drums (membranophones), and other percussion instruments (idiophones).

The two most common types of stringed instruments were the lyre and the harp. Lyres varied in size, shape, and number of strings. Some lyres were small, handheld instruments that could be played while sitting, standing, or walking. Larger lyres could be played only by two standing musicians. Harps were smaller than lyres, but they also varied in size and shape. They could be played by sitting or standing musicians holding the instruments in either a vertical or a horizontal position. Another stringed instrument, the lute, developed much later than either the harp or lyre. Lutes also differed in size, shape, and number of strings. All three stringed instruments were made of wood, sometimes covered with precious materials such as silver and gold.

Wind instruments—flutes, trumpets, and horns—were made of reed, wood, bone, and metal. Like stringed instruments, they varied in size and shape. The earliest flutes contained one or two pipes, but by the first millennium B.C.*, a type of flute with several pipes, known as the panpipe, was introduced from the West. Some flutes had reeds like present-day clarinets and oboes. Flutists generally accompanied singers and dancers. Trumpets and animal horns, because of their loud sounds, were used more often in military contexts and grand processionals and to signal public announcements. The ram's horn, or shofar, is mentioned often in the Hebrew BIBLE in connection with wars and religious rituals.

Drums ranged from small hand drums to giant kettle drums. Smaller drums were an indispensable accompaniment to dancing at banquets and festivals. Small to medium-sized drums also were played in military contexts, such as while troops were marching. Larger drums often played an important role in temple rituals. In Mesopotamia, for example, large kettledrums were often beaten at temples during eclipses of the moon.

Drums are a type of percussion instrument, an instrument that produces sound when a stick, hand, or other object strikes another surface. Other percussion instruments used in the ancient Near East included bells, rattles, cymbals, and "clappers." Made from wood, metal, clay, shell, or bone, these instruments provided background accompaniment to other instruments during religious and secular events. One of the most characteristic percussion instruments of ancient Egypt was the *sistrum,* a type of rattle whose soft sound resembled that of a breeze blowing through papyrus reeds. Egyptians believed that the *sistrum* attracted the attention of the gods and helped ward off evil. (*See also* **Entertainment; Family and Social Life; Feasts and Festivals; Palaces and Temples; Rituals and Sacrifice; Women, Role of.**)

Lost Sound of Music

Very little is known about the "sounds" of ancient Near Eastern music. Some surviving texts include information on musical notation, scales, and musical theory. However, it is difficult to know what this means in terms of present-day musical ideas. Even less understood is the tempo and rhythm of ancient musical works. It is obvious that some music was fast and other music slow and that some music was considered sad while other music was joyful or associated with some other emotion. However, without more information, the true sounds and rhythms of ancient Near Eastern music are lost to the ears of present-day humans.

MYCENAE AND THE MYCENAEANS

Mycenae (my•SEE•nee), the most important city-state* in Late Bronze Age Greece (ca. 1600–1200 B.C.), was located in the Peloponnese, the peninsula that forms the southern part of mainland Greece. According to legend, the city of Mycenae was founded by Perseus, a hero in Greek MYTHOLOGY. Legends about the Mycenaeans (my•suh•NEE•uhnz) have been preserved in Homer's great epics*, the *Iliad* and the *Odyssey.* Whether Homer's stories were based on historical fact or were fictional, is still disputed, but many scholars believe that elements of the stories are true.

* **city-state** independent state consisting of a city and its surrounding territory

* **epic** long poem about a legendary or historical hero, written in a grand style

 See map on inside covers.

History. Greece, including the Peloponnese, was settled as early as 6000 B.C., and by 3000 B.C., the people there began to build multistory houses and to use SEALS to identify ownership of goods. Some scholars believe that beginning around 2000 B.C., the Mycenaeans invaded the region and settled there. The Mycenaeans came from the north of Greece and spoke an INDO-EUROPEAN LANGUAGE. They were more advanced at pottery making, building, and metalworking than the people they displaced. However, this theory is disputed by other scholars, who believe that the Mycenaeans were the original inhabitants of the area.

Notwithstanding their origin, the Mycenaeans were a warlike tribe and set up competing city-states. The city of Mycenae quickly became the most powerful of these. Other major Mycenaean cities included Pylos, Tiryns, Thebes, and Orchomenus. The Mycenaeans fortified the cities with enormous walls to protect them during an attack. Many of the cities also contained magnificent palaces, which were organized around large halls. The entire society, like that of the Minoans, was "palace based." The Mycenaean economy was based on the export of such items as wine, grain, POTTERY, and olive oil. Historians and archaeologists* believe that

* **archaeologist** scientist who studies past human cultures, usually by excavating material remains of human activity

Mycenae and the Mycenaeans

The Mycenaeans were a warlike people. Around the 1400s B.C., they were responsible for the violent destruction of the palace at Knossos on Crete. They also raided both the Egyptian and Hittite Anatolian coasts and colonized many Aegean and Mediterranean islands and the surrounding mainland. This detail from a vase dating from the early 1100s B.C. depicts Mycenaean warriors wearing bronze armor.

Searching for Agamemnon

Heinrich Schliemann was a German merchant who became wealthy in the indigo trade in the mid-1800s.

When he was in his 40s, he gave it all up to search for the sites described in Homer's epics. He first uncovered the city of Troy in northwestern Turkey. In 1876, Schliemann moved to Greece, looking for King Agamemnon's home. He thought that he had found what he was looking for when he discovered some prehistoric tombs at Mycenae. One of these tombs, which Schliemann thought was the location of Agamemnon's burial site contained a golden mask that he thought was Agamemnon's. Although Schliemann was mistaken, he had opened a new understanding of ancient Greece to later archaeologists.

the Mycenaean trade network stretched throughout the Mediterranean because remnants of Mycenaean pottery have been found throughout the region.

From around 1400 B.C. until 1100 B.C., the Mycenaeans colonized the islands of the AEGEAN SEA. This period marked the height of Mycenaean power in the region. In fact, it was during this period that the famous battle of Troy is believed to have taken place. Sometime between 1250 and 1180 B.C., the Mycenaean king, Agamemnon led a coalition of Greek armies against the kingdom of Troy in western ANATOLIA (present-day Turkey) and ultimately destroyed that city. Around 1100 B.C., Mycenae was destroyed. It is not known whether the destruction was caused by fire or an enemy attack.

Relations With Other Aegean Powers. Although the Mycenaeans focused greatly on military conquest, they also established important trade relationships with other empires. Trade with the islands of the Cyclades and with CRETE probably existed as early as 3000 B.C.

From about 1600 to 1400 B.C., there was obviously a great deal of contact between the Mycenaeans and the Minoans. The two societies were probably in competition for the Mediterranean trade, but it seems that there was no ongoing warfare between them until (possibly) the Mycenaean destruction of the palace at KNOSSOS on Crete around 1400 B.C. Thereafter, the city of Knossos remained in Mycenaean control. During this period, the Mycenaeans also established colonies on the islands of the Cyclades and Dodecanese, CYPRUS, Sicily, northern Greece, MACEDONIA, and parts of Asia Minor and Italy. Being more warlike than the Minoans, they also raided the Egyptian and Hittite coasts.

Culture. Although the Mycenaeans built several cities, most continued to live in small villages in the countryside. This was unlike the case of the great civilizations, such as Egypt and Mesopotamia, in the Near East. The

Mycenaeans borrowed their WRITING, pottery, ARCHITECTURE, and palace culture from the Minoans. They used a script called Linear B, which was based on the Minoan script, Linear A, and was an early written form of the Greek language. They built huge palaces with beautiful frescoes* and halls with large columns. Mycenaean pottery, which is similar to Minoan pottery, was known and copied throughout the ancient Near East, particularly in the Levant*.

Unlike the Minoans, however, the Mycenaeans buried their kings in a *tholos,* or large tomb lined with rock and capped with a false dome. Dead leaders were buried with magnificent grave goods, such as golden masks, jewelry, game boards made of ivory, and several weapons.

Many modern scholars, while impressed with the Mycenaean culture, feel that it did not compare with the culture of the Minoans, from whom they borrowed so much. One scholar even goes so far as to call Mycenaean culture "rather dull."

The Fall of Mycenae. The Mycenaean civilization began to decline after 1200 B.C. The city of Mycenae was destroyed around 1100 B.C., and the cities of Tyrins and Pylos were destroyed shortly thereafter. Other settlements on the Peloponnese were also abandoned around the same period.

Most scholars believe that massive invasions and immigrations of the Dorian people were responsible for this. However, it is possible that the abandonment of the smaller sites was caused by the invasions of the SEA PEOPLES, who also invaded Egypt and perhaps the Levant around the same time. Finally, it is possible that environmental factors such as prolonged drought* or earthquakes or internal revolutions brought down the Mycenaean civilization.

Notwithstanding the cause, the city of Mycenae and the Mycenaean civilization lost power in the region. Thereafter, Mycenae was only a village and did not again flourish until several centuries later. Around the 400s B.C., Mycenae reemerged as an independent city-state but soon declined in importance. Later, for a short time during the Hellenistic* period, Mycenae again became an important city, but by A.D. 160, the city had been abandoned and was in ruins.

Modern Discoveries. Remnants of the Mycenaean civilization were excavated in 1876 by German archaeologist Heinrich Schliemann. Schliemann's archaeological work, as well as the research conducted by later scholars, yielded fortification systems, bronze armor and weapons, precious grave offerings, and thousands of pottery fragments. Little remains of the city today, except its main entrance. (*See also* **Greece and the Greeks; Minoan Civilization; Troy.**)

* **fresco** method of painting in which color is applied to moist plaster so that it becomes chemically bonded to the plaster as it dries; also, a painting done in this manner

* **Levant** lands bordering the eastern shores of the Mediterranean Sea (present-day Syria, Lebanon, and Israel), the West Bank, and Jordan

* **drought** long period of dry weather during which crop yields are lower than usual

* **Hellenistic** referring to the Greek-influenced culture of the Mediterranean world and western Asia during the three centuries after the death of Alexander the Great in 323 B.C.

MYTHOLOGY

Mythology is a medium through which a culture expresses its most deeply held values. Myths put into words a culture's vision of its history, its place in the universe, and its relationship with its deities*.

Many types of myths exist in the records of the ancient Near East. Some are CREATION MYTHS, which tell how the world came into being.

Mythology

* **deity** god or goddess

Other myths recount the origin of civilization, the shape of the cosmos, the actions and relationships of the gods, the founding of states or kingships, or the interactions of people and gods.

Role of Mythology. Mythology existed long before writing was invented, and its original purpose was to help people make sense of the world around them. For example, many cultures have a myth that explains the change of seasons as periods of growth and fruitfulness alternating with times of decay and barrenness. In fact, the Sumerian, Babylonian, Greek, and Roman myths explaining seasonal change all feature a goddess of fruitfulness who must spend some time every year in the kingdom of death, resulting in winter. Such similarities, which also exist among other myths, suggest that regions of the ancient Near East may have shared a common heritage of beliefs, stories, and images largely because of their common climatic conditions.

After the invention of writing, myths became a subject of written LIT-ERATURE. Mythology was woven from the same material as religious belief;

Dating from the Old Babylonian period (ca. 1900–1600 B.C.), this clay plaque shows a god with a bow slung over his shoulder bravely killing a solar-headed cyclops (a giant with one eye in the middle of the forehead). Some historians believe that the scene depicts Ninurta, a Mesopotamian war god, killing the monster Asakku.

the gods of the stories were the same gods people worshiped in temples and in daily life.

Mesopotamia. Several myths dating from the 2500s B.C. have survived from ancient Sumer, but they are difficult to decipher* or interpret. Some Akkadian myths recorded during the second millennium B.C.* have also survived. From ancient Babylon, the most notable example of mythmaking is *Enuma Elish,* a creation myth. Its author wove together old mythical themes into a tale of conflict among several gods, explaining how MARDUK, the city god of Babylon, rose to power and became the chief god of Babylonia.

Another Babylonian myth, the *Erra Myth,* is a dialogue between Erra (Nergal), the god of the underworld, and his lieutenant, Ishum. It dates from around 1000 B.C., when invasions by the ARAMAEANS disrupted life in Babylonia. The *Erra Myth* explains the turmoil in Babylonian society as the punishment for the noise produced on earth by humanity, which was out of control.

The Sumerian *Enki and Ninmakh* and the Babylonian *Epic of Atrakhasis* describe the creation of the human race from clay and divine blood. Other Sumerian and Akkadian myths deal with the adventures of legendary heroes such as GILGAMESH, Enmerkar, and Lugalbanda, who were later considered gods.

Egypt. Myths were important in the religion of ancient Egypt. However, they existed more as spoken, not written, literature. Consequently, surviving Egyptian texts include relatively few myths, fragments of which lie embedded in incantations* and spells. It may be that the ancient Egyptian cults* guarded their myths as secrets or mysteries. Still, most people would have known the central myths about their major deities.

A good example of the Egyptians not recording their myths is the story of ISIS and OSIRIS, possibly the best known of Egypt's myths. Countless Egyptian texts and artworks refer to both Isis and Osiris, but no surviving Egyptian document tells the whole story. The myth only survives in a version told by the Greek writer Plutarch in the A.D. 100s.

According to Plutarch, the myth centers around three events: the murder of Osiris by his brother SETH; the birth of Osiris's son HORUS and his protection by his mother, Isis; and the conflict between Horus and Seth. A key element of the myth is the cutting up of Osiris's body into pieces, which were buried at locations throughout Egypt.

The Levant. The ancient Israelites and their neighbors, the Canaanites, shared a great many myths. Elements of their shared beliefs are found in the Canaanite myths that scholars call the BAAL CYCLE. These stories describe the activities of the storm god BAAL and his role in establishing the cosmic*, human, and natural orders. His battles against Sea (Yamm) and Death (Mot) are echoed in the Hebrew BIBLE. The Israelites also used imagery similar to that in the Baal cycle in their mythmaking, even after they officially ceased to worship Baal, EL, and the other Canaanite gods in favor of their national god, YAHWEH.

* **decipher** to decode and interpret the meaning

* **second millennium** B.C. years from 2000 to 1001 B.C.

* **incantation** written or recited formula of words designed to produce a given effect

* **cult** system of religious beliefs and rituals; group following these beliefs

* **cosmic** pertaining to the whole universe

125

Other elements of Canaanite myths focus on relations between humans and deities in days long past. For instance, *Aqhat* tells how the goddess ANAT killed a young man and how his sister avenged his death. *Keret* tells how El helped a king acquire a bride and overcome illness.

The priests and kings of Israel who developed Israelite mythology used old, familiar mythic stories and images, but they added new details to make them their own. One example is the Hebrew Bible's image of Eden, or paradise, which features elements common to both Ugaritic and Mesopotamian myths. The Israelites' greatest story revolves around their central myth about how they were chosen by Yahweh from among their more powerful neighbors.

Iran. All known ancient Iranian myths come from after the 600s B.C., when the religion Zoroastrianism was founded. As a result, it is difficult to determine which myths include elements from the time before Zoroaster and which were Zoroastrian creations. However, historians believe that Zoroastrian mythology was the first to mention a savior who would save the world from evil in the days of the world's end.

Anatolia. The HITTITES of Anatolia (present-day Turkey) blended mythological elements from the Hurrians and Mesopotamians with their own beliefs. For example, a major Hittite god, KUMARBI, was a Hurrian deity. Tales about Kumarbi refer to the Hurrian weather god TESHUB and to EA, the Babylonian god of wisdom. One distinctively Hittite set of myths concerned gods who disappeared from the earth. In each version of this story, the deity's absence brought suffering on earth until someone found the vanished deity. The deity then returned to earth and resumed his duties. (*See also* **Epic Literature; Literature; Religion.**)

Myths That Heal

In the ancient Near East, myths were seen as having the power to heal and drive away evil. A magician dealing with someone suffering from evil causes might call on a myth that described the victory of good over evil. This myth would help drive the evil away. For example, learning how a toothache came to be (a worm refusing any other food but gum tissue) allowed a healer to banish it. In ancient Egypt, when people were sick, part of their medical treatment included listening to mythical stories. This reassured them of their place in the universe, enabling them to get well and to continue to live as part of the cosmic order.

NABONIDUS

ruled 556–539 B.C.
Babylonian king

* **indigenous** referring to the original inhabitants of a region

* **regency** form of government in which a regent rules in place of the rightful ruler, who is absent, too young, or otherwise unable to rule

* **patron** special guardian, protector, or supporter

* **deity** god or goddess

Nabonidus (nab•uh•NY•duhs) was the last indigenous* king of Babylonia. For much of his reign, he lived in Arabia, leaving his son Belshazzar as head of a regency* in BABYLON. Nabonidus also introduced several religious reforms centered on the worship of the moon god Sin, which challenged the superiority of MARDUK, the national god of Babylonia and angered the Babylonians.

Nabonidus was the son of a Babylonian prince and Adad-guppi, a woman from Haran, an important religious center in northern Mesopotamia. Adad-guppi had an avid devotion to Sin, the patron* god of Haran, which might explain her son's support of that deity*. Though not a direct member of the Babylonian royal family, Nabonidus came to the throne in 556 B.C., after the assassination of King Labashi-Marduk. Scholars believe that Nabonidus may have taken part in the conspiracy, but that he did not expect to become king. As king, Nabonidus led successful military campaigns to Cilicia in southeastern ANATOLIA (present-day Turkey). He also began to focus religious attention on Sin. He rebuilt the Temple of Sin in Haran and installed his daughter as high priestess of Sin at the city of UR.

In 553 B.C., Nabonidus left on a military campaign to Lebanon and then to Arabia. During his absence, the Persians under CYRUS THE GREAT began to threaten Babylonia. This growing threat forced Nabonidus to return to Babylon. Thereafter, he continued to carry out his religious reforms with greater fervor, leading to increasing opposition from his subjects. In 539 B.C., the Persians attacked Babylonia and captured Babylon without a fight. Because of their hostility toward Nabonidus, the Babylonians welcomed the Persians as liberators.

The capture of Babylon ended the Babylonian empire, which was incorporated into the PERSIAN EMPIRE. The fate of Nabonidus, however, is disputed. Some historians say that the Persians sent him into exile in Carmania, a Persian province in southeastern IRAN. (*See also* **Babylonia and the Babylonians.**)

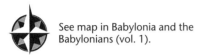

See map in Babylonia and the Babylonians (vol. 1).

NABOPOLASSAR

ruled 626–605 B.C.
Babylonian king

Nabopolassar (nab•uh•puh•LAS•uhr) was the first ruler of the Neo-Babylonian empire and the founder of the so-called "Chaldean" dynasty. During his reign, the Babylonians captured and destroyed a number of important Assyrian cities, including ASHUR, NINEVEH, and KALKHU, and played a leading role in the collapse of the Assyrian empire.

Nabopolassar seized the throne of Babylon after the death of King ASHURBANIPAL in 627 B.C. At first, Nabopolassar encountered resistance from Babylonians as well as the Assyrians. After many years of fighting, however, he finally secured firm control over Babylonia. Nabopolassar then began working to extend his power into surrounding areas while defending Babylonia from the Assyrians.

In 616 B.C., Nabopolassar began to advance into Assyria and gained limited control of some Assyrian provinces. Around the same time, a new power was growing in the region—the MEDES of IRAN. In 614 B.C., the Medes, led by King Cyaxares, attacked and raided the Assyrian city of Nineveh. Nabopolassar marched into Assyria as well and met Cyaxares at Ashur after that city had fallen to the Medes. The two rulers signed a treaty forming an alliance that they secured with the marriage of Nabopolassar's son to Cyaxares' granddaughter.

The Medes and Babylonians together launched devastating attacks against Assyria and took control of several cities there. The fall of Nineveh in 612 B.C. marked the end of the Assyrian empire, although the Assyrians made a few unsuccessful attempts at recovery over the next few years. According to the treaty between Nabopolassar and Cyaxares, the Medes gained control of northern MESOPOTAMIA, leaving the Babylonians in control of the rest of the region.

After the Assyrian conquest, Nabopolassar turned his attention to the Levant*, which had been seized by the Egyptians. In 605 B.C., an aging Nabopolassar sent his son NEBUCHADNEZZAR II to fight the Egyptians. The Babylonians won a decisive victory against the Egyptians at KARKAMISH in SYRIA. Shortly thereafter, Nabopolassar died, and Nebuchadnezzar raced home from Syria to claim the throne. (*See also* **Assyria and the Assyrians; Babylonia and the Babylonians; Chaldea and the Chaldeans.**)

* **Levant** lands bordering the eastern shores of the Mediterranean Sea (present-day Syria, Lebanon, and Israel), the West Bank, and Jordan

Names, Personal

* **deity** god or goddess

* **assimilation** adoption of the beliefs and customs of a society

* **Semitic** of or relating to people of the Near East or northern Africa, including the Assyrians, Babylonians, Phoenicians, Jews, and Arabs

* **matriarchal** society in which women hold the dominant position

* **scribe** person of a learned class who served as a writer, editor, or teacher

* **first millennium B.C.** years from 1000 to 1 B.C.

* **Asiatic** referring to people who come from the Levant, the lands bordering the eastern shores of the Mediterranean Sea (present-day Syria, Lebanon, and Israel), the West Bank, and Jordan

Depending on how the people of a particular culture select names, a personal name may be a link to an individual's ancestors, ethnic heritage, or deities*. Ancient Near Eastern texts contain thousands of names. Historians have looked through these texts to examine how change in a region, such as conquest, assimilation*, or changes in religious beliefs, might be reflected in its personal names.

Customs of Naming. The peoples of the ancient Near East followed a variety of practices in giving personal names. Patriarchal cultures, in which people traced their descent and social status from their father's families, often used patronymics, names based on the father's name. Semitic* cultures generally used personal names followed by a patronym, except when the identity of the father was unclear, such as with slaves. In that case, the mother's name was used. Matriarchal* societies, such as that of the Lycians of ANATOLIA (present-day Turkey) took their names from their mothers.

The people of ancient MESOPOTAMIA named their babies soon after birth. Some children were named for their grandfathers or for their dead relatives whom the new babies were thought to replace. Adults sometimes took or were given new names to reflect events in their lives. Scholars know of one case where the name of a Babylonian governor was changed to a Greek name by a Seleucid king. Slaves might receive a name that emphasized dependence on their owner, such as *I look at her eyes.* Mesopotamian scribes* and scholars signed their works with names that identified them as descendants of famous scribes of earlier generations. The use of ancestral names or occupations for "last names" came into use in Mesopotamia during the middle of the first millennium B.C.*

The Akkadian people had the unique custom of giving names that seemed to reflect the newborn baby's feelings, such as *My god has mercy upon me.* The Sumerians used names consisting of a sentence or phrase, such as *Servant of [king's name].*

Theophoric names, personal names that included the name of a deity, were also common in many cultures. In Elam, people bore names that included the names of their gods. For example, *Manzat,* the name of an Elamite goddess, appeared in male and female names. These personal names usually took the form of sentences, such as *God [name] loves me* or *God [name] may protect me.* When the sentences became too long to be easily used as names, people shortened them until only the name of the god remained.

The religious society of the ancient Egyptians was reflected in their use of theophoric names. For example, the personal name Sebekhotpe meant "[The god] Sebek is satisfied."

When people from other ethnic backgrounds settled in Egypt, they often took Egyptian names. People of foreign origin were well aware of the power of names to identify them as outsiders or members of the community. For such people, taking an Egyptian name was an important step in being accepted by Egyptian society. For example, one royal official from the 1100s B.C. bore both the Asiatic* name *Benazu* and the Egyptian name *Ramessesemperre.* During the Ptolemaic period (305–30 B.C.), however, it was considered a crime punishable by death for an Egyptian to take a Greek name without permission. This was largely because the Greek-speaking Ptolemies were trying to keep the Egyptians separate from themselves.

Nicknames were also common throughout the history of the ancient Near East. Usually, a nickname was given by abbreviating a long name.

Clues to the Past. Many personal names from the ancient Near East appear in texts. Some are the names of kings or generals whose deeds were recorded. Others are the names of ordinary people found on population registers, tax rolls, property deeds, and other documents.

* **linguistic** related to language

The structure and content of names often reflect the ethnic or linguistic* roots of the people who bore those names. The study of the origins and uses of personal names is called onomastics, and it is useful to historians interested in tracing the movements of peoples and the spread of languages.

* **third millennium B.C.** years from 3000 to 2001 B.C.

* **migration** movement of individuals or peoples from one place to another

Researchers investigating population changes toward the end of the third millennium B.C.* in Babylonia believe that there was a migration* of West Semitic peoples (Amorites) into Babylonia. They base this conclusion on the presence of West Semitic names in Babylonian texts, because no such names appear in texts from earlier periods in the same region. Another example of onomastics concerns the spread of Aramaic, the language of the Aramaeans from Syria, across much of the Near East during the first millennium B.C. (years from 1000 to 1 B.C.). Historians have found a high percentage of Aramaic personal names in Mesopotamia, even among non-Aramaean royal families. In these cases, studying personal names provides historians with a means to see the influences one culture had on another.

NARAM-SIN

ruled ca. 2254–2218 B.C.
King of Akkad

* **city-state** independent state consisting of a city and its surrounding territory

* **fortification** structure built to strengthen or protect against attack

* **divinity** state or quality of being a god

One of the greatest kings of Akkad, Naram-Sin (nah•RAHM•seen) ruled for more than 35 years. The Akkadian empire reached its height of power under Naram-Sin, who changed the nature of kingship by claiming the titles of a god. After his death, the empire experienced a swift, irreversible decline.

The grandson of SARGON I, Naram-Sin took the throne on the death of his father, King Manishtushu. He inherited a secure kingdom, which he enlarged by launching military expeditions to SYRIA, ANATOLIA (present-day Turkey), Elam, and Magan (Arabia). Most of his military campaigns were successful, and the Akkadian empire reached its greatest extent. When his power threatened some Sumerian city-states*, which feared for their own independence, Naram-Sin quelled any rebellions that erupted.

Naram-Sin unified the administration of Akkad and appointed members of the royal family to powerful positions in the empire. He encouraged growth in trade and began an extensive building program, constructing temples, fortifications*, and monuments commemorating his military victories and achievements. At some point during his reign, Naram-Sin began using titles usually reserved for the gods. This was the first time in Mesopotamian history that a king had claimed divinity* during his own lifetime. The practice continued under a few later kings in MESOPOTAMIA, but the idea of divine kingship never became as firmly established as in ancient Egypt.

Natural Disasters

In the centuries after his death, Naram-Sin became the subject of many legends. Although most honor him for his military victories, some criticize him as a misfortunate ruler who caused rebellion and invasion because of his pride and unwise decisions. (*See also* **Akkad and the Akkadian Empire; Dynasties; Kings.**)

Natural Disasters

See *Disasters, Natural.*

NAVAL POWER

The major waterways of the ancient Near East—including the Mediterranean Sea, Persian Gulf, RED SEA, NILE RIVER, TIGRIS RIVER, and EUPHRATES RIVER—all served as highways for commerce and conquest. In the early history of the region, naval power was relatively unimportant. Over time, however, developments in ships and weaponry made navies more significant.

The first naval vessels in the ancient Near East were cargo ships, which were used to transport SOLDIERS to the scene of battle. When necessary, troops fought from the ships, standing on the decks and shooting arrows or throwing spears at the enemy. The earliest known depiction of a naval battle, dating from about 3100 B.C., is found on a carved ivory knife handle from Egypt that shows two rows of ships—one Egyptian and one, perhaps, Sumerian—with dead men floating between them. Another early reference to a naval battle dates from the 2200s B.C., when King Shar-kali-sharri of Akkad sent a naval force to conquer the islands and coasts of the Persian Gulf. Yet another reference dates to the Third Dynasty of Ur (ca. 2112–2004 B.C.), when an enemy fleet of 240 ships threatened the city of KISH, located on the Euphrates River. Texts also mention an attack by the Egyptians on the coast of CANAAN in the Levant* during the late third millennium B.C.*

Most powerful states in the ancient Near East eventually developed navies. Even the HITTITES, who were not naturally a seagoing people, assembled a navy when necessary. One of their greatest naval successes was the conquest of the island of CYPRUS in the 1300s B.C. During the same period, the Minoans of CRETE and Mycenaeans of Greece had the strongest navies in the eastern Mediterranean region. During the first millennium B.C. (years from 1000 to 1 B.C.), the Phoenicians were best known for their maritime* skills.

In Egypt during the New Kingdom (1539–1075 B.C.), the navy in Egypt was a separate entity. Egyptian naval forces at this time had officers of various ranks and titles, as well as different classes of ships. The naval officers who sailed the ships were professional sailors. However, the men who served as combat troops and rowers were still land soldiers. In the 1200s B.C., one of the most famous battles in the history of the Near East took place between the Egyptians and the SEA PEOPLES. The Egyptian victory was depicted on a temple wall.

By the 800s B.C., the first true warships appeared. Developed by the Greeks, these ships, propelled by oars and sails, had large, spearlike rams attached to the bow, or front, of the ship near the waterline. These rams

* **Levant** lands bordering the eastern shores of the Mediterranean Sea (present-day Syria, Lebanon, and Israel), the West Bank, and Jordan

* **third millennium** B.C years from 3000 to 2001 B.C.

* **maritime** related to the sea or shipping

See color plate 12, vol. 4.

The Phoenician ships, shown here in an Assyrian bas-relief, date from the 600s B.C. The Phoenicians were among the greatest seafarers and maritime traders of their time. They controlled virtually all maritime trade in the Mediterranean and made many advances in shipbuilding, including building ships that could make longer voyages. In fact, some evidence suggests that the Phoenicians explored the Atlantic coast of Europe as far as Britain and perhaps sailed around Africa.

were designed to damage the hulls, or bodies, of enemy ships, causing them to sink. By the 700s B.C., the Egyptians had begun to build naval ships with rams, and the Phoenicians had adopted the design by the 600s B.C. With the development and improvement of such rams, naval vessels became formidable weapons of war.

During the years between 1000 and 1 B.C., naval power became increasingly important in the Near East and the eastern Mediterranean region. The Persians, who dominated the Near East from at least 500 B.C., employed sailors from Phoenicia, Greece, and Egypt. In the 400s B.C., the Greeks began to achieve naval superiority with Athenian triremes—oar-powered warships that were fast and easy to maneuver—that had crews of up to 200 rowers. By about 300 B.C., the use of such ships allowed the Greeks to overcome both the Persians and the Phoenicians and to become the dominant naval power in the entire region. (*See also* **Armies; Ships and Boats; Wars and Warfare.**)

NEBUCHADNEZZAR II

**ruled 605–562 B.C.
Babylonian king**

The greatest king of the so-called "Chaldean" dynasty* of ancient BABYLON, Nebuchadnezzar II (neb•yuh•kuhd•NEZ•uhr) is known for his military prowess and his role in the history of the Israelites. He is also credited with transforming Babylon into one of the greatest and most magnificent cities of the ancient Near East.

The oldest son of King NABOPOLASSAR, the founder of the dynasty, Nebuchadnezzar began a military career at a young age and became known as a capable leader and administrator. In 607 B.C., he led the Babylonian troops in northern Assyria and later commanded the military expeditions against the Egyptians in SYRIA and the Levant*.

Necho II

* **dynasty** succession of rulers from the same family or group
* **Levant** lands bordering the eastern shores of the Mediterranean Sea (present-day Syria, Lebanon, and Israel), the West Bank, and Jordan

* **tribute** payment made by a smaller or weaker party to a more powerful one, often under the threat of force

* **city-state** independent state consisting of a city and its surrounding territory

* **fortification** structure built to strengthen or protect against attack

Two years later, Nebuchadnezzar led his forces to an impressive victory against the Egyptians at KARKAMISH in Syria. This victory gave Babylonia control over Syria. Nebuchadnezzar then began to pursue the Egyptians toward Egypt. After receiving the news of his father's death in Babylon, however, he returned home to claim the throne. Soon after he secured power in Babylon, Nebuchadnezzar resumed his campaigns. In 604 B.C., he led his forces into the Levant and subdued local states there, including the kingdom of Judah. Gradually, he consolidated his control over the Levant, although pockets of resistance remained.

In 601 B.C., Nebuchadnezzar clashed again with the Egyptians near the borders of Egypt. This time, however, the Babylonians suffered great losses and were forced to retreat. The kingdom of Judah, an ally of Egypt, took this opportunity to rebel, and it stopped paying tribute* to the Babylonians. Nebuchadnezzar remained in Babylon for a few years to strengthen his forces. In 597 B.C., he crushed the revolt in Judah. When the Judeans revolted again, Nebuchadnezzar's response was swift and fierce. He destroyed much of the city of JERUSALEM, including its great temple, and took many Judeans into captivity in Babylonia. Thereafter, Nebuchadnezzar had full control of the Levant.

He continued to extend Babylonian power in other areas. After a 13-year siege of TYRE, he gained control of that Phoenician city-state*. He also gained control of former Assyrian provinces in northern Mesopotamia but failed in his later attempts to invade and conquer Egypt. Nevertheless, Nebuchadnezzar had established Babylonia as the foremost power in the Near East, and the empire reached its greatest extent since the days of King HAMMURABI more than 1,000 years earlier.

Nebuchadnezzar also launched extensive building projects, especially in Babylon. He built and repaired shrines and temples and constructed massive fortifications*, defensive walls, and lavish palaces. Many scholars credit him with building the famous HANGING GARDENS OF BABYLON, considered one of the wonders of the ancient world.

After his death in 562 B.C., Nebuchadnezzar was succeeded by his son Amel-Marduk, the first of several ineffective rulers. Despite Nebuchadnezzar's military successes and the magnificence of Babylon, his successors inherited a politically unstable empire, which began to decline. Within 25 years, during the reign of King NABONIDUS, the Babylonian empire fell to the Persians. (*See also* **Babylonia and the Babylonians; Chaldea and the Chaldeans; Israel and Judah; Judaism and Jews.**)

NECHO II

ruled 610–595 B.C.
Egyptian pharaoh

Necho II was the second pharaoh* of the Twenty-sixth Dynasty, which ruled Egypt between the reigns of Ethiopian and Persian kings. During his reign, Necho II tried unsuccessfully to expand the territorial boundaries of Egypt and to promote Egyptian trade.

Necho came to the throne on the death of his father, Psamtik I, the founder of the dynasty*. Like his father, Necho worked hard to keep Egypt independent of foreign rule and helped the Assyrians as their empire collapsed at the hands of the Babylonians and Medes. In 609 B.C.,

* **pharaoh** king of ancient Egypt

* **dynasty** succession of rulers from the same family or group

* **city-state** independent state consisting of a city and its surrounding territory

* **Levant** lands bordering the eastern shores of the Mediterranean Sea (present-day Syria, Lebanon, and Israel), the West Bank, and Jordan

Necho invaded SYRIA to stop further Babylonian expansion there. Despite early successes, the Egyptians suffered defeat in the city-state* of KARKAMISH in 605 B.C. at the hands of the Babylonian leader NEBUCHADNEZZAR II. Thereafter, Necho was forced to withdraw from Syria and abandon any hope of expanding Egyptian power into the Levant*.

Necho also launched efforts to expand Egyptian trade and commerce. He maintained fleets of ships on both the Mediterranean and Red Seas. To promote Egypt's position as an intermediary in trade, Necho began building a canal between the Nile Delta and the Red Sea. However, technical difficulties forced the Egyptians to abandon that project. According to the Greek historian HERODOTUS, Necho then sought another way to promote Egyptian trade. He sent an expedition of Phoenician sailors to find a sea route around Africa. The expedition was successful, but the route was impractical for trade purposes. At his death in 595 B.C., Necho II was succeeded by his son Psamtik II. (*See also* **Economy and Trade; Egypt and the Egyptians; Trade Routes.**)

NEFERTITI

lived ca. 1370–1336 B.C.
Egyptian queen

* **pharaoh** king of ancient Egypt
* **cult** formal religious worship

* **stela** stone slab or pillar that has been carved or engraved and serves as a monument; *pl.* stelae

* **deity** god or goddess

One of the best-known queens of ancient Egypt, Nefertiti was the chief wife of the pharaoh* AKHENATEN. She supported the religious reforms initiated by her husband and may have served as co-ruler during his reign. It is not known who Nefertiti's parents were or even where she came from. Some historians believe she may have been a princess from Mitanni, a kingdom in upper MESOPOTAMIA.

Nefertiti's husband, originally called Amenhotep IV, came to the throne around 1353 B.C. After a few years, he initiated revolutionary religious reforms that caused great turmoil in Egypt. Mainly, he cast aside Egypt's chief god, AMUN, and established a new cult* of ATEN, a sun god. Amenhotep also built a new capital dedicated to Aten, called AKHETATEN, and changed his own name to Akhenaten.

Nefertiti played an important role in the new cult of Aten. In ancient Egyptian art, she is shown making offerings to the god, a privilege that was generally reserved for kings. Nefertiti's name also appears on stelae* alongside her husband's name and the name of Aten. These stelae were the focus of household worship, and they suggest that Nefertiti was worshiped as a deity* along with Akhenaten and Aten.

Ancient Egyptian art from early in Akhenaten's reign shows Nefertiti wearing the same headdress as that worn by earlier queens. Later she wore a tall blue crown that became unique to her. In the last years of Akhenaten's reign, Nefertiti is shown wearing crowns normally reserved for kings, leading some historians to believe that she may have served as co-ruler. They also believe that she may have ruled as king for a brief time after Akhenaten's death around 1336 B.C.

Nefertiti was not Akhenaten's only wife, but little is known about his other wives. Nefertiti and Akhenaten had six daughters, two of whom later became queens of Egypt.

* **bas-relief** kind of sculpture in which material is cut away to leave figures projecting slightly from the background

Nefertiti is depicted in art and statues more frequently than any other Egyptian queen. She appears in many bas-reliefs* and artworks in the

No other queen has been depicted in art as frequently as Nefertiti. This exquisite, painted limestone bust is the most famous representation of her. Historians suggest that the bust served as a model for artists to use. It was excavated from an artist's workshop at Amarna by German archaeologists in the A.D. 1900s.

* **bust** statue of a subject's head, neck, and shoulders

temples at KARNAK and AMARNA. The most famous representation of the queen is a life-sized painted bust* in which she is wearing her unique blue crown. (*See also* **Egypt and the Egyptians; Queens.**)

NEO-HITTITES

The Hittite empire in ANATOLIA (present-day Turkey) fell shortly after 1200 B.C., when invaders destroyed its capital, KHATTUSHA. The Hittite peoples then began to form independent kingdoms southeast of KHATTI, their homeland. These kingdoms, and the people who inhabited them, are known as the Neo-Hittites, or new Hittites. For nearly 500 years, the

Neo-Hittites preserved the language and traditions of the Hittite empire before they were finally absorbed into the Assyrian empire.

HISTORY

By 1200 B.C., a group known as the SEA PEOPLES may have advanced into Anatolia from the north and west. This migration put tremendous pressure on the Hittite empire there. Taking advantage of the situation, hostile armies from the north—perhaps the Hittites' old enemies, the Kashka people—possibly attacked Khattusha and burned it to the ground in about 1190 B.C.

New States and New Threats. As the Hittite empire disintegrated, many of its inhabitants migrated to southeastern Anatolia and northern SYRIA. They regrouped around old TRADE ROUTES and river crossings and established small independent city-states*. The westernmost of these states were grouped into a kingdom called Tabal. To the east, along the western bank of the EUPHRATES RIVER, lay the states of Melid and Kummukh. South of Kummukh in Syria lay KARKAMISH, the most important Neo-Hittite city-state. Several smaller Neo-Hittite lands lay south of Karkamish.

Between about 1190 and 1110 B.C., the Neo-Hittites strengthened their control on the trade routes that ran through Anatolia. They also established new city-states in the Levant*. Around 1100 B.C., a nomadic* people known as the ARAMAEANS began to move into Syria, perhaps from east of the Euphrates River. The Aramaeans conquered some of the existing Neo-Hittite city-states and stopped Neo-Hittite expansion in the south. Notwithstanding their conquests, it was not the Aramaeans but the Assyrians who posed the greatest threat to the Neo-Hittites.

The Assyrians. Around 1110 B.C., King Tiglath-pileser I of Assyria crossed the Euphrates River and attacked Melid and Karkamish. These kingdoms became vassals* of Assyria and paid tribute*, but they were not absorbed into the Assyrian empire. The Assyrians allowed the local Neo-Hittite kings to retain control in exchange for their loyalty.

The Assyrians were not strong enough to advance as far as Tabal, which remained free of Assyrian influence for several hundred years. Finally, in the 840s B.C., the Assyrian king SHALMANESER III attacked Tabal, destroyed many of its cities, and forced the kingdom to pay tribute. By about this same time, a number of hill peoples north of Assyria had established a powerful new kingdom there, called URARTU. Thereafter, Melid, Karkamish, and many other Neo-Hittite states severed their alliances with Assyria and joined forces with Urartu.

Around 745 B.C., King TIGLATH-PILESER III of Assyria launched the first of several campaigns to regain the lands lost to Urartu. During the next 30 years, the Assyrians conquered Tabal, Karkamish, Melid, and finally, Kummukh. The conquerors dealt harshly with the Neo-Hittites; they destroyed their cities, sold much of the population into slavery, and made the former kingdoms provinces of the Assyrian empire.

The Assyrians were resettled in the newly conquered Neo-Hittite states, which remained under Assyrian control until the Assyrian empire

---

* **city-state** independent state consisting of a city and its surrounding territory

* **Levant** lands bordering the eastern shores of the Mediterranean Sea (present-day Syria, Lebanon, and Israel), the West Bank, and Jordan

* **nomadic** referring to people who travel from place to place to find food and pasture

* **vassal** individual or state that swears loyalty and obedience to a greater power

* **tribute** payment made by a smaller or weaker party to a more powerful one, often under the threat of force

Inscription of Azatiwada

In the A.D. 1940s, archaeologists excavating the site of ancient Azatiwadiya in southern Turkey found bilingual inscriptions in Phoenician and in Luwian hieroglyphics. These inscriptions were commissioned by the Neo-Hittite ruler Azatiwada, who ruled in the 700s B.C. The inscriptions celebrate Azatiwada as the founder of Azatiwadiya. The complete Phoenician version has survived and is the longest Phoenician document known to scholars. The accompanying Luwian text has aided scholars in the study of the Luwian language and in deciphering the hieroglyphic script.

collapsed some 100 years later. Although some of the remote Neo-Hittite states in the west and north regained a degree of independence, the Assyrian conquest marked the end of the Neo-Hittite period.

CULTURE

Many historians consider the period following the collapse of the Hittite empire as the Anatolian Dark Ages. Nevertheless, the Neo-Hittites preserved much of the culture and traditions of the empire during that period, making contributions of their own.

Language and Religion. The Hittites spoke two main LANGUAGES: Nesite, which was spoken in Khattusha and central Anatolia, and Luwian, which was spoken in the west and south. The Neo-Hittites abandoned the Nesite language but continued to use Luwian for official writings, such as INSCRIPTIONS, and for everyday texts, such as letters and contracts. Unlike Nesite, which was written in cuneiform*, the Luwian language used a type of HIEROGLYPHICS, in which pictures represented words and syllables. Many Luwian inscriptions have been found by archaeologists*, providing a significant amount of information about Neo-Hittite life and culture.

The Neo-Hittites retained many of the religious traditions of the Hittites. They worshiped the storm god TESHUB, the sun goddess KHEPAT, and ISHTAR, the goddess of love and war. In the north, religious traditions were similar to those in Khattusha, while Syrian traditions prevailed in the south. In the kingdom of Karkamish, for example, the Syrian goddess Kubaba was the city's main deity for hundreds of years.

Like the Hittites, the Neo-Hittites incorporated foreign gods into their religious system. For instance, the rulers of the state of Hamath worshiped the Semitic* goddess Baalat in addition to traditional Hittite deities. One new religious development among the Neo-Hittites was the belief in an AFTERLIFE for humans.

Architecture and Art. Neo-Hittite cities were centered on a high citadel, or fortress, containing palaces and temples. The surrounding town consisted of residences and other public buildings. Most buildings were constructed of mud brick* and heavy wooden beams. The bases of the buildings were covered with carved stone. Massive walls and towers to protect against enemy attack surrounded both the city and the citadel.

Neo-Hittite art consists largely of SCULPTURE from temples and public buildings and relief* carvings on walls, gates, and doors. These artworks usually portray religious, military, and mythological themes. Some freestanding sculptures have also been found, most of which are figures of deities or funeral monuments to dead leaders.

While Neo-Hittite art has various distinct features, many of its elements can be traced back to the art of the Hittite empire. It also seems likely that early Neo-Hittite art influenced the art of both the Assyrians and the Aramaeans. (*See also* **Assyria and the Assyrians; Cities and City-States; Indo-European Languages; Luwians; Religion.**)

* **cuneiform** world's oldest form of writing, which takes its name from the distinctive wedge-shaped signs pressed into clay tablets

* **archaeologist** scientist who studies past human cultures, usually by excavating material remains of human activity

* **Semitic** of or relating to people of the Near East or northern Africa, including the Assyrians, Babylonians, Phoenicians, Jews, and Arabs

* **mud brick** brick made from mud, straw, and water mixed together and baked in the sun

* **relief** sculpture in which material is cut away to show figures raised from the background

ARCHITECTURE AND TOMBS

Plate 1

During the New Kingdom period, Egyptian tombs typically featured decorated burial chambers. This burial chamber from Thebes belonged to an official during the Twentieth Dynasty (ca. 1190–1075 B.C.) and depicts figures from Egyptian mythology. Anubis, the god of cemeteries and embalming, is depicted on the walls to the left and right. Among the figures on the back wall are the falcon of the sky god Horus, and Osiris, god of the dead, who is shown seated.

Plate 2

The architectural design and decoration of Persian palaces were aimed to reveal the power and majesty of the ruler. The palace at Susa was built by King Darius I (ruled 521–486 B.C.), who made the city one of his capitals. Among the palace's magnificent features were large halls that were decorated with glazed bricks, depicting images such as the one above of a lion with horns, wings, and an eagle's feet.

Plate 3

During the Neo-Babylonian period (612–539 B.C.), the walls of the inner city of Babylon were broken by eight gates. Most impressive was the huge gate dedicated to the goddess Ishtar, a reconstruction of which is shown here. The Ishtar Gate, which had 50-foot-high foundation walls, was built of brick and ornamented with blue tiles and colored figures of bulls and dragons. It opened on a wide avenue called the Processional Way, which was also decorated with colored figures of lions.

Plate 4

The mortuary temple of the Eighteenth Dynasty Egyptian female king Hatshepsut (ruled ca. 1472–1458 B.C.) is a unique structure in New Kingdom architecture. The temple, built near Thebes, was partially cut out of cliffs. Measuring 250 by 700 feet, the temple contains several courtyards, terraces, and a hypostyle (columned hall) carved with reliefs that reflect Egyptian religious beliefs.

Plate 5

Made of terra-cotta and dating from between 1400 and 1150 B.C., these sarcophagi (ornamental coffins) were excavated from a large cemetery south of Gezer in Israel. More than 50 such sarcophagi were found there, and they often contained more than one body buried along with grave goods. Although archaeologists are not certain, some believe that these sarcophagi were made by the Philistines.

Plate 6
The great hypostyle, or columned hall, at the Egyptian temple of Amun at Karnak (near Thebes) was constructed by Nineteenth Dynasty pharaoh Sety I (ca. 1294–1279 B.C.). The hall features 134 columns that were carved to look like papyrus plants with either closed or opened buds. The columns are organized in 16 rows, with up to 9 columns in each row. The temple itself is a T-shaped structure surrounded by four walls enclosing more than seven acres.

Plate 7
Sculpted guardian figures were often a part of gates in the ancient Near East. Dating from the 700s B.C., this relief from Sargon II's palace at Khorsabad shares features with the other Assyrian guardian figures. They were often sculpted with the body of a bull (sometimes a lion) and the head of a human and were crowned with a divine tiara with horns.

Plate 8

Dating from the early third millennium B.C., this clay model of a round house was found at Mari in Syria. It contains four small rooms surrounding a square central room. The central room contains a hearth and built-in benches and is connected by passages to the surrounding rooms. One of the outer rooms is covered by a roof with a chimney. Some scholars believe that this model, which measures about two feet in diameter, represents a shrine or a fort rather than a house.

Plate 9

During the Twenty-first Dynasty (ca. 1075–945 B.C.), wealthy Egyptians buried the dead in an inner and an outer coffin, both of which were often painted with religious scenes. The inner coffin shown here, containing the mummy of a Twenty-first Dynasty priestess, is painted in red and dark and light blue on a yellow background. Its scenes portray the deceased's journey to the underworld.

Plate 10

As a formerly nomadic people, the Persians did not have a strong architectural tradition. Consequently, they adopted and adapted from other great powers of the ancient Near East. This 10-foot-high capital, or top section of a column, which dates from the Achaemenid period (538–331 B.C.), shows influences from other cultures. The spiral scrolls underneath the bulls reflect a technique used in Greek columns, and the use of floral images was inspired by Egyptian capitals. The main part of the capital consists of the front sections of two bulls that are placed together.

Plate 11

The Urn Tomb at Petra, shown here, was constructed during the A.D. 100s and 200s in Jordan. The sculptured facade of this temple-like tomb was carved entirely out of rock as was an inner chamber measuring 59 by 65 feet. The tomb was built by the Nabataeans, who came to Petra from Arabia.

Plate 12

Seven gateways, including the famous Lion Gate shown here, led into the Hittite capital of Khattusha (present-day Boğazköy, Turkey). Dating from the 1600s B.C., the lions were sculpted to protect the city from evil influences, a feature common in ancient Near Eastern architecture. When viewed from the front, the lions in the Lion Gate appear to be coming out from the gate.

Plate 13

This clay model of a house may come from western Syria and date from the third millennium B.C. Typically, houses in Syria and the Levant were built of sun-dried mud bricks on two or three layers of stone foundations. They also had one or more upper floors. This 16½-inch-tall model might have been used as an offering.

Plate 14

This building is a reconstructed version of the ziggurat at Ur, built by King Ur-Nammu around 2100 B.C. It represents the earliest true ziggurat known and consisted of three platforms stacked on top of each other and topped by a temple. The base of Ur-Nammu's ziggurat is believed to have measured 210 by 160 feet, and the completed building may have been nearly 50 feet high. Earlier Sumerian ziggurats, built before 3000 B.C., consisted of a single large platform on top of which sat a temple.

Plate 15

Scholars consider the Lycian house tombs to be one of the most impressive surviving features of the Lycian culture of ancient Anatolia (present-day Turkey). Both freestanding and cut into rock, these tombs, built in the 400s and 300s B.C., resemble the wooden houses in which the Lycians lived. The tombs were generally built for multiple burials and could be accessed by means of a sliding door that moved along grooves cut into the rock.

See map in Egypt and the Egyptians (vol. 2).

The Nile River of Africa is the longest river in the world, covering a distance of more than 4,000 miles. Beginning near the equator, the river flows northward through northeastern Africa and passes through Egypt before emptying into the Mediterranean Sea. The Nile River was extremely important to ancient Egypt. Without the Nile, Egypt would be nothing but desert, because the region receives very little rainfall. The Nile has provided Egypt with fertile land since ancient times, allowing one of the greatest civilizations of the ancient world to develop.

The ancient Egyptians were well aware of their dependence on the Nile River. Their name for Egypt, *kemet,* means "black land," and refers to the rich, black soil carried and deposited by the river. In fact, because of the river's importance to Egyptian civilization, the ancient Greek historian HERODOTUS wrote that Egypt was "the gift of the Nile."

Geography of the Nile. The Nile River consists of three major waterways: the Blue Nile and the Atbara River, which originate in the highlands of ancient Nubia (present-day Ethiopia), and the White Nile, which originates in Lake Victoria in present-day Uganda. The Blue Nile and White Nile join in the present-day Sudan to form one river. The Atbara River joins that river about 200 miles farther downstream.

Before the Nile River flows into Egypt it passes through six rapids called the Nile Cataracts. These cataracts occur where the river flows between steep cliffs, causing the current to become swift and rough. The Sixth Cataract is downstream from the present-day city of Khartoum in the Sudan. The First Cataract is hundreds of miles farther north at a place known in ancient times as Elephantine. This cataract was the traditional southern boundary of ancient Egypt and served as a natural barrier to outsiders trying to enter Egypt from the south.

North of the First Cataract, the river forms three fertile regions that have been intensively farmed and heavily populated since ancient times: the Nile Valley, the Nile Delta, and the Faiyûm Depression. The Nile Valley consists of a long, narrow strip of land running along both sides of the river from the First Cataract to the head of the Nile Delta near the ancient city of MEMPHIS. In ancient times, the Nile Valley ranged between 1 and 13 miles in width. Barren desert stretched outward for hundreds of miles on both sides of the valley.

The Nile Delta was formed of soil deposited by the river as it flowed into the Mediterranean Sea. In ancient times, the delta began north of Memphis, where the river fanned out into several branches. The Nile Delta covers an area stretching about 100 miles from north to south and about 150 miles from east to west. The entire delta has a very low elevation, enabling the land there to remain wet long after floodwaters recede. Many areas within the delta remain swampy year-round. Because of its great size and abundant water supply, the Nile Delta has always had more fertile land than the Nile Valley.

Southwest of Memphis, the Faiyûm Depression—a broad, low-lying area—is fed by the Bahr Yusuf, a branch of the Nile River. Since ancient times, this region has contained a lake whose level rises and falls with that of the Nile. Surrounding this lake is an area of fertile land where,

Puzzling Behavior of the Nile

The behavior of the Nile puzzled the people of ancient Egypt, as well as ancient Greeks and Romans. The Nile overflowed its banks each summer, no matter how little rain fell in Egypt. Explanations for this were many and varied. For example, Thales, a Greek philosopher, suggested that strong winds blowing south from the Nile Delta in summer held back the waters of the river, causing floods upstream. Another ancient Greek, Oenopides of Chios, thought that heat stored in the ground dried up underground water in winter, causing the river to recede. It was not until the 100s B.C. that the correct explanation was offered by a Greek astronomer and mapmaker named Eratosthenes. He was the first to learn about the heavy rains at the headwaters of the Nile.

in ancient times, the Egyptians built CANALS and systems of IRRIGATION to use the water of the Faiyûm Depression and expand the area of fertile farmland.

Impact on Agriculture. Ancient Egypt was dependent on the Nile River for AGRICULTURE, which was based on the flood patterns of the river. Egyptians also marked the season by the different phases of the Nile.

The Nile flooded in a more or less predictable pattern. Each year in late June, the Nile began to rise because of heavy rains in the highlands of Ethiopia and farther south. The river continued to rise gradually, and by August, it overflowed its banks. The floodwaters spread slowly over the narrow plain on both sides of the river, depositing a thick layer of rich black silt* on the land and soaking into the soil. After the floodwaters subsided, Egyptians could plant crops in the moist floodplain, which remained wet long enough for the crops to grow for harvest about three months later.

The flooding of the Nile River irrigated the land naturally. Natural levees* formed along the banks of the river because more silt was deposited there than in the outlying floodplain. Ancient Egyptians built homes and other structures on these areas of higher ground and cultivated DATE PALMS and other trees on these natural ridges.

Around 3000 B.C., Egypt's rulers began to build irrigation systems to bring more land under cultivation and increase production. Projects included repairing and reinforcing the natural levees, building artificial levees around fields to contain floodwaters, and maintaining channels to control the flow of water.

Impact on Transportation, Government, and Society. The Nile was a convenient means of transportation in ancient Egypt because of its natural features. North of the First Cataract, the Nile flows slowly and smoothly all the way to the Mediterranean Sea. In addition, the north-flowing current of the river is matched by highly reliable south-blowing winds. Consequently, ancient boats and barges could float north with the current and sail south with the wind. Transportation along the Nile was easy, quick, and cheap, and the river served as the major highway of Egypt. The ease of transportation on the Nile promoted trade, which became an important part of the economy of ancient Egypt.

The narrow width of the Nile Valley and the fact that the river runs the full length of Egypt enabled Egyptian rulers to extend their control over the entire realm. By about 3000 B.C., this had led to the establishment of a strong centralized government in Egypt. Because people clustered along the Nile, the rulers found it relatively easy to control the population and keep Egypt united.

Although the Nile's flood patterns were quite regular, abnormal FLOODS caused serious problems in ancient Egypt. Unusually low floods caused food shortages and FAMINE, while high floods damaged crops and destroyed villages. Such fluctuations in Nile flooding may account for the periodic declines in the power of Egypt's central government, as people lost faith in the ability of their leaders to please the gods and guarantee prosperity. (*See also* **Climate; Egypt and the Egyptians; Environmental Change; Euphrates River; Geography; Nubia and the Nubians; Rivers; Tigris River.**)

* **silt** soil or other sediment carried and deposited by moving water

* **levee** embankment or earthen wall that helps prevent flooding

NINEVEH

* **sixth millennium B.C.** years from 6000 to 5001 B.C.

* **second millennium B.C.** years from 2000 to 1001 B.C.

* **cult** formal religious worship

The last great capital of the Assyrian empire, Nineveh was also the oldest and most populous city in ancient Assyria. Located in northern MESOPOTAMIA on the east bank of the TIGRIS RIVER, the city was continuously inhabited from as early as the sixth millennium B.C.* until the A.D. 1500s.

Attracted by fertile land and a strategic location, early peoples established a settlement at Nineveh. During the Uruk period (ca. 4000–3000 B.C.), the city developed much like those in southern Mesopotamia. In the second millennium B.C.*, Nineveh became famous as the main center for the cult* of the goddess ISHTAR. In the 800s B.C., Nineveh underwent significant expansion. King ASHURNASIRPAL II (ruled 883–859 B.C.) and his successors built and repaired palaces and temples there. However, Nineveh did not reach its height of power and prestige until the 600s B.C., when King SENNACHERIB made it the new capital of the Assyrian empire.

As seen in this plan of the ancient city of Nineveh, two mounds dominate the ruins: Tell Kuyunjik, the site of Sennacherib's palace, and Tell Nebi Yunus, the imperial armory where tribute and arms were stored. The drawing suggests that the city was surrounded by 7.5 miles of wall intersected by 15 impressive gates built of mud brick and stone.

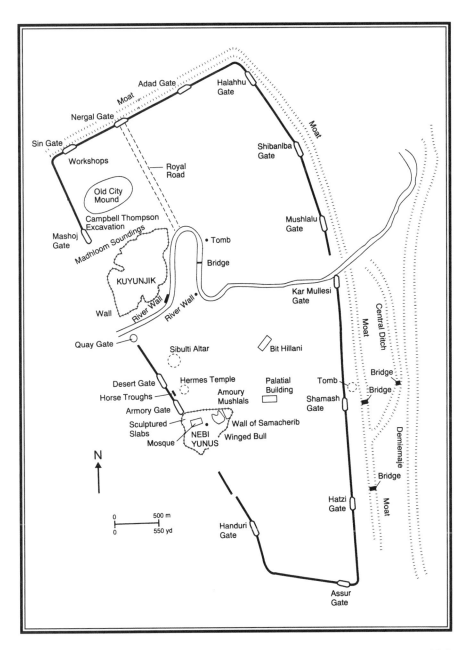

Nippur

See map in Assyria and the Assyrians (vol. 1).

* **bas-relief** kind of sculpture in which material is cut away to leave figures projecting slightly from the background

* **artifact** ornament, tool, weapon, or other object made by humans

Sennacherib transformed Nineveh into a magnificent city. He constructed an enormous, lavishly decorated palace, enlarged the city square, and built impressive avenues. He also created acres of parks and open spaces, including a great wildlife park with exotic plants and animals. Sennacherib also built canals and aqueducts to bring water from mountain streams many miles away. The pace of construction in Nineveh slowed during the reigns of ESARHADDON and ASHURBANIPAL, although both kings continued to build new structures and modify existing ones. Ashurbanipal is noted for the library he established at Nineveh, which contained thousands of CLAY TABLETS on many subjects, and for the magnificent bas-reliefs* that decorated the walls of his royal palace.

Nineveh became a symbol of the power, prestige, and wealth of the Assyrians, but it was short-lived. In 612 B.C., the Babylonians and MEDES attacked and sacked Nineveh during the last stages of their conquest of Assyria. The city survived but sank into obscurity. Parts of it continued to be inhabited for another 1,000 years, until they were absorbed into the city of Mosul.

The ruins of ancient Nineveh consist of several mounds, the main one of which is known as Tell Kuyunjik. Excavated in the A.D. 1800s, these ruins have yielded evidence from many periods in the city's history. Among the most famous artifacts* recovered there are more than 20,000 tablets from Ashurbanipal's library and bas-reliefs from his palace. (*See also* **Assyria and the Assyrians; Cities and City-States; Hanging Gardens of Babylon; Libraries and Archives; Palaces and Temples; Sculpture.**)

NIPPUR

* **city-state** independent state consisting of a city and its surrounding territory

* **pantheon** all the gods of a particular culture

* **deity** god or goddess

* **cult** formal religious worship

* **dynasty** succession of rulers from the same family or group

* **scribe** person of a learned class who served as a writer, editor, or teacher

An ancient city-state* in southern MESOPOTAMIA, Nippur (ni•POOR) was the site of the main temple of ENLIL, the supreme god of the Mesopotamian pantheon*. Nippur was occupied as early as the 5000s B.C. The city's religious importance dates from about 2100 B.C., when King Ur-Nammu of UR constructed a temple dedicated to Enlil called the Ekur. The city also contained temples to other deities*, including the goddess Inanna.

As the center for the cult* of Enlil, Nippur played an important role in Sumerian and Babylonian religion and politics. For instance, according to Sumerian tradition, the roots of kingship came from Enlil. Thus, Nippur was considered the seat of kingly power, and kings sought legitimacy through official recognition from the priests of Enlil. Yet Nippur never became a political capital, and no king or dynasty* from that city ever dominated Mesopotamia.

Nippur grew into a large city, attracting people from throughout the region because of its religious significance. The city also became a center of learning, with an academy for training scribes*, founded by King SHULGI. Around the 1700s B.C., Nippur began to experience periods of prosperity and decline. The city was nearly abandoned several times but experienced a rebirth each time. The final period of decline began in the A.D. 200s, which led to the city's complete abandonment several centuries later. (*See also* **Cities and City-States; Palaces and Temples; Religion; Sumer and the Sumerians; Ziggurats.**)

NITOKRIS

ruled ca. 2100s B.C.
Egyptian queen

* **famine** severe lack of food due to failed crops

* **dynasty** succession of rulers from the same family or group

Nitokris was one of just a few queens of ancient Egypt to serve as the ruler of her country and not just as the wife of a king. She was the sister of King Merenre II of the Sixth Dynasty (ca. 2350–2170 B.C.). When Merenre was killed at the hands of his subjects, who blamed him for the famine* Egypt suffered during his reign, Nitokris took over the throne.

Much of what is known of Nitokris's reign comes from the writings of later historians Manetho and HERODOTUS. Manetho claimed that Nitokris built the third pyramid at GIZA, but later historians have discovered that the monument preceded her reign.

Nitokris is best known for avenging the death of her brother. According to the Greek historian Herodotus, she had a huge underground room constructed and connected by a hidden pipe to the NILE RIVER. She then invited all those she believed responsible for killing her brother to a banquet. While they feasted in the chamber, Nitokris opened the pipe and water flooded the room, drowning everyone present. She then committed suicide. Nitokris was the last person in her family to rule Egypt, so with her death, a dynasty* ended.

Two other women named Nitokris are known from ancient times. One, as described by Herodotus, was a queen of BABYLON, who may have ruled during the 500s B.C. and been responsible for the construction of many public works. The other was an Egyptian princess who was named the wife of the god AMUN by her father, King Psamtik I, around 650 B.C. (*See also* **Dynasties; Egypt and the Egyptians; Queens.**)

NOMADS AND NOMADISM

* **domesticated** adapted or tamed for human use

The term *nomad* refers to people who travel from place to place in search of food and pasture. Most nomads are pastoralists, which means that their lifestyle is based on breeding and herding livestock. They live such a life because of the need to find new pastures in which to graze their herds of SHEEP, GOATS, CATTLE, or other animals. Nomads and nomadism existed throughout the ancient Near East, and they played an important role in shaping the history and culture of the region.

NOMADISM IN THE NEAR EAST

Pastoral nomadism probably arose in the Near East sometime after 9000 B.C., when AGRICULTURE began to develop. Despite the differences between nomadism and farming, modern scholars believe that the two lifestyles may always have been intertwined and that they probably developed together rather than independently.

Origins of Nomadism. The earliest agricultural settlements in the Near East consisted of farmers who tilled the soil and individuals who cared for domesticated* animals. At first, the animals probably grazed in pastures close to the fields and villages. Some animals, especially goats, which grazed on crops as well as pasture, probably did a great deal of damage to land that was valuable for crops as well.

The practice of herding animals in lands away from farming communities probably began for the purpose of conserving nearby land for

141

crops. Moving herds to and from distant pastures became the main task of individuals and families who specialized in tending the animals. Over time, these people developed a nomadic lifestyle separate from that of agriculturists and their communities.

By about 3500 B.C., the largest agricultural settlements in the Near East had developed into the first cities. The urban populations needed wool, milk, hides, and meat. The nomadic peoples and their herds supplied these animal products in exchange for manufactured goods from cities. By about 2300 B.C., nomadism had become a feasible alternative to agriculturalism. Pastoralists and agriculturists remained in contact with each other and often moved between the two lifestyles. Farmers turned to nomadic pastoralism when raising crops became difficult or impossible because of DROUGHTS or other problems. Likewise, some nomads practiced HUNTING, trading, and farming in addition to herding animals.

The relationship between nomads and sedentists (people who live in one place) was often mutually beneficial, but this did not prevent the occasional outbreak of hostilities between the two groups. Sedentists sometimes waged war against nomads, and nomads frequently raided settled communities. The interaction of these two groups played a major role in the politics and economy of the ancient Near East.

In 1973, American archaeologist Frank Hole set out to study ancient pottery at a site in southwestern Iran. However, a land-leveling project altered the site before Hole got a chance to study the pottery. He was disappointed until he noticed that the leveling had inadvertently exposed a nearly 9,000-year-old nomad tent camp.

ЭYƎ◁1ϿꓘZ∓Y⼂W⼂⼂⼂ (decorative script border)

Notable Nomadic Groups. Among the earliest nomads mentioned in Near Eastern texts were the Gutians from the Zagros Mountains of IRAN. The Gutians are credited with destroying the Akkadian empire of MESOPOTAMIA in the 2100s B.C. Like many other nomadic groups that lived close to urban civilization, they became absorbed into settled societies and adopted many of the traditions and customs of the people they conquered.

The nomads most often mentioned in Mesopotamian texts are the AMORITES, a group of peoples from northern Mesopotamia and SYRIA, who spoke a Semitic* language. Shortly before 2000 B.C., the kings of UR considered the Amorites a threat and built a wall to protect their kingdom. Yet records also indicate that many Amorites settled in Mesopotamian communities. After the collapse of the Third Dynasty of Ur in about 1950 B.C., the Amorites took control of several Mesopotamian cities. One Amorite leader, SHAMSHI-ADAD I, established a kingdom that included almost all of northern Mesopotamia. The Babylonian king HAMMURABI is also believed to have descended from the Amorites.

Another important group of nomadic people were the ARAMAEANS of Syria. First mentioned in texts from the late 1100s B.C., the Aramaeans established many small states west of the Assyrian empire. The Aramaeans and Assyrians clashed frequently until the Aramaean states were finally defeated by Assyria in the early 700s B.C. Nevertheless, Aramaic, the language of the Aramaeans, became the lingua franca* of the Assyrian empire. It remained in widespread use throughout the ancient Near East for more than 1,000 years, even following the introduction of Greek by Alexander the Great and his successors.

Yet another nomadic group, the Arabs, first appeared in written records around 850 B.C. Arabs controlled important TRADE ROUTES through the Arabian peninsula on which CARAVANS carried luxury goods, such as frankincense and myrrh*, from southern Arabia to the Near East. Fearing that Assyrian expansion would disrupt trade, the Arabs often allied themselves with other groups in campaigns against Assyria. At the same time, Arab rulers paid tribute* to Assyrian kings who, in turn, relied on the Arabs to ensure the flow of goods through their lands.

The Arabs played an important role in Assyrian campaigns against Egypt in the mid-600s B.C. Arab leaders provided King ESARHADDON with CAMELS and supplies to invade Egypt through the deserts. Still, the Assyrians continued to raid Arab territories to weaken the tribes, extract tribute from them, and ensure their loyalty and cooperation.

Around the 500s B.C., two nomadic groups from southern Russia caused much destruction in the ancient Near East region. These were the Cimmerians and the Scythians. The Cimmerians were warriors who invaded the kingdom of URARTU and ANATOLIA (present-day Turkey) in the 700s and 600s B.C. The Scythians, were warrior horsemen who invaded Assyria, Syria, the Levant*, and Egypt in the 600s B.C. Their attacks contributed to the fall of the Assyrian empire and Urartu in the 600s and 500s B.C. Yet another tribe of nomadic people who had a strong impact on the ancient Near East were the Parthians, a horse-riding tribe who were originally from CENTRAL ASIA. The Parthians seized Iran during the 200s B.C. and Mesopotamia during the 100s B.C.

Frozen in Time

Archaeological work has shown that nomadic lifestyles have remained much the same for thousands of years. For example, in 1973, American archaeologist Frank Hole studied an ancient nomadic campsite in southwestern Iran with the help of local nomads. Based on their modern practices, one of Hole's nomadic assistants was able to determine the size and arrangement of the site, the season in which it was occupied, and whether a tent site belonged to a leader or an average person. He also told Hole where to dig to uncover the locations of the fireplace and ash dumps of the ancient site. The assistant's accurate assessment of the site suggests that the layout of nomadic campsites has remained the same for nearly 9,000 years.

* **Semitic** of or relating to a language family that includes Akkadian, Aramaic, Arabic, Hebrew, and Phoenician

* **lingua franca** language that is widely used for communication among speakers of different languages

* **frankincense and myrrh** fragrant tree resins used to make incense and perfumes

* **tribute** payment made by a smaller or weaker party to a more powerful one, often under the threat of force

* **Levant** lands bordering the eastern shores of the Mediterranean Sea (present-day Syria, Lebanon, and Israel), the West Bank, and Jordan

143

Nomads and Politics. The relationship between nomads and sedentists ranged from distrust and hostility to trust and cooperation. The leaders of Near Eastern kingdoms considered nomads a threat because they were suspicious of any group whose movements they could not control. Not only did their wandering make nomads a security problem, but it also made them difficult to tax. On the other hand, nomads played an important part in the trade and economy of Near Eastern states. Expert animal breeders, they supplied donkeys to MERCHANTS, farmers, and soldiers. Nomads also hired themselves out as shepherds to farming communities. Nomadic herds were often allowed to graze on fallow* fields, where their wastes fertilized the soil.

Nomads controlled trade routes between Mesopotamia, Egypt, and the Levant. This was especially true after the domestication of the camel, which was better adapted to desert conditions than the donkey. Their knowledge of safe routes through deserts and other wilderness areas made nomads invaluable to merchants.

NOMADIC LIFESTYLE AND CULTURE

Because ancient nomads did not live in settled communities, historians have found it difficult to reconstruct their history and culture. Nevertheless, by studying artifacts* and written records and by looking at the life of present-day nomadic peoples, they have been able to piece together a picture of ancient nomadic lifestyle and culture.

Migration. The most prominent feature of ancient nomadism was the nomads' migration between winter and summer grazing lands. The climate of the Near East made such movement necessary. From November to March or April, the rainy season brought abundant water to many areas, allowing herds to graze on lands that could not support crops as well as near desert oases*. During the dry season, from April to October, these areas could no longer support enough vegetation to graze large herds of animals, forcing the nomads to drive their herds to other pasturelands.

There were two basic types of nomadic migration: vertical and horizontal. Vertical migration involved movement from lowland grazing areas in the rainy season to highland pastures in the dry season. This pattern was typical of nomads who lived near mountains, such as in northern Iran, southeastern Anatolia, and northern Syria. In horizontal migration, nomads grazed their herds in desert areas or grasslands in the rainy season and moved closer to agricultural zones during the dry season. Horizontal migration was common among groups who inhabited the fringes of desert regions in the Levant and the SINAI PENINSULA.

Lifestyle and Culture. Nomads made their living by trading animal products. They also relied on hunting, gathering, and trade with agriculturists for grains, fruits, and other goods to supply other needs. Nomadic people sometimes raided agricultural settlements to obtain the goods they needed. Usually, however, they enjoyed peaceful relations with their settled neighbors, and the two groups learned to rely on and benefit from each other's special skills.

* **fallow** plowed but not planted, so that moisture and organic processes can replenish the soil's nutrients

* **artifact** ornament, tool, weapon, or other object made by humans

* **oasis** fertile area in a desert made possible by the presence of a spring or well; *pl.* oases

ƎYꙄ◁1ꙄꟾᛕZꙶYƚWꟼФ7ОꙅWᒣᛕꟾꙄƎYꙄ◁1ꙄꟾᛕZꙶY

Iranian nomads are seen here breaking their winter camp in preparation for the spring migration. The stone walls that surround the camp shield the interior from wind and cold. Archaeological assessments have revealed that the layouts of present-day nomadic campsites such as the one shown here are the same as they were thousands of years ago.

* **clan** group of people descended from a common ancestor or united by a common interest

* **hierarchical** referring to a society or institution divided into groups with higher and lower ranks

Most nomadic groups were organized into tribes whose members belonged to various clans*. Each group claimed descent from a common ancestor. Politically, they ranged in organization from small, decentralized groups to large chiefdoms. In small groups, most individuals held equal status, while larger groups were more hierarchical*. (*See also* **Animals, Domestication of; Arabia and the Arabs; Economy and Trade; Family and Social Life; Land Use and Ownership.**)

NUBIA AND THE NUBIANS

* **arable** suitable for growing crops

Nubia was the Arabic name for the region that comprises present-day southern Egypt and northern SUDAN. The ancient Greeks and Romans called the region Aethiopia. During their long history, the Nubians were periodically involved in the affairs of Egypt and the Mediterranean world. Nubia also became the homeland of a great civilization, the oldest in Africa south of Egypt.

Land and Early History. Physically, Nubia was primarily desert and not arable* except for narrow strips along the NILE RIVER. However, the region was rich in gold and other valuable minerals. Moreover, the Nile provided an important trade route between Egypt and the rest of Africa. Nubia's minerals and trade goods brought the region great wealth.

Nubia and the Nubians

The Egyptians were not the only ancient Near Eastern people to build pyramids At least 300 pyramids can be attributed to the kings, queens, and nobles of the Nubian kingdom of Kush. However, Kushite pyramids were much smaller than those of the Egyptians. While Egypt's largest pyramid covered more than 173,000 square feet, the largest Kushite pyramid covered only about 2,900 square feet.

See map on inside covers.

ca. 3500 B.C.
First Nubian kingdom is established.

ca. 2000 B.C.
Egypt conquers Lower Nubia.

ca. 1700 B.C.
Kush takes control of Lower Nubia.

ca. 1540 B.C.
Egypt regains control of Nubia.

ca. 800 B.C.
Nubians establish an empire centered at Napata.

ca. 760 B.C.
King Piye unites Egypt and Nubia.

ca. 660 B.C.
Assyrians expel Nubian rulers from Egypt.

Early farmers raised crops in seasonally dry channels of the Nile River and established the earliest permanent settlement in the region by about 5000 B.C. By about 3800 B.C., the people of Nubia had established several trading centers along the Nile. Gold, copper, IVORY, shells, semiprecious stones, INCENSE, and other luxury goods were traded northward to Egypt in exchange for Egyptian manufactured goods and agricultural products.

First Nubian Kingdom. Sometime around 3500 B.C., a small kingdom emerged in northern Nubia, a region that later became known as Lower Nubia. The Egyptians called this first Nubian kingdom Ta Sety (land of the bow), a name that reflected the fame of Nubian archers.

This early kingdom was greatly influenced by Egypt. The kings of Ta Sety modeled themselves after Egyptian rulers, a tradition continued by later Nubian kings. Like Egyptian kings, Nubian rulers built large tombs and monuments for themselves, and they were buried with many objects of wealth. At this time, the Nubian economy was based on a mix of herding and farming, while contact with Egypt focused on a regular trade in luxury items and manufactured goods.

Nubia was prosperous between about 3500 and 3100 B.C., but this period was followed by a shadowy period of nearly 1,000 years about which little is known. During this time, northern Nubia lost much of its population, and the distinctive culture of the region disappeared suddenly. It is possible that Egyptian raids may have caused the decline in northern Nubia. Around 2300 B.C., a new Nubian culture appeared, and Nubia again began to prosper. This culture was noted for the importance it placed on CATTLE raising, its fine POTTERY, and increased trade with Egypt.

Egyptian Rule and the Rise of Kush. Around 2000 B.C., the Egyptians conquered Lower Nubia, but the Nubians there managed to retain their cultural identity. The Egyptians built a series of forts along the Nile River in Nubia to protect trade and guard against a kingdom in southern Nubia (Upper Nubia) called Kush. The kingdom of Kush, which remained independent of Egyptian rule, was developing into a major power that began to rival Egypt and its dominance of the Nile.

Egypt controlled Lower Nubia until about 1700 B.C., when the Egyptian government collapsed due to internal strife. Taking advantage of the situation in Egypt, Kush took control of Lower Nubia. The capital of Kush at this time was the city of Kerma, located on the Nile between Upper and

146

⟨YƎ⊣⊲⇃⊲⋉⟨Z∓Y†W⊲Φ⌿O⟨Ш⟋⋋⅂⅂⅃BYƎ⊣⊲⇃⊲⋉⟨Z∓Y⟩

Nubia and the Nubians

Lower Nubia. Kerma soon became an urban center with large temples, manufacturing sites, and huge tombs. Its people included metalworkers and potters, whose goods were exported throughout Egypt.

By 1540 B.C., strong kings had reunited Egypt, regained control of Nubia, and extended their rule farther south to include Kush. Egypt also made a determined effort to "Egyptianize" Nubia and the Nubians, which led to their adoption of Egyptian culture. Nubian customs and artifacts* became almost indistinguishable from those of Egypt, and wealthy Nubians adopted Egyptian deities* and their system of writing, called hieroglyphics*. The Egyptian rulers built great temple complexes in Nubia that became important centers of religion, politics, culture, and economy. The best known is the famous temple complex at ABU SIMBEL.

The Empire of Kush. Little is known about the history of Nubia and the Nubians in the years between 1100 and 800 B.C. By the end of this period, a new kingdom had emerged in Upper Nubia, centered at the city of Napata on the Nile River. This kingdom, which arose from the earlier kingdom of Kush, soon developed into a great empire.

As the new empire of Kush expanded and gained power, the Egyptians experienced another period of political upheaval, during which northern Egypt fell to the LIBYANS. Taking advantage of this situation, the new rulers of Kush extended their control into Egypt as far north as the city of THEBES. Controlling Thebes, the old imperial* capital of Egypt, was an accomplishment. The city was the center of the cult* of AMUN, the state god of Egypt and later of Kush.

Around 760 B.C., a Kushite king named Piye gained control of all of Egypt and united it with Nubia to form one of ancient Africa's greatest states. Piye and his successors ruled Egypt for about 100 years, a period known as the Twenty-fifth Dynasty. Kings of this so-called "Ethiopian" dynasty led Egypt through its last era of great achievements, which included a massive building program under King TAHARQA. Around 660 B.C., invaders from Assyria advanced into Egypt and drove out the last Nubian king of the Twenty-fifth Dynasty. However, Kush remained a powerful state in Nubia for another 1,000 years.

The Rise of Meroë and the Fall of Kush. By about 300 B.C., the capital of Kush had moved to Meroë, a city on the right bank of the Nile several hundred miles south of Napata. Meroë and Kush developed a culture that reflected Egyptian traditions as well as Greek, Roman, and African ideas. Nubian art and architecture became distinct and original, and Nubians used their own language and writing instead of Egyptian hieroglyphics. During this period, Egypt faced a succession of foreign rulers: the Persians, the Macedonians, and the Romans. The Nubians tried to help the Egyptians revolt against foreign rule, but they came under Roman rule themselves in about 20 B.C. In the A.D. 200s, Meroë came into conflict with Axum, a kingdom in Ethiopia. Around 350, invaders from the west known as the Noba overran most of Kush, ending the Kushite state. (*See also* **Dynasties; Economy and Trade; Egypt and the Egyptians; Kush and Meroë; Trade Routes.**)

* **artifact** ornament, tool, weapon, or other object made by humans
* **deity** god or goddess
* **hieroglyphics** system of writing that uses pictorial characters, or hieroglyphs, to represent words or ideas

* **imperial** pertaining to an emperor or an empire
* **cult** formal religious worship

Opposing Views of the Nubians

The Nubian people did not develop a written language of their own until quite late in their history. Therefore, most of what we know about them today comes from the ancient Egyptians, Greeks, and Romans, each of whom had biased views. The Egyptians viewed the Nubians as culturally inferior to themselves. Consequently, early Egyptian scholars dismissed Nubian civilization as a crude copy of the Egyptian civilization. The Greeks and Romans viewed the Nubians as a morally and culturally superior people beloved by the gods. The Greek historian Herodotus even believed that Nubia was the source rather than a copy of the Egyptian civilization.

147

Numbers and Numerals

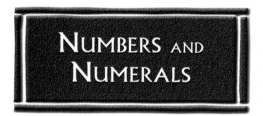

NUMBERS AND NUMERALS

Numbers are units of quantity and the basis of counting. As elements of mathematical systems, they enable people to perform simple arithmetic and complex mathematical operations. Numerals are the symbols used for writing numbers. In ancient times, the peoples of the Near East developed systems for counting and expressing numbers—a necessary step toward the growth of mathematics, engineering, and astronomy.

Counting and Writing Numbers. Even before writing was invented, Near Eastern peoples counted with small objects called tokens. Each token represented one of a particular type of item, such as a sheep. A clay packet found in the ruins of the Mesopotamian city of URUK contained six egg-shaped tokens, each representing a jar of oil. Scholars believe that before 3000 B.C., the people of the ancient Near East did not have a conception of numbers independent of the commodities* they counted. The signs included both the commodity and the measurement. In other words, abstract numbers such as one, two, or three, referring to any set of items was unknown.

* **commodity** article of trade

Once people began to write, they developed images for numerals. Some experts believe that the written symbols were imitations of the counting marks that people had made earlier by pressing tokens into wet clay. For instance, a CLAY TABLET found at Godin Tepe, IRAN, expresses the idea "33 jars of oil" with an egg-shaped symbol for a jar of oil preceded by three circles (three tens) and three wedges (three ones)—much easier than collecting and storing 33 tokens.

The Egyptians developed a decimal system based on multiples of ten. They used distinctive symbols for 1, 10, 100, and 1,000. To write a number, they wrote down each symbol as many times as it appeared in the number. The numeral for 48, for example, was written with four symbols for 10 and eight symbols for 1. The Sumerians also wrote numerals by adding as many symbols as necessary. Their counting system alternated between units of ten steps and units of sixty steps. Number sequences ran from 1 to 60, 61 to 600, and 601 to 3,600. They used the number 3,600 to indicate any very large but indefinite number, as we might say "a zillion."

* **second millennium** B.C. years from 2000 to 1001 B.C.

The Babylonians, who dominated Mesopotamia during the second millennium B.C.*, developed new methods of counting and writing numbers. Like the Sumerians, their counting system was sexagesimal, or based on units of 60. They had symbols for every number between 1 and 10 as well as symbols for 20, 30, 40, and 50. To write numbers of 60 and above, they developed a place-value method. Instead of repeating symbols as many times as necessary to reach a given total, they assigned a value to each position, or place, in the numeral. For example, the symbol for 1 could also represent 60 or 3,600, depending on its position within the numeral. Modern number systems also use place value—a single numeral represents units of one, a numeral to the left of it represents units of 10, and so on. By the 300s B.C., the Babylonians began to use a special sign for zero.

Today, much of the world uses a decimal system that expresses numbers with the numerals 1 through 9. Called Arabic numerals, they originated in southern India before A.D. 500. Shortly thereafter, the Indians began using the zero as a multiplier and placeholder. The Arabians adopted the Indian numeral system in the 700s or 800s, and through Spain, introduced it to the European world.

Mystical Meanings of Numbers. Numbers also held religious and magical significance in the Near East. Mesopotamians regarded seven as a powerful number, and many magical spells or ritual actions were repeated seven times. They used numerals to write the names of their gods in shorthand—EA, for example, was 40 and ENLIL was 50. Numerals could also represent deities* and heavenly bodies—the number 15 stood for both the goddess ISHTAR and the planet Venus. Numerals were also used by scribes* to indicate colors or the cardinal points of the compass, or to convey messages intended only for other scribes.

Near Eastern peoples also gave mystical significance to numbers in a system called alphabetic numeration, where each letter of the alphabet corresponded to a number. In the Hebrew method, *aleph,* the first letter, equaled one. *Beth,* the second letter, equaled two, and so on. Jewish religious scholars used this method to find what they believed were hidden meanings in biblical texts. For example, they claimed that when the Hebrew BIBLE said that 318 men accompanied Abraham it really meant that his servant Eliezer accompanied him, because the numerical value of Eliezer's name was 318. During the 200s and 100s B.C., Greek letters were similarly used on the SEALS of certain officials and tax officers of the SELEUCID EMPIRE to indicate the year the seals were issued. (*See also* **Mathematics.**)

* **deity** god or goddess

* **scribe** person of a learned class who served as a writer, editor, or teacher

NUZI

* **second millennium B.C.** years from 2000 to 1001 B.C.

* **provincial** having to do with the provinces, outlying districts, administrative divisions, or conquered territories of a country or empire

* **archaeologist** scientist who studies past human cultures, usually by excavating material remains of human activity

* **artifact** ornament, tool, weapon, or other object made by humans

Nuzi (NOO•zee) was a town in northeastern MESOPOTAMIA. During the period of the Akkadian empire, the town was called Gasur. In the second millennium B.C.*, when the town was controlled by the HURRIANS, it was renamed Nuzi. The town reached its height of prosperity in the 1500s B.C., when it was an administrative center in the kingdom of Mitanni. By the 1200s B.C., the Assyrians had attacked and destroyed Nuzi.

Inhabited by the Hurrians, KASSITES, Assyrians, and Babylonians, Nuzi was an ordinary town. Its economy was based on AGRICULTURE and trade. Nuzi's population consisted of a mix of rich and poor residents, including farmers, merchants, craftspeople, and slaves. The town was governed by provincial* officials of regional kingdoms. At its height, the city's population was estimated at 1,600. Despite its small size, Nuzi possessed all the characteristics of major Mesopotamian cities, including defensive walls, temples and government buildings, outlying settlements, and surrounding agricultural lands. The town had several neighborhoods housing various classes of people.

Archaeologists* began to excavate the ruins of Nuzi in the early A.D. 1900s. The ruins and artifacts* they found—including temples dedicated to ISHTAR (goddess of love, fertility, and war) and TESHUB (storm god), government buildings, canals and IRRIGATION systems, homes, and public

Obsidian

A large temple devoted to the goddess Ishtar was located in the center of Nuzi. Glazed nails, strings of beads, and glass plaques decorated the walls of the temple. A statue of the goddess, an altar for sacrificing animals, and statuettes of lions (shown here) were located inside the temple. The lion was a symbol associated with Ishtar.

See map in Mesopotamia (vol. 3).

and private documents—have provided one of the most complete pictures of the economy and society of a typical provincial town in ancient Mesopotamia. (*See also* **Walled Cities.**)

O bsidian (uhb•SI•dee•uhn) is a natural, glasslike rock formed by the rapid cooling of volcanic lava. Slightly harder than window glass, it generally is black in color. However, the presence of certain minerals in the rock can produce red, brown, and green varieties of obsidian.

Obsidian is a brittle rock that chips easily, creating smooth surfaces bordered by extremely sharp edges. Since prehistoric time, humans have used sharp-edged pieces of obsidian to make cutting TOOLS and weapons. They sometimes used the rock to make JEWELRY and decorative ornaments as well. Some ancient cultures, such as that of the Greeks, made mirrors from obsidian by polishing its smooth, glassy surfaces.

In the ancient Near East, one of the most important sources of the rock was in central ANATOLIA (present-day Turkey). As early as about 6000 B.C., inhabitants of the settlement of ÇATAL HÜYÜK used local sources of obsidian to make tools and weapons. In fact, archaeological* evidence suggests that much of that community's prosperity centered on an obsidian trade with other regions.

Obsidian was an important item of trade, and archaeologists have uncovered extensive trade networks over which the rock was carried. Obsidian artifacts* found in SYRIA and the Levant*, for example, can be traced to sources in central Anatolia. Others in southwestern IRAN can be traced to sources in the CAUCASUS region near the Black and Caspian Seas. It is unclear whether obsidian was carried by traders or was passed from village to village through exchanges of goods. In either case, obsidian

* **archaeological** referring to the study of past human cultures, usually by excavating material remains of human activity

* **artifact** ornament, tool, weapon, or other object made by humans

* **Levant** lands bordering the eastern shores of the Mediterranean Sea (present-day Syria, Lebanon, and Israel), the West Bank, and Jordan

rock and tools made from obsidian reached areas far from the sources. (*See also* **Caravans; Economy and Trade; Glass and Glassmaking; Trade Routes; Weapons and Armor.**)

OFFERINGS

* **city-state** independent state consisting of a city and its surrounding territory

Food of the Gods

The gods of the ancient Near East had to eat just like humans did, so offerings of food and drink were common in religious rituals and ceremonies. In some places and time periods, meals were regularly served to the gods in temples, often twice a day, in the morning and evening. Such offerings included bread, cakes, beer, wine, fish cakes, meats, and all sorts of fruits and vegetables. In order to supply these offerings on a regular basis, temples often had their own gardens, wineries, and herds of livestock. They also relied on regular contributions from the people in the community.

* **consecrate** to declare sacred or holy by means of a religious rite

* **Levant** lands bordering the eastern shores of the Mediterranean Sea (present-day Syria, Lebanon, and Israel), the West Bank, and Jordan

People in the ancient Near East gave offerings to gods, rulers, temple officials, dead ancestors, and spirits, such as the ghosts of loved ones. These offerings might consist of food or other necessities of daily life, luxury items, or an animal or human sacrifice.

Caring for the Gods. A scholar who studied ancient MESOPOTAMIA coined the phrase "care and feeding of the gods" to describe the temple rituals of ancient Mesopotamia. The phrase can also be applied to religious rituals performed throughout the Near East. These rituals, which included making offerings of food and drink to the gods, were believed to be vitally important. Without them, the city-state* or kingdom might lose the favor of the gods, resulting in disaster for the society.

During major festivals, the responsibility of making offerings to the gods fell largely on the king. This formal activity emphasized his duties as ruler and his obligation to maintain a good relationship between the gods and his land and people. Kings made such offerings in special ceremonies, using stone bowls and other containers to present offerings of food and drink.

Offerings were also an important part of daily religious worship. Temple priests prepared and offered meals and drinks to the gods each day, generally in the form of a banquet. In ancient Mesopotamia and Egypt, offerings included cooked meat, fish, bread, grains, fruits and vegetables, flour mixed with oil, honey, wine, and milk. Offerings might also include images, INCENSE, CLOTHING, COSMETICS, PERFUMES, and decorative objects. The daily offerings were intended for the gods, but the priests and worshipers who presented them partook from the food once it was consecrated*. In Israel, however, the offerings were burned and converted into smoke, which then reached YAHWEH in heaven.

Throughout the ancient world, blood offerings were an essential part of worship. Such offerings involved the sacrifice of animals, where the blood was drained and offered to the gods. Although rare, human sacrifice was also performed to atone for sins or to avert major disasters. Evidence suggests that the Phoenicians sacrificed children at the city-state of CARTHAGE in North Africa as did other Canaanites in the Levant*. There is also evidence of human sacrifice dating from the earliest periods in Egypt and Mesopotamia, especially in royal burial sites.

Offerings to the Dead. In Mesopotamia, Egypt, and ANATOLIA (present-day Turkey), people believed that it was important to make offerings to the spirits of the dead. Called funerary offerings, they consisted of things the spirit would need for the afterlife. The spirits of dead kings might receive offerings of delicious meat dishes and baked goods as well as fine clothing, furniture, perfumes, and other luxury items. Ordinary people might receive cold water, hot broth, beer, flour, oil, wine, honey,

151

Olives

This painted stela, dating from around 2500 B.C., portrays an Egyptian named Wepemnofret seated before a table of offerings. Excavated from Wepemnofret's tomb at Giza, the inscriptions on the stela list his name and titles in large hieroglyphics. The stela also contains lists of offerings in a table with five columns.

See color plate 7, vol. 1.

and occasionally the ribs of a sacrificed animal. These offerings were made to please the dead and to make their existence in the afterlife more comfortable. If the spirits failed to receive the offerings due them, they could return as troublesome ghosts to bother the living. (*See also* **Afterlife; Book of the Dead; Priests and Priestesses; Religion; Rituals and Sacrifice.**)

OLIVES

* **Levant** lands bordering the eastern shores of the Mediterranean Sea (present-day Syria, Lebanon, and Israel), the West Bank, and Jordan

One of the first fruits cultivated by peoples of the ancient Near East, the olive was well suited to the types of CLIMATE and soil found in many parts of the region. Olive groves thrive in cool, wet winters and hot, dry summers, which are typical of the eastern Mediterranean region. They also require little rainfall and flourish in sandy, rocky, well-drained soil. Because the olive is so well adapted to the region's land and climate, it became one of the most important crops of the ancient Near East.

The oldest evidence of olives in the Near East comes from the Levant* and dates to about 3700 B.C. Olive trees were also native to southeastern ANATOLIA (present-day Turkey) and the Mediterranean coast of SYRIA. Around 3000 B.C., the cultivation of olives spread to many regions in the Near East. Local growers began to plant olive groves with cuttings taken from wild olive trees. Because it takes several years after planting for an olive tree to bear fruit, olives were not grown to satisfy immediate needs for food. In many places, olives and olive oil, obtained by pressing the ripe fruit, became important trade goods.

Olives and olive oil had many uses and were an important part of the diet, partly because they can be easily preserved. When stored in brine (saltwater), olives keep for long periods and can be transported across great distances. Olive oil was used as a fuel as well as to make COSMETICS and PERFUME. The oil was also used in political and religious rituals. Israelite and Hittite kings were anointed* with olive oil as a sign of their

* **anoint** to bless by applying oil or some other substance

152

authority. Priests, too, were anointed with olive oil, and it was used in purification ceremonies and as a part of animal sacrifices. (*See also* **Agriculture; Food and Drink; Rituals and Sacrifice.**)

OMAN PENINSULA

* **oasis** fertile area in a desert made possible by the presence of a spring or well; *pl.* oases

See map in Arabia and the Arabs (vol. 1).

* **commodity** article of trade

* **archaeological** referring to the study of past human cultures, usually by excavating material remains of human activity

The Oman peninsula in southeastern Arabia was an important center of trade in the ancient Near East. Although much of the peninsula is desert, it also contains oases*, mountains, and a plateau, which have enough water to support AGRICULTURE. The Omani Mountains contain large deposits of copper and two kinds of black stone—diorite and olivine-gabbro—which were popular for use in ancient SCULPTURE.

Hunting, gathering, and fishing societies existed on the Oman Peninsula for thousands of years. By about 3000 B.C., permanent agricultural settlements had begun to emerge in the region. Around the same time, local inhabitants began to mine copper in the mountains. Around the 2500s B.C., cities in MESOPOTAMIA began to import copper from Oman, a land they called Magan. This is evident in texts found in the city of Akkad that mention that ships from Magan docked at its harbors.

Early relations between Akkad and Magan were peaceful, but the two regions later went to war. Around 2250 B.C., an Akkadian fleet crossed the Persian Gulf to attack Magan, and texts mention a later campaign as well. By about 2100 B.C., trade had resumed between Mesopotamia and Magan. Commodities* included copper, black stone, IVORY, and semiprecious stones. The last two items probably came to Magan from MELUKKHA (in India), and archaeological* evidence suggests close trade links between the Oman peninsula and the Harappan civilization of western India. Shortly after 2000 B.C., for reasons that remain unclear, trade links between Mesopotamia, Magan, and Melukkha broke down. Thereafter, their names came to refer to distant places. Evidence also suggests that Oman was independent throughout most of its early history. (*See also* **Arabia and the Arabs; Metals and Metalworking; Trade Routes.**)

OMENS

* **divination** art or practice of foretelling the future
* **astrologer** person believed to be able to foretell earthly events by studying the motions of heavenly bodies

An omen is a natural phenomenon or other occurrence that is believed to be a sign that a good or bad event is to happen in the future. Reading omens is a form of divination*. Many texts from the ancient Near East refer to omens, and everyone from kings to peasants and slaves took the observation and interpretation of omens very seriously. Priests, diviners, and astrologers* were responsible for explaining omens.

Belief in omens emerged from the notion that gods created and operated the universe in a meaningful way. People who knew how to read the patterns in natural phenomena could peer into the supernatural secrets of the gods. In ancient MESOPOTAMIA, the *baru*, Akkadian for examiner, asked the gods for omens and interpreted them. Most of the *baru* mentioned in the records worked for the crown; they were either palace scholars or were attached to a branch of local government or the army.

One of the *baru*'s standard methods of divination was extispicy, or reading omens in the liver and intestines of a sacrificial animal, usually a

Oracles and Prophecy

In ancient Mesopotamia, diviners, or sooth-sayers, practiced extispicy, the process of deriving omens from the liver of a sacrificial animal. This clay model of a sheep's liver, dating from between 1900 and 1600 B.C., is inscribed with notes to aid the diviner in "reading" the organ for omens. Diviners used these models as well as handbooks that listed every mark, discoloration, and deformation, along with its significance, to interpret omens.

* **archaeologist** scientist who studies past human cultures, usually by excavating material remains of human activity

sheep. Archaeologists* have found clay models of livers with notes describing and locating features important in divination. These models have been found not only in Mesopotamia but also in Anatolia and Canaan, where extispicy was also practiced.

Such practices produced "solicited" omens, or omens requested by individuals at a particular time to find the answers to specific questions. Diviners also found omens in such things as the movement of a drop of water placed in a dish of oil (lecanomancy) or the patterns in a cloud of INCENSE smoke (libanomancy). Usually, the client asked for a yes or no answer to a question. If the omen was unclear, the diviner could repeat the process. A diviner might also provide advice on how to avoid a bad outcome foretold by the omen.

Not all omens were solicited. Any abnormal or unusual event, such as the birth of a deformed animal or an earthquake, was seen as an omen, often signaling looming evil or danger. Such unsolicited omens usually differed in their significance. For example, an untimely thunderstorm might be interpreted as an omen affecting a city or district. A larger event, such as an eclipse of the sun or a large earthquake, was an omen of national importance, perhaps signaling an invasion or the death of a king. Divine messages might also come to people in DREAMS or trances.

Among the most common unsolicited omens were astral omens, which dealt with such events as eclipses, meteor showers, and the movements of the planets and stars. In ancient times, astronomers closely watched heavenly objects in the sky, and the observation of astral phenomena led to the development of astrology, the belief that the movements of heavenly bodies correspond to events on earth.

Over the course of time, omens were gathered and organized into handbooks, which people used as aids in interpreting divine signs. Omen handbooks from Mesopotamia contain long lists of divine signs written in a specific format: "If this is the sign: this is what will happen." Many of these signs dealt with situations in everyday life—for example: "If a man washes himself with water in the corridor of the house: he will become old." The use of such books became an important part of daily life to discover and control the supernatural forces of the gods. (*See also* **Astrology and Astrologers; Oracles and Prophecy.**)

ORACLES AND PROPHECY

In the ancient Near East, RELIGION and MAGIC were two closely related expressions of the relations between people and the supernatural world. Both were concerned with obtaining certain types of knowledge: those that interpreted the will of the gods and foresaw the future. Many Near Eastern peoples believed that with the right methods and the aid of a trained priest, magician, or other practitioner, they could uncover the hidden knowledge that was all around them, waiting to be revealed.

Oracles, which are communications from the gods in answer to questions, and prophecies, which are messages from the gods that may predict the future, were two avenues by which supernatural or divine knowledge reached humans. The term *oracle* also refers to people who deliver the communications from the gods and who operate within the religious, royal, or social structures of society. They included priests or priestesses at temples and shrines. Prophets, in contrast, believed they were called—or commanded—to prophecy by their gods. They were driven by strong feelings to share their prophecies, which could be unexpected or even unwelcome. Like oracles, many prophets also worked for the temple or state, although some prophets appeared outside these establishments, driven by the urgency of their messages.

DIVINATION AND ORACLES

Many ancient Near Eastern societies practiced divination, or the technique of interpreting signs to tell the future. Oracles often served as diviners because they could respond to people's questions about the future or about the meaning of certain occurrences.

Types of Divination. Diviners in the ancient Near East helped explain the meaning of signs, including OMENS, or indications of coming events, either good or bad, and DREAMS. In ancient Egypt and Mesopotamia, diviners looked for omens using ASTROLOGY, in which the movements of the sun, moon, visible planets, and stars were thought to correspond to events or conditions in earthly life.

Almost all cultures practiced divination through dreams. People regarded dreams as a channel through which the gods or dead ancestors communicated with individuals in the living world. However, the person who received the dream could not be the one who interpreted it; the process required separate individuals. Kings could receive divine commands through dreams. People sometimes slept in temples in the hope that the gods would appear in their dreams to give advice, a practice called incubation. Hittite texts contain descriptions of dreams along with omens and oracles. For example, one text describes how King Murshili II asked the gods to send a dream that would explain why his people were dying of a plague*. The Israelites also believed that dreams could contain communications from their god, YAHWEH.

* **plague** contagious disease that quickly kills large numbers of people

Oracular Process. An omen or a dream could appear on its own, but an oracle could be heard only when someone posed a specific question to the gods about the future or the meaning of events or things. Records of consultations with oracles provide the best documentation for Egyptian divination. According to these records, the general procedure was to present a prepared question that could be answered yes or no. The process of presenting the question was called "reaching the god." The subjects of questions varied widely and included such matters as nominations for offices and accusations of theft. The methods of acquiring the answer also differed from place to place.

The Hittites relied on oracles to predict the success of almost all important undertakings in public and private life. Hittite texts contain references to oracular inquiries about such matters as the course of a military campaign and illnesses in the royal family.

PROPHETS AND PROPHECIES

Prophecy in the ancient Near East was associated mainly with Israel, although prophets lived in other places as well. A prophet believed that a deity* had chosen him to communicate important information to an individual or a community. The prophet could obtain that information from his or her deity or from other supernatural beings—in the case of the Jewish prophet Zechariah, an angel—through a dream, a vision, or ecstasy. Prophets are described as inspired, sometimes even frenzied by the urgency with which divine messages are conveyed.

In Mesopotamia, Egypt, and Iran. Texts unearthed at the Mesopotamian city of MARI include prophecies from the reign of ZIMRI-LIM, around 1760 B.C. Prophets claimed to be speaking for the god Dagan, who at the time had a broad regional appeal. Some of the prophecies deal with the safety of the king and military affairs, while others relate to the temple. Men and women could be prophets, but their message was conveyed to the king through intermediaries, such as the queen or governors.

Very little evidence exists for prophecy in ancient Egypt. Several narratives dating back to the Old Kingdom and First Intermediate periods (ca. 2675–1980 B.C.) contain prophecies, but they are all set after the predicted event had occurred. Although these documents contain messages and predictions, they do not attribute their statements to the gods.

In IRAN, the religion called Zoroastrianism was founded by the prophet Zoroaster around 600 B.C. Zoroaster spoke out against the priests and religious practices of his time and declared that the god AHURA MAZDA had revealed sacred truths to him.

In Israel. The largest surviving collection of prophetic writings and stories about prophets is in the Hebrew BIBLE. The prophets of the Israelites received messages from Yahweh in dreams, in trances, or while awake. Among the best-known biblical prophets are ISAIAH, JEREMIAH, and Ezekiel, who left records of their utterances, while others, such as Elijah and Elishah, are known mostly through stories that involved them. There were also women prophets, such as Miriam, Huldah, and Deborah. Like Zoroaster, some of the prophets of ISRAEL AND JUDAH criticized the religious establishments of their eras for wandering from the path of true and righteous worship. They claimed to be speaking for Yahweh and often began their prophecies with the words "Thus says the Lord."

The Israelite prophets may have answered a divine call, but they also fulfilled earthly functions. They advised kings on matters of foreign policy and directed their oracles at enemy nations. In the biblical Book of 2 Kings, prophets are even credited with initiating revolutions and appointing rival kings to the throne. They also analyzed and criticized royal actions from the point of view of the common people, helping to keep

* **deity** god or goddess

The Prophecy of Neferti

Composed during the reign of King Amenemhet I of the Twelfth Dynasty, *The Prophecy of Neferti* praises the king and celebrates his success in ending a chaotic period in Egyptian history. Set fictitiously in the court of Fourth Dynasty king Sneferu, Neferti, a skilled scribe, sage, and priest, predicts the future. He foretells calamities for Egypt until a king from the south—Ameny (Amenemhet I)—takes the two crowns of Upper and Lower Egypt and establishes stability and joy.

kingly power within limits. The prophets, like all diviners and oracles, gave expression to the universal belief that the affairs of this world were linked to higher levels of existence. (*See also* **Witchcraft.**)

* **deity** god or goddess

See color plate 10, vol. 1.

* **cult** formal religious worship

One of the most important deities* of ancient Egypt, Osiris (oh•SY•ruhs) was the god of the dead, lord of the underworld, and protector of the deceased in the AFTERLIFE. He was also associated with rebirth, which was linked to human resurrection and the annual cycles of vegetation and flooding of the Nile River.

Osiris and ISIS, his sister and wife, played a central role in the best-known Egyptian myth. Osiris was king of Egypt until he was killed by his evil brother SETH, who wanted to take the throne. Osiris was brought back to life by Isis, who gave birth to their son HORUS. Osiris then went to live in Duat, the Egyptian underworld. When Horus grew up he fought Seth and became king, and Isis joined Osiris in Duat.

Some scholars believe that this myth was created to explain the death of an Egyptian king, who was considered a god, and to pave the way for the rightful successor. The Egyptians believed that their king was the "living god" Horus. When the king died, he was reborn as Osiris in Duat, and his son became Horus and thus the legitimate heir.

The oldest and most important cult* center of Osiris was at ABYDOS. Because of his connection with death and kingship, Osiris was often depicted as a mummy wearing a crown and carrying a royal scepter, or staff. Although originally associated only with Egyptian kings, the myth of Osiris was later seen to offer the promise of resurrection for all people. The cult of Osiris became very popular and even spread beyond Egypt to the Greek and Roman worlds. (*See also* **Amun; Cults; Egypt and the Egyptians; Gods and Goddesses; Religion.**)

Painting

See *Art, Artisans, and Artists; Pottery; Wall Paintings.*

* **millennium** period of 1,000 years; *pl.* millennia

* **archaeologist** scientist who studies past human cultures, usually by excavating material remains of human activity

Palaces and temples were by far the most important buildings constructed in the ancient Near East. Ranging from modest structures to the largest and most magnificent ones, these buildings were the homes of kings and gods. They were the major centers of power in Near Eastern societies. Palaces and temples not only played crucial roles in the politics, GOVERNMENT, economy, and RELIGION of societies, but they also served as powerful symbols of both earthly and heavenly kingdoms.

Because of their importance, palaces and temples were built to last. While many ancient buildings vanished into dust over the course of millennia*, the remains of a number of palaces and temples have survived, providing archaeologists* with evidence to reconstruct the history of ancient Near Eastern cultures. These structures provide information about ancient ARCHITECTURE and building techniques, and the artworks found within them have helped increase our knowledge of ancient ART, ARTISANS, AND ARTISTS. Moreoever, the LIBRARIES AND ARCHIVES excavated at these sites provide firsthand knowledge of ancient Near Easterners' political and business activities as well as their religious beliefs.

PALACES OF THE ANCIENT NEAR EAST

The palaces of the ancient Near East were the residences of kings and their families, as well as the centers of royal administration and government. The dual functionality was reflected in their layout and design, and a specific palace architecture was developed to meet the special needs and demands of these functions.

Functions of Palaces. As the home of a king, the palace was equipped with kitchens, storage areas, dining areas, and living quarters. The size and level of comfort of these facilities varied according to the wealth of the ruler and his family. While the residences of some local rulers could be modest, the palaces of kings were large, magnificent structures. Decoration and artwork provided enjoyment for the king and served as symbols of his wealth and power. WALL PAINTINGS and bas-reliefs* depicted the king as a great warrior, protector, and builder.

Palaces also served as the center of government and often contained large complexes of official rooms to serve the needs of the state. One of the most important official rooms was the throne room, where the king presided over the royal court and exercised his power. Palaces might also contain other ceremonial rooms, as well as workshops, treasuries, storerooms, and workrooms for scribes* and other members of the government bureaucracy*. Because the king played a central role in religion, palaces were often connected to temples and shrines.

History of Palaces. Palaces did not always exist in the ancient Near East. In very early periods, the homes of local rulers were probably much like those of other people, though larger. However, as civilizations developed and the power of rulers grew, their residences became larger and more impressive.

With the rise of large territorial states, the wealth, power, and responsibilities of kings expanded greatly. The size and splendor of their residences grew as well, becoming the first true palaces. Over the centuries, palaces became larger and more complex to meet the requirements of growing kingdoms and empires. This was especially evident in the palaces of great kings in imperial* capitals.

Mesopotamian Palaces. The first true palaces in Mesopotamia were built in the early third millennium B.C.*, when large secular* buildings that were clearly different from temples and other official structures appeared. Among the earliest palaces of this period were ones built in the Sumerian cities of KISH and ERIDU. A classic example of an early Mesopotamian palace is the Babylonian Palace of the Governors at ESHNUNNA. Connected to a large temple complex, this building had an outer

* **bas-relief** kind of sculpture in which material is cut away to leave figures projecting slightly from the background

* **scribe** person of a learned class who served as a writer, editor, or teacher

* **bureaucracy** system consisting of officials and clerks who perform government functions

* **imperial** pertaining to an emperor or an empire

* **third millennium** B.C. years from 3000 to 2001 B.C.

* **secular** nonreligious; connected with everyday life

courtyard for public affairs, an inner courtyard for more private functions, and a throne room used as an audience hall by the king.

One of the best-preserved Mesopotamian palaces is the palace at MARI, which dates from the 1700s B.C. Much larger than the Palace of the Governors, it had more than 260 rooms on the ground floor and covered an area of more than five acres. The palace at Mari clearly reflected the dual function of Near Eastern palaces, with lavish and extensive living quarters for the king and his family, as well as a large complex of official areas. The official areas on the ground level of the palace included a richly decorated royal courtyard, a large throne room, a temple, ceremonial rooms, and storerooms for food and other goods. The second floor of the palace contained offices from which the king, officials, and bureaucrats governed the state.

Among the largest Mesopotamian palaces were those of the Assyrians. Assyrian palaces have a design similar to that of the Palace of the Governors at Eshnunna, but they are much more extensive. The largest is the citadel* of SARGON II, built between 717 and 707 B.C. This palace had two outer courtyards, an enormous throne room, and living quarters. Assyrian palaces were usually single-story buildings, but there is some evidence that the king carried out religious ceremonies on the roof. The inner walls of rooms in the palace were covered with stone reliefs* showing scenes of the court, religious symbols, hunting scenes, and records of the king's military campaigns.

The most magnificent palace of the Neo-Babylonian period (612–539 B.C.) was the Southern Citadel of BABYLON. In fact, King NEBUCHADNEZZAR II called it "the marvel of mankind, the center of the land, the shining residence, the dwelling of majesty." This great palace had a series of five courtyards, numerous reception rooms, a large throne room, and the other areas typical of large palaces. Its facade* was covered with glazed

* **citadel** fortified place or stronghold that commands a city

* **relief** sculpture in which material is cut away to show figures raised from the background

* **facade** front of a building; also, any side of a building that is given special architectural treatment

---

Ninurta, a war god, was worshiped by ancient Mesopotamians. His principal cult center was the temple Eshumesha at Nippur, built during the first half of the second millennium B.C. From excavations at the ancient site of Nippur, archaeologists have obtained a great deal of information about the temple's activities, including the kind of staff it employed.

This chart provides a list of some of the workers, whose responsibilities fell into three categories—religious, administrative, and domestic. While religious workers attended to the needs of the god, administrative and domestic workers oversaw the managerial aspects and upkeep of the temple. Some of these workers were considered specialists and worked at the temple on long-term appointments. Workers whose jobs did not require a high level of skill and training were probably replaced regularly.

STAFF OF THE TEMPLE AT NIPPUR	
Religious Staff	**Domestic Staff**
high-priest	miller
lamentation-priest	cow herder
purification-priest	oil-presser
high-priestess	water-carrier
naditu [cloistered] priestess	fuel-carrier
diviner	mat-maker
snake charmer	weaver
	stonecarver
Administrative Staff	(copper)-smith
	courtyard-sweeper
house supervisor	barber
treasurer	guard
accountant	
scribe	
overseer of the oil pressers	

Palaces and Temples

ceramic bricks depicting lions and trees. In one corner of the building was an unusual arrangement of rooms identified by some scholars as site of the fabled HANGING GARDENS OF BABYLON.

Egyptian Palaces. Little has been preserved from the earliest palaces of ancient Egypt. Evidence suggests, however, that the architectural style of these palaces probably originated in northern Egypt, perhaps influenced by Mesopotamia. When northern and southern Egypt were united at about 2000 B.C., the architectural style was adopted throughout the kingdom.

The basic form of Egyptian palaces was a mud brick* enclosure wall, within which were numerous buildings. The enclosure wall had an elaborate pattern of recesses and projections on the facade that formed niches. These niches were plastered, painted white, and decorated with colored patterns and designs. The high walls of the palace enclosure dominated the skyline and were visible from great distances.

The royal residences and buildings within the enclosure wall were built of brick as well. They included columned halls, reception areas, courtyards, private living quarters, artists' workshops, and areas for administration, storage, and other activities. The importance of the palace—and its symbolic role as the seat of kingship—was reflected in the term *pharaoh* ("great house"), which became the title of Egyptian kings during and after the Eighteenth Dynasty (ca. 1539–1292 B.C.).

One of the most significant and best-preserved Egyptian palaces is the palace of Amenhotep III at THEBES. This palace, situated next to a vast artificial lake, contained an extensive complex of buildings focusing on a series of rooms organized around columned halls and open assembly areas. The structure was one story, but the halls were higher than the surrounding rooms, and their upper walls contained windows to let in air and light. In addition to official rooms, the palace contained apartments for the pharaoh and for royal women of different ranks. Many of the interior

* **mud brick** brick made from mud, straw, and water mixed together and baked in the sun

This drawing is a reconstruction of the plan of the extensive Khorsabad citadel built between 717 and 707 B.C. for Assyrian king Sargon II. Surrounded by fortifications, it contained the royal palace and temples, which were built on a platform, and the residences of high officials, which were on a lower level. The palace occupied three-quarters of the citadel and had two outer courtyards, an enormous throne room, and living quarters.

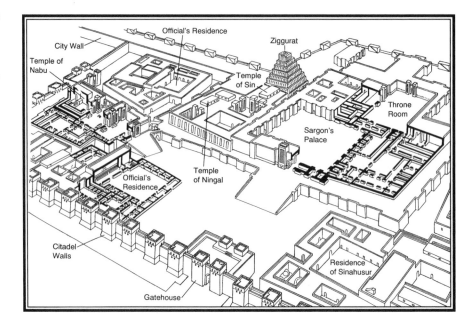

160

walls and floors of the palace were decorated with brightly colored paintings related primarily to the world of nature. The ceilings of the public halls also had decorations, but they were more formal, often consisting of sacred symbols and designs.

In ancient Egypt, a palace also served as an administrative center for high officials acting on behalf of the king. For instance, during the 1700s B.C., a palace at Avaris in the Nile Delta was used by an Egyptian official of the Thirteenth Dynasty. Bearing the title "overseer of foreign lands," this official used the palace to conduct diplomatic* relations with the Minoans from CRETE and the Canaanites and other Semitic* peoples from the Levant* and SYRIA.

Palaces in Other Regions. Palaces also were built by other groups in the ancient Near East, including the Hittites of Anatolia, the rulers of ancient Canaan and Israel, and the Persians. Although these structures different somewhat in layout and design, they all contained the same basic features and served the same purposes as Mesopotamian and Egyptian temples.

A distinctive feature of palaces in Syria was a "half-timbered" construction, which consisted of a stone foundation with the walls above built of wooden beams and plaster. A number of Hittite palaces were built on fortified hill sites. The Persians often reoccupied the palaces of the rulers they conquered as they extended their empire.

TEMPLES OF THE ANCIENT NEAR EAST

Temples in the ancient Near East were residences of the gods—the places where deities* lived and where humans served them. Temples also became important economic and social institutions. They controlled vast agricultural lands and other resources, providing products and work for members of the community. As centers of religious ritual and economic activity, temples also helped bring order and stability to the society and contributed materially and spiritually to its prosperity.

Functions of Temples. Unlike churches, mosques, and synagogues of today, most of the temples of the ancient Near East were not places where ordinary people went to worship. Because they were thought to be the actual residences of the gods, temples were sacred sites and entrance was restricted to the king and the priests of the temple.

In Near Eastern societies, the king was considered the chief priest of the state religion, and he was responsible for building and maintaining temples, performing religious rites and ceremonies, and supporting worship of the gods. How well he performed his duties was thought to have a significant impact on society, bringing prosperity or hardship to the kingdom because of the favor or displeasure of the gods. The day-to-day functioning of the temple was in the hands of the priests and other temple workers. The priests performed daily rituals involved with taking care of all the needs of the gods, whose presence in the temple was represented by statues and cult* images.

To serve the gods properly, temples were equipped like households, with kitchens, tables (in the form of altars), receptions rooms, living and

Palatial Living

Ancient Near Eastern rulers spared no expense in building, decorating, and maintaining their palaces. These buildings were not only the homes of the most important individuals in society and the seats of government, but they were also powerful symbols of the prosperity and prestige of the state. The luxury of palaces was an obvious benefit to the ruler and his family. Yet the size and beauty of structures were meant to inspire awe in citizens—and perhaps fear in enemies because of the great power and wealth the buildings represented.

* **diplomatic** relating to the practice of conducting peaceful negotiations between kingdoms, states, or nations

* **Semitic** of or relating to people of the Near East or northern Africa, including the Assyrians, Babylonians, Phoenicians, Jews, and Arabs

* **Levant** lands bordering the eastern shores of the Mediterranean Sea (present-day Syria, Lebanon, and Israel), the West Bank, and Jordan

* **deity** god or goddess

* **cult** formal religious worship

161

Palaces and Temples

* **hierarchy** division of society or an institution into groups with higher and lower ranks

Temples to the Sun God

In ancient Egypt, a special type of temple was dedicated to the worship of the sun god Ra. These solar temples were very different in design from the temples dedicated to the other gods. They consisted of an enormous open courtyard that had an altar in the center for making animal sacrifices. As early as the Fifth Dynasty (ca. 2500–2350 B.C.), solar temples were built in connection with pyramid complexes. A thousand years later, the growing dominance of Amun, the god of the sun-disk, under pharaoh Akhenaten led to the construction of huge solar temples that were among the largest temples ever built in ancient Egypt.

* **sanctuary** most sacred part of a religious building

sleeping quarters, and storage rooms. The operation of the temple "household" required a large staff of priests, craftspeople, scribes, and servants, many of whom lived within the temple or in surrounding buildings. Temple staffs, including priests, were organized according to a hierarchy* of roles and responsibilities. In many ways, the large staffs that administered the affairs of temples were very similar to the palace bureaucracies that ran the government of the states.

Maintaining the temple and its staff required not only a complex administrative apparatus but also enormous economic resources. Some of the resources needed for the temple came as offerings and gifts from the king and worshipers. However, temples also controlled land, large herds of livestock, and workshops for the manufacture of various goods. Control of such resources brought great wealth to the temples and their administrators, making temples among the most important economic institutions of society and their administrators among the wealthiest.

History of Temples. Temples were built in the Near East long before the first palaces. The earliest known remains of temples in Mesopotamia date from before 5000 B.C., although some archaeologists have discovered wall decorations and statues several thousand years older that may suggest the existence of temples at a much earlier time. In Egypt, the earliest evidence for sanctuaries* dates from only about 3000 B.C.

The earliest temples were small, simple shrines. Nevertheless, their design and structure show certain elements that remained basic features of temples throughout ancient times, including altars and niches for god statues and cult images. Over time, temples increased in size and complexity, but they always kept various features that were unique and that distinguished them from palaces, their earthly counterparts.

Mesopotamian Temples. Temples throughout Mesopotamia, no matter what their size, had several elements that distinguished them as sacred buildings. The most sacred part of a temple was the inner sanctuary, a large room where the statue of the deity stood in an alcove set in one of the building's short walls. An offering table stood nearby. One or more rooms, perhaps used for religious purposes or for storage, flanked the inner sanctuary along the temple's long walls. Often a staircase led to the roof, where some rituals were performed.

The layout of the temple's sacred spaces generally followed a pattern that remained relatively unchanged over time. In addition to sacred spaces, temple complexes had courtyards and rooms designed for use by the priests in their daily life. Large complexes also had surrounding buildings with living and working areas for temple staff. The entire complex might be surrounded by a wall.

Many Mesopotamian temples were build on platforms approached by sets of stairs. Shortly before 2000 B.C., this design feature had developed into platforms consisting of several raised terraces with a temple on top. Known as a ziggurat, this type of structure was a distinctive feature of Mesopotamian temple architecture and was found in nearly every important city. One of the latest and tallest, the ziggurat at Babylon, was built by King Nebuchadnezzar II and is believed to have risen nearly 300 feet high.

Egyptian Temples. Most early temples in Egypt were of rather modest size and made from simple materials. Like Egyptian palaces, these temples often had enclosure walls decorated with niches. The focus of each temple was a shrine to its god located in the enclosure. Some temples were built on platforms filled with clean sand, which may have symbolized the purity of creation. The walls and doorways often were decorated with elaborate scenes, either painted or carved in relief.

In later centuries, the Egyptians built enormous temple complexes, such as the great temple at KARNAK dedicated to the god AMUN. These temple complexes featured massive enclosure walls surrounding the temple, storehouses, residences for priests, and other buildings. The temples themselves were long buildings that featured a series of large courtyards surrounded by columned halls. The inner sanctuary, which held the statue of the god, was set apart from the other temple areas by a surrounding corridor. It also had a raised floor and a separate roof, forming a virtual temple within a temple.

While early temples were built primarily of mud brick, later temples were often built of stone. Some temples were even carved out of rock, such as the great temples of ABU SIMBEL. Temples continued to be colorfully decorated with both realistic scenes and symbolic designs. Most of the elements of temple design, including building materials and the placement of a temple on its site, had various symbolic meanings.

Temples in Other Regions. Temples in other areas of the Near East, such as Anatolia, Syria, and the Levant, served functions similar to those in Mesopotamia and Egypt. Their basic architectural elements were similar as well, although certain design and decorative elements reflected regional differences.

One of the characteristic features of Hittite temples was an elaborate gateway that contained small chambers on each side for gatekeepers and attendants. A distinctive feature of some Levantine temples, called bench temples, was a series of low mud brick benches around the walls of the sanctuary and near the central altar. This bench was not for seating but was used for presenting offerings.

With the rise of small nation-states in Canaan after 1200 B.C., temple architecture increasingly reflected local religious differences. Several temples in Israel, for example, had open courtyards containing sacrificial altars. Sometimes a staircase at the front of a temple led to an open porch whose roof was supported by two columns. The porch led into the large main chamber and behind that was the "holy of holies," a small chamber at the back of the temple that contained the cult statue. Only high priests were allowed to enter this chamber.

The most famous temple of the region, the fabled Temple of Solomon in Jerusalem, no longer exists. The close association between that temple and the royal palace of King Solomon—which was part of a huge temple-palace complex—reflected the close connection between temple and state that existed throughout the ancient Near East. (*See also* **Archaeology and Archaeologists; Bas-Reliefs; Cults; Economy and Trade; Gods and Goddesses; Land Use and Ownership; Priests and Priestesses; Property and Property Rights; Religion; Rituals and Sacrifice; Ziggurats.**)

The Temple of Solomon

One of the most famous temples of the ancient Near East—and perhaps the most mysterious—was the Temple of Solomon in Jerusalem. Built in the 900s B.C., during the reign of King Solomon, the temple was destroyed by the Babylonians in the 500s B.C. Nothing of this fabled temple has survived to the present day except descriptions of it in the Hebrew Bible. Modern archaeologists have the skills to excavate the site of the temple—known as the Temple Mount—but they cannot do so because of religious tensions and opposition from Jews, Muslims, and Christians, all of whom claim the site as a holy place. Excavations of other temples have helped confirm that the biblical descriptions are probably accurate and that the Temple of Solomon was rather modest in size. Though no trace of the temple exists, it remains a powerful symbol of Jewish faith.

See
color plate 9,
vol. 1.

Palestine

See *Canaan; Philistines.*

PAPYRUS

* **Levant** lands bordering the eastern shores of the Mediterranean Sea (present-day Syria, Lebanon, and Israel), the West Bank, and Jordan

Papyrus was the main writing material of ancient Egypt. Manufactured as early as 3000 B.C., it remained in use for some 4,000 years. By about 2000 B.C., the use of papyrus had also spread to Syria and parts of the Levant*, and much later, found its way to ancient Greece and Rome.

Papyrus is a paperlike material made from the stems of the papyrus plant, a reed that grew widely in marshes and swamps in Egypt. Although stronger than paper, papyrus cannot survive rough handling, dampness, or fire. As a result, very few ancient papyri still exist. Most of those that survive were excavated at BURIAL SITES AND TOMBS in the desert regions bordering the Nile River in Egypt, where the dry climate helped preserve them from decay. A number of ancient papyri have also been found in the desert regions of the Levant and Mesopotamia.

Manufacture of Papyrus. The basic method of making papyrus remained unchanged for thousands of years. It required a great deal of skill, and the production of the material generally was left in the hands of specialized craftsmen, most of whom worked for the government.

After the papyrus reeds were harvested, the long stems of the plant were cut into shorter pieces. The rough outer coating of these pieces was then removed, and the soft fiberlike material inside was cut or torn into long strips about an inch wide. A dozen or more of these strips were laid side by side, to form a layer. A second layer of strips was placed perpendicular to and over the first layer. The two layers were then covered with a cloth and pounded with a wooden mallet until they merged into a single sheet. This sheet was pressed under a heavy weight and left to dry. Dried sheets were often polished—perhaps by rubbing them with a smooth stone—to create a smooth finish. Finally, the edges of the sheets were trimmed.

Several sheets of papyrus (20 was a standard number) were joined together to form a roll. To make this roll, the sheets were placed end-to-end, with each sheet overlapping the next by about half an inch. The overlapping edges were sealed with a starch paste. After drying, the pasted sheets were rolled up and tied with strings of papyrus fibers. Manufacturers almost always made rolls rather than separate sheets. If a single sheet of papyrus was required, it was cut from a roll.

Ancient Medical Knowledge

One of the oldest known medical works is a collection of Egyptian medical texts that were recorded on a papyrus roll around 1550 B.C. Named after the German scholar George Ebers, who acquired the document in the late A.D. 1800s, the Ebers Papyrus contains hundreds of magical spells and folk remedies for various health problems, ranging from toenail pain to crocodile bites. It also contains an amazingly accurate description of human blood vessels and the functioning of the heart. In addition to its medical advice, the Ebers Papyrus contains directions for getting rid of such household pests as scorpions, rats, and flies.

* **scribe** person of a learned class who served as a writer, editor, or teacher

Use of Papyrus. Papyrus was used for writing many types of documents, from personal letters to government records, religious documents, and literary works. In ancient Egypt, scribes* usually wrote on complete rolls of papyrus rather than on separate sheets, which were used for letters. The rolls came in various heights, and rolls of different sizes were used for different types of documents. Typically, the more important the document, the taller the roll. Except for very important documents, most rolls were less than 16 inches in height, and many were less than 8 inches high.

This painted relief from Egypt's Fifth Dynasty (ca. 2500–2350 B.C.) depicts men gathering papyrus plants. Harvested papyrus stems were used to make not only writing material, but also baskets, rope, and even boats.

Most literary works and government documents took up a complete roll of papyrus. If a work was too long to fit on a standard roll (about 15 feet), additional sheets were pasted together to make the roll longer. One ancient Egyptian document that records temple donations during the reign of Ramses III was a papyrus roll 141 feet long. If a work was too short to fill a standard roll, excess sheets were cut off. In the case of school texts and private copies of literary works, several works were often written on one roll.

Completed papyri were rolled and retied with papyrus strings. Such rolls often were sealed with a small amount of clay, which might be marked with identifying SEALS. Completed single sheets of papyrus were folded to form a small package and then tied and sealed. The contents of the roll—or the address in the case of a letter—were written on the outside. Sets of completed papyrus rolls were tied together and stored in boxes, baskets, pots, or bags, and the containers were labeled to indicate their contents. In some temples and government buildings, specific rooms were set aside for the storage of papyrus rolls.

Papyrus was relatively expensive, costing about one-fifth of a skilled worker's monthly wages. It was also in short supply during the seasons of the year when papyrus plants were not yet ready for harvest. Because of cost and seasonal shortages, it was common practice to recycle papyrus by washing off old text and writing new text on it.

Importance of Papyrus. Nearly all ancient Egyptian documents were written on papyrus. Many scholars think that the invention of this writing material accompanied the development of bureaucracy* in Egypt, which necessitated the maintenance of extensive government records. Papyrus was a more convenient and flexible writing material than the CLAY TABLETS used in ancient Mesopotamia, although it was not as durable.

By about 2000 B.C., papyrus had become an important export commodity* in Egypt, and its manufacture was monopolized* by the royalty. Light in weight, easily transported, and conveniently stored, it remained the most important writing material in the Mediterranean world until the Middle Ages*, when it was replaced by parchment and vellum, which were made from animal skins. (*See also* **Books and Manuscripts; Egypt and the Egyptians; Record Keeping; Scribes; Writing.**)

* **bureaucracy** system consisting of officials and clerks who perform government functions

* **commodity** article of trade

* **monopolize** to control exclusively or dominate a particular type of business

* **Middle Ages** period between ancient and modern times in western Europe, generally considered to be from the A.D. 500s to the 1500s

PARTHIA

See map in Persian Empire (vol. 3).

* **satrapy** portion of Persian-controlled territory under the rule of a satrap, or provincial governor

* **dialect** regional form of a spoken language with distinct pronunciation, vocabulary, and grammar

* **Hellenistic** referring to the Greek-influenced culture of the Mediterranean world and western Asia during the three centuries after the death of Alexander the Great in 323 B.C.

* **aristocracy** privileged upper class

* **dynasty** succession of rulers from the same family or group

Parthia (PAHR•thee•uh) was the ancient name for the region that corresponds to present-day northeastern Iran. The term also is used to refer to the Parthian empire, which flourished there between 247 B.C. and A.D. 224. The empire served as a link between the Near East and the Far East and a bridge between the ancient world and the world of Islam.

Nothing is known about Parthia before the 550s B.C. except that the Parthians were members of horse-riding tribes from CENTRAL ASIA and that Parthia was a satrapy* of the PERSIAN EMPIRE. In 330 B.C., when the Persian empire was conquered by ALEXANDER THE GREAT, Parthia became a satrapy of his Macedonian empire. When Alexander died in 323 B.C., it became a satrapy of the succeeding SELEUCID EMPIRE.

In 247 B.C., a Parthian satrap named Arsaces I revolted against the Seleucids and founded the Parthian empire and the Arsacid dynasty. Although he was not Parthian, Arsaces spoke the Parthian dialect* and adopted the region's Hellenistic* culture. Later kings expanded the empire, and by 124 B.C., it included all of Iran and territory from MESOPOTAMIA to India. The empire was divided into provinces and ruled by a small aristocracy*. The Parthian king was the supreme ruler, but the outlying provinces had a considerable degree of independence.

The empire prospered and expanded during the reigns of Mithradates I (ruled 171–138 B.C.) and Artabanus II (ruled 128–124 B.C.). Artabanus was succeeded by Mithradates II, also known as Mithradates the Great. During his reign, Parthia was attacked repeatedly by Armenians from the northeast and Scythians from the northwest. Mithradates defeated both groups and further expanded the empire. When he died in 88 B.C., rival dynasties* struggled to take control of the empire until 70 B.C., when Phraates III took over the throne and restored stability. Beginning in 54 B.C., the Romans launched repeated attacks against Parthia for about 200 years, weakening the empire. Finally, in A.D. 224, the Parthians were overthrown by the Persians of the Sasanian dynasty, and the Parthian empire ended.

Because of the Parthians' location and large territory, they controlled most of the trade routes between Asia and the Mediterranean. They used the wealth they gained from this trade to implement and fund their extensive building programs. In both their buildings and their artworks, the Parthians showed an interesting blend of Asian and Greek influences. (*See also* **Iran; Scythia and the Scythians.**)

PATRIARCHS AND MATRIARCHS OF ISRAEL

The patriarchs and matriarchs of Israel are considered the most influential ancestors of the Israelites. These men and women whose stories are told in the Hebrew BIBLE include Abraham and his wife, Sarah; their son Isaac and his wife, Rebecca; Isaac's son Jacob and his wives, Rachel and Leah; and Jacob's son Joseph. The stories of the patriarchs and matriarchs explain the origins of the Israelites and why they were selected as their god YAHWEH's "chosen people."

Abraham and Sarah. The first patriarch, Abraham (also known as Abram), lived in Ur of the Chaldees (city and district in Mesopotamia). According to the Bible, Yahweh commanded Abraham to leave Ur and travel to CANAAN. In return for Abraham's obedience, Yahweh promised him that his descendants would inherit Canaan—the Promised Land. Abraham believed Yahweh's promise of an heir, but his wife, Sarah, was doubtful. Childless, she believed that she was too old to have children.

To fulfill Yahweh's promise, Sarah urged Abraham to father a child by her slave, Hagar, whom she could claim as her own. Sarah herself later gave birth to a son, Isaac, and forced Hagar and her son Ishmael to leave the household. In Islamic tradition, Ishmael is considered the father of the Arabs. Abraham is thus revered as an ancestor by Muslims as well as by Jews and Christians.

One important story about Abraham concerns the potential sacrifice of Isaac. While Isaac was still a boy, Yahweh commanded Abraham to prove his obedience by sacrificing Isaac. At the last moment, however, Yahweh gave Abraham a ram to sacrifice in Isaac's place. This story reemphasizes Abraham's faith in Yahweh, who rewards him by promising him future power and glory.

Isaac and Rebecca. When Sarah died, her death was a terrible blow to Isaac. To relieve his son's grief, Abraham sent a messenger to Mesopotamia to find Isaac a wife. The messenger left it up to God to choose the proper wife for Isaac: Rebecca.

After 20 years of marriage, Rebecca gave birth to twins named Esau and Jacob. Yahweh tells Rebecca that both of her sons will establish great nations, but that the older son (Esau) will serve the younger one (Jacob). When her sons became young men, Jacob secured the right of firstborn from Esau, and Rebecca tricked Isaac, who had gone blind, into giving his blessing to Jacob instead of to Esau because she believed that Jacob would make the better leader. When Esau realized he had been deceived, he became angry, and Jacob was forced to flee for his life. During this journey, Yahweh appeared to Jacob and confirmed the promise originally made to Abraham, that Jacob would have numerous descendants who would possess much land.

Jacob, Rachel, and Leah. Jacob went to live with his uncle Laban in Upper Mesopotamia, where he fell in love with Rachel, Laban's younger daughter. To win her as his wife, Jacob worked for Laban for seven years. At the wedding ceremony, Laban substituted his older daughter Leah for Rachel. Jacob was also given Rachel but then worked another seven years to deserve her.

* **concubine** mistress to a married man

Jacob had 13 children by his two wives and their two servants, Zilpah and Bilhah, who became his concubines*. After many years in Upper Mesopotamia, Jacob returned to Canaan with his family. On the way, he had a physical struggle with a divine being—either Yahweh or an angel—after which his name was changed to Israel. This name was later used for the nation of Israel. Once back in Canaan, Jacob made up with Esau. Jacob's sons were ancestors to the 12 tribes into which the Israelite people were later divided.

Joseph. Joseph was the son of Jacob and Rachel. Joseph was also his father's favorite son. When Jacob gave him a splendid "coat of many colors,"

⁊ℬＹⳈ◁◁⅄ℬⳄℤ⅁Ⓨ†Ⱳ⅄φ⟅◁ℴⳄℳⳄℵℇℬＹⳈ◁◁ℇⳄℤ⅁

Peasants

* **pharaoh** king of ancient Egypt

* **famine** severe lack of food due to failed crops

* **second millennium B.C.** years from 2000 to 1001 B.C.

Joseph's brothers became jealous and sold him as a slave to a group of traveling merchants, who took him to Egypt.

After many episodes in Egypt, Joseph gained the pharaoh's* favor by interpreting the ruler's dreams. Joseph warned that the dreams referred to a coming famine* and advised the pharaoh to store the grain from a preceding period of good harvests. This advice saved Egypt from the famine and earned Joseph the pharaoh's gratitude and an important position in the kingdom.

The same famine drove Joseph's brothers to Egypt in search of food. They met Joseph but did not recognize him because more than 20 years had passed since they sold him. He recognized them, however. Joseph finally revealed himself to his brothers and forgave them. He then invited them all to settle in Egypt, where the family grew, becoming the Israelites. After many generations, the Israelites (known to the Egyptians as the Hebrews), who had become slaves, left Egypt under the leadership of MOSES. They eventually resettled in Canaan and established the nation of Israel.

History and Meaning of the Stories. Scholars debate whether the patriarchs and matriarchs are actual historical figures. Those who do believe that they are place their origins in Upper Mesopotamia during the second millennium B.C.* Some scholars argue that the patriarchs and matriarchs symbolize the earliest people who accepted Yahweh. From a religious standpoint, the stories reinforce the early Israelite belief that they were a "chosen people" and that the blessing and protection of Israel and its people depends on obedience to and faith in their god, Yahweh. (*See also* **Egypt and the Egyptians; Hebrews and Israelites; Israel and Judah; Judaism and Jews; Monotheism; Religion; Theology.**)

PEASANTS

* **illiterate** unable to read or write

Peasants were free laborers—agricultural laborers, craftspeople, and herders—who worked outside urban centers. They comprised the majority of the population of the ancient Near East and played a crucial role in AGRICULTURE, the basis of every economy. Despite their importance to the prosperity of early civilizations, scholars know very little about peasants. They were illiterate* and could not keep records of their lives. The literate classes did not write about peasants except for administrative purposes, such as recording taxes collected from them. Consequently, much of the information scholars possess about peasants is based on inferences from other sources.

Peasant Work. Most peasants in the ancient Near East were tenant farmers, who toiled in fields owned by temples, kings, or other members of the ruling class. They were paid with rations, which consisted of a portion of the crops they harvested, or products from the animals they tended. Most peasants worked under overseers, who managed the land for its owner and often had complete control over the peasants.

Peasants' duties were not limited to working the fields. Under a system of forced labor known as corvée, peasants had to perform work for

168

the state for one or two months each year. In the Hittite kingdom of KHATTI, this could include building public works, such as fortifications*, temples, or roads. In addition to these duties, peasants in Egypt were required to perform military service as well.

The role of the peasant in ancient Mesopotamian society changed over time. From about 3500 to 2000 B.C., most peasants worked for the temples, receiving rations in return. In the early second millennium B.C.*, lands were held by private individuals who paid the peasants in rations. Some peasants traveled and hired themselves out as workers or sold themselves into slavery. By the late second millennium B.C., when the economies of Mesopotamia began to disintegrate, peasants who could no longer handle their burden and lack of rights went to live on royal land.

Ancient Near Eastern peasants who worked as farmers and those who worked as herders depended on each other for survival. In order for crops to grow, farmers needed the herders to bring their animals, such as oxen, to the fields to plow them.

Peasant Life. The life of a peasant in the ancient Near East was difficult. Between the long hours tending crops and the corvée system, peasants had little free time. They rested on the occasional festival day, at which time the landlord might give them extra food or a jar of beer or wine. Most peasants struggled to survive on the food and produce they received as wages. Some peasant households owned poultry and goats that helped meet some of their food needs.

Peasants in Egypt typically lived in tiny mud huts clustered together in villages that often lacked fresh water or sanitation. Despite their poverty, peasants were taxed regularly and faced being beaten if they failed to pay the tax. After suffering years of poor living conditions, some peasants abandoned the land and their families and moved to cities. Others formed outlaw bands and roamed the countryside assaulting travelers and isolated villages. (*See also* **Land Use and Ownership; Labor and Laborers; Taxation.**)

PERFUMES

* **fortification** structure built to strengthen or protect against attack

* **second millennium B.C.** years from 2000 to 1001 B.C.

* **frankincense and myrrh** fragrant tree resins used to make incense and perfumes

* **incense** fragrant spice or resin burned as an offering

H ow fragrant your perfumes, more fragrant than all other spices," wrote the author of the Song of Songs in the Hebrew BIBLE. Many ancient texts reveal an appreciation for perfumes, fragrant substances worn for personal adornment or used to beautify the air. Ingredients in perfumes, especially frankincense and myrrh*, became major trade items in the ancient Near East.

Perfumes originated in the ancient Near East after people there had formed the custom of burning incense* at religious and healing rituals. Kings began to use fragrant woods in the construction of their palaces. Eventually, people started using aromatic spices and other fragrances in everyday life, although such delights were very costly.

Ancient perfumes generally consisted of plant oils or animal fats to which aromatic substances were added. Sometimes they combined ingredients such as roses, myrtle, sandalwood, cinnamon, blue water lilies and henna flowers (especially in Egypt), and hyacinth and saffron (prized by the Israelites) to create distinctive scents.

Perfumes were used in rituals, as medicinal treatments, and in cosmetics. The Egyptians used aromatic creams and oils to prepare MUMMIES for entombment. They also wore scented cones of fat on wigs for special occasions. As the warmth of their bodies melted the fat, the perfume spread.

In MESOPOTAMIA, perfumes were often made by women and were used in medicine, magic, rituals, and cosmetics. For instance, herbalists sold scented medical resins and perfumed cosmetic creams. The ancients created a variety of jars and spoons for storing and handling perfumes, scented body creams, bath oils, and other fragrances. Such containers are among the finest decorative objects of the ancient world. (*See also* **Cosmetics; Economy and Trade; Hair; Incense.**)

PERSEPOLIS

See map in Persian Empire (vol. 3).

The city of Persepolis (puhr•SE•puh•lis), also known as Parsa, was the capital of the PERSIAN EMPIRE under the Achaemenid dynasty. The city was founded around 518 B.C., by Persian king Darius I to replace the former Persian capital of Pasargadae. It was completed by Darius's successor, XERXES. Other Persian kings also made additions to the city, but most of it was built by Darius and Xerxes over a period of nearly 60 years.

Because Persepolis was located in a remote, mountainous region, it was not convenient for the royalty to reside there. Persian kings and their families probably only lived there in the spring. Much of the administration of the empire was carried out in other cities. Thus, it is likely that Persepolis was mainly a ceremonial center where coronations, royal burials, and other important ceremonies took place.

At Persepolis, valuables were stored in the Treasury. When Alexander the Great looted the city in 330 B.C., the Treasury was emptied. However, details such as these, from a relief adorning the audience hall at Persepolis, provide modern historians with a picture of the glorious metalwork of the Achaemenid dynasty.

The city was built on a huge stone terrace almost 50 feet high and measuring about 1,400 feet from north to south and 1,000 feet from east to west. Two stone staircases led from the plain to a single gatehouse at the top of the terrace. Palaces, audience halls, and other structures were constructed atop the terrace. The largest structure was the audience hall of Darius and the 100-column throne hall of Xerxes. Both were located in the center of the terrace, dividing it into two halves. The northern half of the terrace was devoted to the military. The southern half contained the palaces of Darius and Xerxes, living quarters of the royal family, and the state treasury building, where most of the empire's wealth was stored. All the buildings and other structures, including the staircases, were extensively decorated with bas-reliefs* and inscriptions.

Around 330 B.C., Persepolis was captured and partially burned by ALEXANDER THE GREAT. The city then became a provincial* capital in the Macedonian empire, but it declined in importance during the succeeding SELEUCID EMPIRE. Today Persepolis lies in ruins, and the remains of the royal palaces and other colossal structures are the only evidence of its former grandeur.

* **bas-relief** kind of sculpture in which material is cut away to leave figures projecting slightly from the background

* **provincial** having to do with the provinces, outlying districts, administrative divisions, or conquered territories of a country or empire

PERSIAN EMPIRE

The Persian empire flourished in the ancient Near East from 550 to 330 B.C. The empire began in ancient IRAN and came to include a vast territory stretching from Greece to India. It was the largest empire of the time, and its extent was unsurpassed until the advent of the Roman Empire, which reached its peak many centuries later. The Persian empire was a model for later empires because it demonstrated how a centralized government could bring together different peoples and cultures.

HISTORY

People of Indo-European origin began to settle in Iran more than 1,000 years before the Persian empire was founded. The empire itself can be divided into two periods: the period of the first Persian empire, from 550 to 522 B.C., and the period of the Achaemenid dynasty*, from 521 to 330 B.C.

* **dynasty** succession of rulers from the same family or group

Early History of the Persians in Iran. Around 1200 B.C., people who spoke Indo-European languages began arriving in northeastern Iran from the CAUCASUS region between the Caspian and Black Seas. By the 900s B.C., two groups, the Persians and the MEDES, had gained control of most of Iran. The Medes lived in northern Iran, which was called Media, and the Persians lived in southern Iran, which was called Persia.

Around 700 B.C., according to later traditions, the Persians were ruled by a king named Achaemenes. His descendants, known as the Achaemenid family, later became the royal family of the Persian empire. Achaemenes divided his kingdom between two of his sons, who later formed the two branches of the Achaemenid family. Each branch produced a line of Persian kings. The first line included CYRUS THE GREAT, founder of the first Persian empire. The second line of kings began with Darius I, also known as Darius the Great, founder of the Achaemenid

Persian Empire

* **vassal** individual or state that swears loyalty and obedience to a greater power

* **city-state** independent state consisting of a city and its surrounding territory

* **nomad** person who travels from place to place to find food and pasture

---

In 559 B.C., after defeating the Medes, Cyrus the Great founded the Persian empire. During his reign, he greatly expanded the empire, establishing Persian dominance in the region. Within 50 years, the empire had reached its height. Around the mid-300s B.C., however, troubles with Greece and Egypt caused the empire to lose some territory. Finally, in 330 B.C., the Persian capital of Persepolis fell to the armies of Alexander the Great of Macedonia, and the Persian empire came to an end.

dynasty. Around the same time, according to Greek historian HERODOTUS, the Medes were unified by their king Deiokes and formed the Kingdom of Media. By the late 600s B.C., the Medes had conquered Persia and made it a vassal*.

The First Persian Empire. In the 500s B.C., Persia was ruled by a king named Cambyses I, who was among the earliest Achaemenid kings. When Cambyses died in 559 B.C., his son, Cyrus II, later known as Cyrus the Great, took over as ruler of Persia. Cyrus II was very ambitious and set out to gain power and improve the position of the Persians in Iran. He also negotiated an alliance with the Babylonians against the Medes. In 550 B.C., he led a revolt against the Medes with help from the Babylonians. The Medes were defeated, and the Persians took control of the Median kingdom, marking the beginning of the first Persian empire.

Cyrus immediately began to increase the territory of his empire. He attacked Lydia and captured its capital, SARDIS, in 547 B.C. Then he led his army in capturing all the Greek city-states* along the western coast of ANATOLIA (present-day Turkey). In 540 B.C., he turned on his former Babylonian allies and captured BABYLON the following year. This conquest gave Cyrus control of all the land west of Iran to Egypt. Cyrus died in 529 B.C. while trying to defeat a tribe of nomads* in Central Asia, although the exact circumstances are in dispute.

Cyrus's successor, his son CAMBYSES II, launched a successful attack against Egypt and established Persian forts along the NILE RIVER. Then he mounted unsuccessful attacks against CARTHAGE, Nubia, and Amon, an oasis in the Egyptian desert. In 522 B.C., hearing of an uprising in Iran,

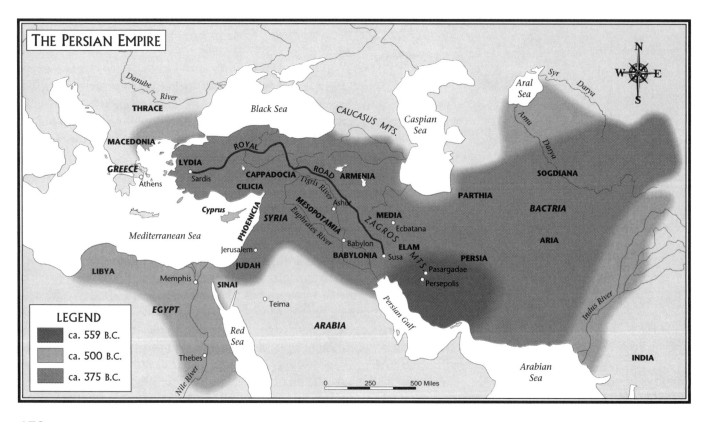

172

B Y Ǝ ◁ ٦ ◁ ≮ Z ∓ Y ✝ W ◁ φ 7 O ◢ M ∠ Ⅺ ⴹ B Y Ǝ ◁ ٦ ◁ ≮ Z ∓ Y

Persian Empire

Cambyses set out to return home to regain control of his kingdom. However, he died on the way, and one of his generals, later known as Darius I, went on to Iran to end the revolt. It took Darius and his troops more than a year to gain control. In 521 B.C., Darius succeeded to the throne.

The Achaemenid Dynasty. Although Darius was from the Achaemenid family, he did not belong to the branch that had produced the first line of Persian kings. He was from the second branch of the family, which became known as the Achaemenid dynasty. It was during the reign of this dynasty that the Persian empire grew to its largest extent.

Darius undertook an expansionist policy and gained control of large sections of northern India, as well as land previously controlled by the Scythians to the west and north of the Black Sea. He led his troops into Europe as far as the Danube River, although he failed to conquer any new lands there. Darius also invaded Greece, but he was defeated in the battle at Marathon in 490 B.C. Darius planned to return to Greece with a much larger force, but a revolt in Egypt and Darius's own death in 486 B.C. prevented him from carrying out his plan.

Darius was succeeded by his son XERXES, who quickly put down the revolt in Egypt. Xerxes also ended a revolt in Babylonia in 482 B.C. Unlike Cyrus and Darius, who had ruled foreign lands with tolerance, Xerxes ruthlessly imposed his will. He next turned his attention to Greece, conquering northern Greece after the battle at Thermopylae in 480 B.C. He then led his troops to Athens, where they burned down the Acropolis. Shortly thereafter, Xerxes returned to Iran. His troops were later defeated by the Greeks in the battle of Plataea, and with that defeat, the Persian invasion of Greece came to an end. In the later years of his rule, Xerxes lost interest in foreign conquests and focused on domestic problems. He was assassinated in 465 B.C.

The death of Xerxes marked a turning point in the history of the Achaemenid dynasty. The kings who followed Xerxes—Artaxerxes I, Xerxes II, and Darius II—were weak and struggled to retain control of the empire. Their reigns were plagued by rebellions, including one in Egypt that took five years to bring under control. Xerxes II was assassinated in a court intrigue after ruling for less than two months. Darius II was faced with several rebellions, including one by the Medes.

In 404 B.C., Artaxerxes II succeeded Darius II. During his 45-year reign, Persia fought a 13-year war with the Greek city-state of Sparta. In the peace treaty that was signed at the end of the war, Greece gave up its claims in Anatolia to the Persians. Also during Artaxerxes' reign, Egypt revolted against Persia. The Egyptians were successful, and Egypt regained its independence. Artaxerxes tried to regain control of Egypt but failed. In 370 B.C., several satraps* mounted an unsuccessful revolt against him. Although these uprisings were put down, the Persian state was weakened, and Artaxerxes was assassinated in 359 B.C.

Artaxerxes III took over the throne on the death of Artaxerxes II. He ordered the deaths of many of his relatives, whom he feared might challenge his rule, but revolts continued. He tried to regain control of Egypt, but without success, encouraging rebellions in other parts of the empire, including the Levant*. In 343 B.C., Artaxerxes led another attack on

Life in Iran Before the Persians

The Persians were not the first people to settle in Iran. Archaeologists have found sites in Iran that were settled at least 5,000 years before the Persians arrived. One site, Ali Kosh, has more than 20 feet of accumulated deposits. Deposits from the lowest layer, which dates back to 7500 B.C., show that the earliest inhabitants gathered wild plants, cultivated wheat and barley, and herded goats and sheep. Deposits from higher layers are more recent, dating from about 6500 B.C. They show that by this time the inhabitants were living in well-built houses, making baskets and pottery, and taking part in a far-reaching trade network.

* **satrap** provincial governor in Persian-controlled territory

* **Levant** lands bordering the eastern shores of the Mediterranean Sea (present-day Syria, Lebanon, and Israel), the West Bank, and Jordan

173

The Story of the Fake Bardiya

According to Darius the Great, in 521 B.C., when King Cambyses was fighting in Egypt, he was informed that his brother Bardiya had led a revolt and seized the throne in Iran. Cambyses died before he could return home and reclaim the throne, but as he lay dying, he revealed to his troops that the Bardiya who had seized the throne was a fake. Apparently, Cambyses knew that the real Bardiya was not on the throne because he had already had the real Bardiya killed. Ironically, Cambyses had arranged his brother's death because he feared he would try to seize the throne while Cambyses was away.

* **bureaucracy** system consisting of officials and clerks who perform government functions

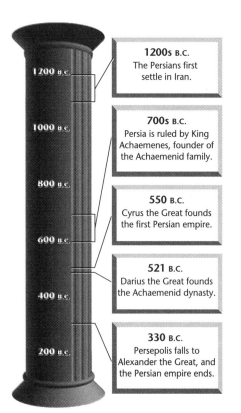

1200s B.C.
The Persians first settle in Iran.

700s B.C.
Persia is ruled by King Achaemenes, founder of the Achaemenid family.

550 B.C.
Cyrus the Great founds the first Persian empire.

521 B.C.
Darius the Great founds the Achaemenid dynasty.

330 B.C.
Persepolis falls to Alexander the Great, and the Persian empire ends.

Egypt. This time he was successful although the Egyptian king escaped to Nubia, where he established an independent kingdom. In 338 B.C., Artaxerxes III was poisoned by an administrator named Bagoas.

After Artaxerxes' death, Bagoas attempted to become the power behind the Persian throne and appointed an Achaemenid prince named Arses king. However, Arses failed to be a puppet king, and he was was killed and replaced on the throne by Darius III, who had Bagoas put to death. In 336 B.C., Darius suppressed a rebellion in Egypt. However, Persian success was short-lived, and the end of the Persian empire was near.

In 334 B.C., ALEXANDER THE GREAT of MACEDONIA launched an attack on the Persian empire with an army of 40,000 troops. Four years later, the Persian capital of PERSEPOLIS fell to Alexander, and the Persian empire came to an end. Darius III was the last king of the Achaemenid dynasty. He was murdered while fleeing from Alexander.

ORGANIZATION AND ADMINISTRATION OF THE PERSIAN EMPIRE

The Persian empire was ruled by a supreme king who was assisted by a royal court and a large bureaucracy*. The empire was divided into satrapies, each ruled by a satrap. Both the military and law were important elements of the empire.

The Central Government. The king was at the center of the Persian empire. His traditional title was "king of kings" because he ruled as the supreme authority. The king also was considered divine.

The royal court was composed of wealthy landowners, high-ranking military officers, priests, government officials, and the wives and relatives of the king. The king and his court usually resided at Susa, but moved to Ecbatana in the summer and Persepolis in the spring. On occasion, the court moved to Babylon. A smaller version of the court traveled with the king when he visited distant provinces.

The government's work was carried out by a large bureaucracy. Most government workers were scribes*, the majority of whom worked at the royal treasuries. The bureaucracy was highly organized, and all government workers were managed by a hierarchy* of officials headed by the king.

Satrapies and Satraps. The number of satrapies into which the empire was divided and their boundaries varied over time. There were just 20 satrapies at the beginning of the reign of Darius the Great. As the empire grew, the number increased. At first, the satraps were appointed by the king, often from among his relatives. In the later years of the empire, a number of satraps inherited their positions. Although many satraps were very powerful, they were watched by officials from the king's court, known as the "king's eyes."

The Military. The Persian army was responsible for conquering and retaining the far-flung lands that comprised the empire. Troops were stationed permanently at strategic locations throughout the empire to put

The tombs of Achaemenid king Darius I and three of his successors were carved into this rocky and imposing cliffside at Naqsh-i Rustam near Persepolis. A stone tower facing the tombs stands to the far left. The site, which was excavated in the A.D. 1930s, was originally held sacred by the Elamites for its ancient spring.

* **scribe** person of a learned class who served as a writer, editor, or teacher

* **hierarchy** division of society or an institution into groups with higher and lower ranks

* **tribute** payment made by a smaller or weaker party to a more powerful one, often under the threat of force

down rebellions and protect trade routes. At the beginning of the empire, the army was composed only of Persian soldiers who were drafted to fight for the king. Later it was composed of hired professional soldiers. During wartime, soldiers were drafted throughout the empire.

Law. The Persians were noted for their justice. One of their greatest achievements was the formulation and implementation of a unified code of laws that applied to everyone in the empire. This system of laws made an important contribution to their ability to rule their vast empire for more than two centuries. Darius the Great, in particular, came to be known as a great lawgiver and legal reformer. He reformed the tax laws of the empire and instituted a tax on agricultural produce, which varied according to the size of the harvest.

Economy. Agriculture was the main source of wealth in the Persian empire. Landholdings varied in size, from plots too small to support more than a single individual to estates owned by wealthy families and worked by hundreds of peasant farmers. Much of the produce from farming went to the central government for taxes, rents, and tribute*. Therefore, the government took an active role in boosting agricultural productivity. It invested state resources in building irrigation works, improving crops, and developing better farming techniques.

Another source of royal wealth was trade. The government took steps to promote this sector of the economy. It sponsored voyages to seek new trading partners, encouraged the development of ports on the Persian Gulf, standardized weights and measures, and developed and circulated coins. The government also built and maintained a superior system of roads that linked Persia with its major trade partners. The roads also served vital administrative and military purposes.

Persian Society and Culture

Society and culture were as varied as the peoples who had been brought together under Persian rule. The tolerance of most kings allowed this variety to flourish. The society and culture of the Persians themselves were based on Iranian traditions. However, the Persians were greatly influenced by the peoples who became part of the empire.

Language. The Persians spoke a dialect* of Iranian called Old Persian. The language was first written when Darius the Great ordered that a script be invented so that he could leave a lasting record of his rise to power on the Behistun inscription. However, Old Persian was never the language of the administration of the empire. Instead, the language most widely used for administrative purposes was Aramaic. The adoption of a single language as the official language of the empire no doubt contributed to the empire's success. Many other languages were spoken throughout the empire, including Elamite, another language that was used for administrative purposes.

Religion. The earliest Persians to enter Iran worshiped many deities*. These deities were associated with fundamental aspects of nature and daily life and with basic concepts such as truth and justice. Traditional rituals included sacrificing animals, drinking alcoholic beverages, and using fire.

Around 600 B.C., a great Iranian religious prophet* and teacher named Zoroaster emerged in northeastern Iran. Zoroaster's teachings stressed moral behavior and truthfulness. He taught that the only true god was Ahura Mazda, the traditional Persian god of goodness, and demoted the other traditional deities to demons. A new religion, called Zoroastrianism, which was based on Zoroaster's teachings, emerged and became the religion of the Achaemenid dynasty.

Art and Architecture. Some of the finest examples of art and architecture in the Persian empire were created for the kings. The most extensive building programs, such as the building of the capital city of Persepolis, were carried out primarily by Darius the Great and Xerxes. Persepolis is considered one of the great artistic achievements of the ancient world. It is praised for its well-proportioned ground plan, rich architectural ornamentation, and magnificent bas-reliefs*.

Persian kings brought together artists, architects, craftspeople, and materials from all over the empire to create their magnificent buildings, monuments, and artworks. Although the finished products are distinctly Persian, almost every detail can be traced to a foreign source. One of the few exceptions is the columned hall, an Iranian invention dating to the first millennium B.C.*

The Persians themselves were especially skilled in metalworking, jewelry making, seal cutting, and pottery making. Their gold work is especially noteworthy for its fine quality. (*See also* **Artaxerxes I, II, and III; Babylonia and the Babylonians; Darius I and Darius III; Elam and the Elamites; Lydia and the Lydians; Susa and Susiana; Zoroaster and Zoroastrianism.**)

* **dialect** regional form of a spoken language with distinct pronunciation, vocabulary, and grammar

* **deity** god or goddess
* **prophet** one who claims to have received divine messages or insights
* **bas-relief** kind of sculpture in which material is cut away to leave figures projecting slightly from the background
* **first millennium B.C.** years from 1000 to 1 B.C.

Imperial Imports

The royal architecture of the Persian empire was created from the most expensive materials and by the most highly skilled workers in the empire. This is clear from a description of the construction of the palace at Susa that was written by Darius the Great. It lists timber from Lebanon, Gandara, and Carmania; gold from Sardis and Bactria; lapis lazuli and carnelian from Sogdiana; turquoise from Chorasmia; silver and ebony from Egypt; ornamentation from Ionia; ivory from Ethiopia, Sind, and Arachosia; stonecutters from Ionia and Sardis; goldsmiths from Media and Egypt; woodworkers from Sardinia and Egypt; and brickworkers from Babylonia.

T he Persian Wars were a series of conflicts between the PERSIAN EMPIRE and Greece that took place between 492 and 449 B.C. In these wars, an alliance of small Greek city-states* defended their homelands against conquest by the Persians. The ultimate victory of the Greeks humiliated the Persians and helped ensure the survival of Greek culture and traditions.

* **city-state** independent state consisting of a city and its surrounding territory

Background of the Wars. During the mid-500s B.C., the Persian kings CYRUS THE GREAT and his son CAMBYSES II began extending Persian rule westward toward the AEGEAN SEA. After defeating the Lydians in ANATOLIA (present-day Turkey) in 547 B.C., the Persians gradually conquered several small Greek city-states in Ionia, a region in western Anatolia.

In 499 B.C., the Ionian Greeks began to rebel against Persian rule. They received some support—a small fleet—from the city-states of Athens (located on the Greek mainland) and Eretria (located on the island of Euboea). The Greek fleet attacked the city of SARDIS, the main Persian stronghold in Anatolia, but the Persian satrap* there defended the city until more Persian troops arrived and forced the Greeks to retreat. Although the Ionian Revolt gained strength the following year, the Persians ultimately triumphed.

* **satrap** provincial governor in Persian-controlled territory

The Ionian Revolt had important consequences for mainland Greece. The Persian king, DARIUS I, was angered by the Athenians' participation in the revolt. He planned to punish the Greeks and extend his empire by invading the Greek mainland.

History of the Wars. In 492 B.C., Darius sent a large army and a fleet of 600 ships to attack Greece. However, the invasion faltered when part of the Persian fleet was wrecked by a storm off the Greek coast. Two years later, Darius assembled a stronger fleet and launched another invasion. This time, the Persians reached the coastal plain of Marathon and started to advance toward Athens, about 25 miles to the southwest. The Athenians asked Sparta for help, but before the Spartans could arrive, the Athenians seized an opportunity to attack and won a stunning victory over the Persians. After losing more than 6,000 men in this defeat, the disgraced Persians returned home.

Ten years passed before the Persians were prepared to invade again. In 480 B.C., King XERXES, Darius's son and successor, arrived in Greece with a large army and navy. The Persians began marching to Athens, but a small Greek force led by King Leonidas of Sparta held them for two days at a narrow mountain pass called Thermopylae. Xerxes and his army found another route through the mountains and circled back to attack the Spartans from behind. Realizing what was happening, Leonidas sent most of his men away, but those who remained fought until their deaths.

The Persians then moved on to Athens, which they captured and burned without a fight because the Athenians had abandoned the city while the Persians were delayed at Thermopylae. Meanwhile, the Greeks decided that their best chance against the Persians was at sea. Some Persian ships had already been destroyed in a storm, and the Greek naval commander Themistocles devised a plan to defeat the rest of the fleet.

* **strait** narrow channel that connects two bodies of water

Pretending to retreat, Themistocles lured the Persian navy into a narrow strait* off the island of Salamis, near Athens. When the Persians entered the strait, the Greek fleet attacked, destroying and capturing many enemy ships. Xerxes, who was watching from a hilltop, saw the remnants of his mighty fleet sail away in defeat.

Xerxes returned to Persia after the defeat at Salamis, but he left a military force in Greece to continue the Persian conquest. These troops invaded and devastated the region of Attica in eastern Greece, but when a Greek army began advancing against them, the Persians withdrew northward into the neighboring region of Boetia. In 479 B.C., Greeks forces defeated the Persians in Boeotia at the battle of Plataea. The same year, the Greeks also defeated a Persian fleet at Mycale, off the coast of Anatolia.

The Greek victories at Plataea and Mycale ended the threat of a Persian invasion of mainland Greece, but the wars continued in Anatolia for another 30 years. In 478 B.C., a number of Greek city-states formed an alliance called the Delian League to defend themselves against further Persian threats. Led by the Athenians, the league also launched an attack on the Persians in Ionia to regain independence for the Greek city-states there.

Between 478 and 449 B.C., the Greeks waged war almost continuously against the Persians in Anatolia. By the end of that period, they had strengthened Greek power in Ionia and prevented any further Persian attempts at conquest in the Aegean. Hostilities between the Greeks and Persians finally ended in 449 B.C., when the two sides signed the Peace of Callias, which marked the formal end to the Persian Wars. (*See also* **Greece and the Greeks; Lydia and the Lydians; Wars and Warfare.**)

PHARAOHS

Pharaohs were the KINGS of ancient Egypt. The word *pharaoh,* which means "great house" in Egyptian, originally referred to the royal palace. Starting in the late Eighteenth Dynasty (ca. 1300s B.C.), the term was used as a synonym for the Egyptian king. Since then, the word *pharaoh* has come to mean any ancient Egyptian king. The discussion below refers to ancient Egyptian kings in general, whether or not they were called pharaohs in their own times.

Learning About the Pharaohs. A great deal of information about Egyptian pharaohs comes from numerous monuments and other structures built and inscribed with facts about their lives and reigns. Because of Egypt's dry climate, many of these structures are amazingly well preserved. Other sources of information are the KING LISTS, chronological lists of Egypt's pharaohs. In the 200s B.C., these lists served as sources for a Greco-Egyptian priest named Manetho, who used them to compile a complete chronology of Egyptian rulers up to his time. Although neither complete nor accurate, the lists are still considered the best sources of information about the pharaohs of ancient Egypt.

In addition to reading about the pharaohs in these sources, scholars have actually *seen* some of the pharaohs. Because the ancient Egyptians believed in life after death, they preserved the bodies of many ancients, especially pharaohs, as MUMMIES. The bodies of some of the pharaohs are

The *Sed*-Festival

One of the earliest known royal festivals in ancient Egypt was the *Sed*-festival. The purpose of this festival was to reaffirm the pharaoh's divine power. It was supposed to occur 30 years after the pharaoh took the throne and then at various times after that. The festival lasted several weeks, during which the pharaoh, priests, and high government officials visited and honored one another and the pharaoh offered gifts to the gods. A number of important rituals also took place during the festival, the most important of which was a symbolic reenactment of the pharaoh's coronation.

* **vizier** minister of state

* **tribute** payment made by a smaller or weaker party to a more powerful one, often under the threat of force

* **artisan** skilled craftsperson

See color plate 2, vol. 4.

so well preserved that scholars have been able to compare the pharaohs' facial features to help settle disputes about whether or not they were related to each other. One of the best-preserved bodies is that of the pharaoh TUTANKHAMEN, who ruled Egypt in the 1300s B.C.

The Pharaoh's Role. The pharaoh was the absolute ruler of ancient Egypt. In principle, this meant that he owned and controlled everything in Egypt, including the land, its resources, and its people. Although the power and reputation of the pharaohs changed over time, the idea of the nature of kingship remained relatively the same throughout ancient Egypt's long history. This stability of the pharaoh's role helped preserve the unity of Egypt and promote its great civilization.

As absolute ruler, the pharaoh governed by royal decree. This meant that, in theory, all commands originated with him and were carried out, without question, by his appointed officials. The pharaoh's chief aid and the government's highest-ranking official was the vizier*, who reported directly to him.

As the "owner" of Egypt, the pharaoh was entitled to most of its wealth. This entered the royal treasury primarily in the form of agricultural produce, which was paid to the pharaoh as taxes and rents. He also had the right to draft soldiers for his military campaigns and laborers for his building projects. In addition, the pharaoh received tribute* from foreign lands Egypt had conquered. All this wealth supported the pharaoh and his family in grand style. Some pharaohs kept an entire community of artisans* busy creating palaces for this world and tombs for the next, both for themselves and for their families.

The role of pharaoh was traditionally reserved for men. Although a QUEEN might have held a great deal of power, normally only a king could be pharaoh. Of ancient Egypt's 300 or so pharaohs, only 4 were women. Through a combination of personality, circumstances, and luck, they were able to break the mold and play a man's role in society. One of the most famous female pharaohs was HATSHEPSUT, who was co-ruler of Egypt with her stepson, THUTMOSE III. Hatshepsut named herself pharaoh while Thutmose was still a boy. She later took on the traditional titles of the pharaoh and exercised absolute power. Although she was portrayed in art and architecture wearing pharaonic dress, including the ceremonial false beard that symbolized the king's power, it is not known whether she dressed as a man in real life.

Egyptians and the Pharoah. Ancient Egyptians held several important beliefs about the pharaoh that supported his role as absolute ruler. The Egyptians believed the pharaoh was both all-knowing and all-powerful. Being all-knowing, the pharaoh was a supremely wise ruler. He was the source of all laws and the essence of moral behavior. Being all-powerful, the pharaoh was the trusted protector of the Egyptian people. It was said that he could defeat any foe by crushing thousands of enemy soldiers on the battlefield and that the snake on his crown could spit flames at his enemies. Without the pharaoh, the ancient Egyptians believed, there would be chaos instead of order on earth. He also said to be a shepherd to his people, who ensured the well-being of his subjects and protected all, rich and poor.

ᚦᛒᛦᛂᚴᛈᚿᚵᛍᛉᚾᛏᛟᚹᚽᛣᚩᛯᚮᚴᛘᛘᛉᛤᚦᛒᛦᚴᛈᚿᚵᛍᛉᚾ

Pharaohs

* **coronation** act or ceremony of crowning a leader

Co-regencies

The transition from a pharaoh to his successor was not always smooth. To avoid potential conflicts over succession, some pharaohs named their successors as co-regents, that is, as co-rulers. Although both were called pharaoh, the younger of the two pharaohs usually served as a junior partner until the older pharaoh died. Often the younger pharaoh was assigned more strenuous duties, such as leading military campaigns, while the older pharaoh stayed at the royal palace and managed the affairs of state.

* **prostrate** to stretch oneself out, with face on the ground, usually in submission or respect

* **dynasty** succession of rulers from the same family or group

Probably the most important belief the ancient Egyptians held about the pharaoh was the belief that he was divine. This meant that he was a representative of the gods and that he was godlike himself. A pharaoh received his divine power at his coronation*, and it was reaffirmed through other ceremonies, most importantly the *Sed*-festival. The pharaoh's divine status was supported by the belief that the first pharaoh appeared at the beginning of time, when gods ruled the earth. Other myths established the pharaoh's relationship with the gods. He was believed to embody the falcon god Horus and to be the son of the sun god Amun-Ra. After death, the pharaoh was identified with Osiris, who was god of the dead and father of Horus.

Although the pharaoh was considered a godlike representative of the gods, he was not believed to be a god. However, after he died, he was believed to rise to the kingdom of the gods and live among them. For this reason, many of the later pharaohs were worshiped as gods after they died. Some pharaohs also built gigantic, elaborately decorated PYRAMIDS as tombs for themselves and filled them with riches so that they would be properly outfitted for their AFTERLIFE among the gods. Many of these pyramids still stand in Egypt. The largest, the Great Pyramid at GIZA, was built by a pharaoh named KHUFU, around 2585 B.C.

Because the pharaoh was believed to be divine, he had absolute power and was shown great respect. For example, all people approaching the pharaoh had to prostrate* themselves before him. The pharaoh's divine status also made him the high priest of ancient Egypt. In this role, it was his job to serve the gods on behalf of the Egyptian people. He did this by building new temples and maintaining old ones and by observing daily rituals in the worship of the gods. These acts ensured that the gods would look favorably on the Egyptian people and bring them peace and prosperity.

Evidence suggests that sometimes the divinity of a particular pharaoh was questioned. For example, if there were a series of poor harvests or if Egypt was successfully attacked by an enemy, the people sometimes lost faith in the pharaoh. Some pharaohs were removed or even assassinated for this reason.

How the Pharaoh Was Chosen. The role of pharaoh was hereditary, and most pharaohs were succeeded by their oldest son. Many pharaohs had several wives, but only one was the chief wife, or queen. Ideally, the oldest son of the chief wife was the pharaoh's successor. This type of succession was paralleled by ancient Egypt's most widespread myth, that of Osiris. In the myth, Osiris dies and is succeeded as king of the gods by his son Horus.

When a succession of pharaohs came from the same royal family, they formed a dynasty*. A new dynasty began when a pharaoh died without a suitable heir and the throne was taken over by a rival family or seized by a foreign conqueror. Ancient Egypt was ruled by more than 30 different dynasties in its 3,000-year history. Sometimes, to help ensure the continuity of a dynasty, a pharaoh married a member of his own family, such as his sister or niece. Such marriages were common among Egyptian pharaohs but not among the rest of the Egyptian people.

Symbols of the Pharaoh. In the ancient Egyptian system of writing called HIEROGLYPHICS, symbols were used to represent people and things. The main symbol used to represent the pharaoh was a double crown. This combined the white crown of Upper Egypt (the Nile River valley south of the delta*) with the red crown that represented Lower Egypt (the delta region). Thus, it symbolized the pharaoh's control over the entire realm. This was important because Lower Egypt and Upper Egypt had a long history of rivalry and independence. Other symbols used to represent the pharaoh were the scepter, or royal staff, and the throne. Both symbolized the pharaoh's authority and power. In addition, the pharaoh's name and title were always written inside an oval, called a cartouche, that symbolized the pharaoh's rule over the entire world.

In art, the pharaoh was portrayed in ways that represented his position between the people and the gods. In scenes with ordinary people, the pharaoh was shown as young, strong, and larger than life size to indicate his superior position. In scenes with the gods, the pharaoh was shown kneeling before the gods to reflect his inferior position or standing face-to-face or side by side with the gods to show his godlike status. (*See also* **Ahmose; Akhenaten; Cleopatra; Djoser; Dynasties; Egypt and the Egyptians; Government; Necho II; Nefertiti; Nitokris; Ptolemy I; Ramses II; Ramses III; Sety I.**)

* **delta** fan-shaped, lowland plain formed of soil deposited by a river

PHILISTINES

See map in Israel and Judah (vol. 3).

The Philistines (FI•luh•steenz) were a people of eastern Mediterranean origin who settled in the Levant (present-day Syria, Lebanon, Israel, the West Bank, and Jordan) around 1200 B.C. Perhaps best known as enemies of the ancient Israelites, the Philistines were portrayed negatively in the Hebrew BIBLE. Partly as a result, the word *Philistine* came to mean "uncultured" or "uncouth." In fact, they were a diverse and creative people who flourished in the land of CANAAN for 600 years.

Origins. Historians are uncertain about the origins of the Philistines. Most believe they were one of a group of tribes known as the SEA PEOPLES, who invaded Egypt during the reign of Ramses III (ruled ca. 1187–1156 B.C.). Some evidence suggests that they may have come from an island in the AEGEAN SEA—possibly the island of CRETE—and were forced eastward because of disruptions within their civilization. The Hebrew Bible says that the Philistines were descended from the Caphtorites, who some scholars believe referred to Cretans.

After unsuccessful attempts to invade Egypt in about 1190 B.C., the Philistines settled in Canaan in the Levant. They came to the region primarily as hostile invaders, destroying the Canaanite towns and cities that lay in their path and establishing their own. It is also possible that Egypt sent the Philistines to Canaan to serve as mercenaries* in fortified, Egyptian-controlled towns.

After settling in Canaan, the Philistines founded many towns and five major cities in the region, including Gaza, Ashkelon, Ashdod, Gath, and Ekron. These cities eventually developed into small city-states* and

* **mercenary** soldier who is hired to fight, often for a foreign country

* **city-state** independent state consisting of a city and its surrounding territory

181

Philistines

* **confederacy** group of cities or states joined together for a purpose; an alliance

formed a confederacy* that was later called the Pentapolis. The entire region under Philistine control became known as Philistia, and the Philistines became a major political and commercial power.

Philistines and Israelites. Soon the Philistines began to expand into surrounding areas, which brought them into conflict with their neighbors, the Israelites. From about 1150 to the 900s B.C., the Philistines were the main enemies of the Israelites, and the Hebrew Bible contains a number of stories about the struggles between them.

By the early 1000s B.C., the Philistines had gained control over much of Israel. Although they suffered setbacks at the hands of the Israelite hero Samson, they soon regained the advantage and held a military superiority that lasted several decades. Conflict erupted periodically during this time. One well-known biblical story concerns a Philistine victory over the Israelites and their capture of the ARK OF THE COVENANT, which held the sacred tablets of the TEN COMMANDMENTS that MOSES had brought to Canaan centuries earlier.

Although the Philistines initially had greater military success than the Israelites, the tables eventually turned. In the early 900s B.C., the Philistines suffered a number of significant defeats at the hands of King DAVID of the Israelites. According to the Hebrew Bible, in David's first encounter with the Philistines, he killed a giant Philistine warrior named Goliath.

Despite Israelite victories, the city-states of Philistia survived and remained independent, but the confederation collapsed. The Philistines ceased to be a major military threat. In the mid-900s B.C., when Israelite territory was divided into two separate kingdoms—ISRAEL AND JUDAH—the

The pottery fragments shown here were recovered from the site of the Philistine city of Ashdod. The use of birds as a decorative element on Philistine pottery was borrowed from the Mycenaeans, who may have been the Philistines' ancestors. Mycenaean influence is also evident in Philistine metalworking, sculpture, and even burial tombs.

Philistines reasserted their commercial power and began to regain some of their political might. For about the next 300 years, the Philistines engaged in periodic struggles with Israel and Judah.

Later History. In the 700s B.C., some Philistine cities experienced great economic growth and prosperity. However, this era also marked the beginning of the end of the Philistines, who could not withstand the power of the Assyrians and Babylonians as they each expanded into the Levant. By 700 B.C., the Assyrians had conquered many Philistine cities and made them their vassals*. The Assyrians demanded tribute* and forcibly moved some of the inhabitants of Philistia to other parts of the Assyrian empire and settled other people in their place. Despite the loss of their independence, some Philistine cities continued to prosper during the period of Assyrian dominance. The city of Ekron, for example, remained important and became wealthier than ever. Assyrian rule also established new economic and political systems and exposed Philistia to new ideas that undermined Philistine culture and society.

Around 600 B.C., the Babylonian ruler NEBUCHADNEZZAR II conquered all of Philistia and incorporated it into his empire. The Babylonians destroyed any remnant of the Philistine culture and independence that had remained after the Assyrian conquest. Like the Assyrians, they forcibly moved huge numbers of Philistines to other areas of their empire. The Babylonian conquest largely destroyed what was left of a separate and unique Philistine culture.

Some cities in Philistia flourished in later periods under Persian, Greco-Macedonian, and Roman rule. However, their heritage was no longer Philistine. In later centuries, the Greek historian HERODOTUS and other travelers called the region Palaistium, a name based on accounts by descendants of the Philistines. In A.D. 135, the Romans incorporated Philistia, Judah, and Syria into a single province called Syria-Palestina. Later the region became known simply as Palestine.

Economic Life and Towns. The Philistines were manufacturers, traders, and farmers. Among their most important crops were grapes, OLIVES, and grains, with which they made WINE, olive oil, and flour. Despite a healthy system of AGRICULTURE, the Philistines based their economy on manufacturing and trade.

The city of Ashdod manufactured a purple-dyed cloth that was prized by royalty throughout the Near East. Ashdod also had one of the largest POTTERY workshops in the Levant. At the height of its power, the city of Ekron was the largest producer of olive oil in the Near East. The Philistines were best known for their metalwork, which included iron axes and plows as well as bronze armor and weapons.

The Philistines were an urban people, and most of the population of Philistia lived in towns and cities. Divided into separate zones—a manufacturing zone, a central area with temples and public buildings, and residential areas—the cities were surrounded by mud brick* walls. Houses consisted of central courtyards encircled by kitchens, living quarters, and storerooms. Philistine towns had sophisticated drainage systems and public garbage dumps outside their walls.

* **vassal** individual or state that swears loyalty and obedience to a greater power

* **tribute** payment made by a smaller or weaker party to a more powerful one, often under the threat of force

* **mud brick** brick made from mud, straw, and water mixed together and baked in the sun

Phoenicia and the Phoenicians

* **deity** god or goddess

Culture and Religion. The culture of the Philistines originally reflected their Aegean origins. For example, Mycenaean-style pottery has been found at the earliest Philistine sites. Initially, the Philistines also remained faithful to the deities* of the Aegean world, especially the Great Goddess.

However, by the late 1000s B.C., outside influences had greatly influenced the Philistines, and they began to adopt many of the local customs of other groups. They adopted various Canaanite gods, such as Dagon, and practiced burial customs that reflected Canaanite and some Egyptian influences. A royal inscription from Ekron shows that by the 600s B.C., they were speaking a Phoenician-like dialect* and writing in a Hebrew-like script. By incorporating cultural influences from different times and places, the Philistines gradually developed a new and distinct culture that was quite different from that of their Aegean ancestors. (*See also* **Egypt and the Egyptians; Hebrews and Israelites; Mycenae and the Mycenaeans.**)

* **dialect** regional form of a spoken language with distinct pronunciation, vocabulary, and grammar

PHOENICIA AND THE PHOENICIANS

* **Levant** lands bordering the eastern shores of the Mediterranean Sea (present-day Syria, Lebanon, and Israel), the West Bank, and Jordan

* **Semitic** of or relating to a language family that includes Akkadian, Aramaic, Arabic, Hebrew, and Phoenician

* **maritime** related to the sea or shipping

* **first millennium B.C.** years from 1000 to 1 B.C.

* **city-state** independent state consisting of a city and its surrounding territory

* **archaeological** referring to the study of past human cultures, usually by excavating material remains of human activity

Phoenicia (fi•NEE•shuh) was the name given by the ancient Greeks to the coastal region of the eastern Mediterranean that included part of CANAAN in the Levant*. The Canaanite inhabitants of this region, known to the Greeks as the Phoenicians (fi•NEE•shuhnz), spoke a Semitic* language and were among the greatest maritime* traders of the first millennium B.C.* Although the Phoenicians shared a common culture, they never formed a unified state. Instead, Phoenicia consisted of a series of independent city-states*, including BYBLOS, SIDON, and TYRE.

The independent Phoenician city-states were frequently threatened by the various empires that arose around them. Still, the Phoenicians dominated sea trade in the region and exerted influence on their neighbors. They also became great colonizers, establishing colonies in North Africa, ANATOLIA (present-day Turkey), CYPRUS, and distant Spain. One of the greatest of these colonies was CARTHAGE in North Africa, which became one of the chief commercial and maritime powers in the western Mediterranean region and a powerful rival of ancient Rome.

History. Ancient Phoenicia consisted of a narrow coastal strip that included parts of present-day Lebanon, southern SYRIA, and northern Israel. Archaeological* evidence has revealed that humans lived in this region as early as 10,000 B.C., and by 4000 B.C., the people of the region were producing distinctive POTTERY and copper metalwork.

Little is known about the early history of the region. Evidence shows that Byblos had commercial contacts with Egypt as early as the 2600s B.C. In fact, the earliest known image of the region's inhabitants appears on a sculpture in an Egyptian tomb dating from the early 2500s B.C. In about 2150 B.C., the AMORITES invaded the region and destroyed Byblos. Amorite control lasted several hundred years, during which time the region continued to maintain close contact with Egypt.

In the 1700s B.C., the HYKSOS from western Asia invaded Phoenicia, ending Amorite rule there. The Hyksos controlled the region until the

1500s B.C. Thereafter, Egypt conquered almost all of Canaan and dominated the area for a few hundred years. However, by the 1100s B.C., Egyptian power in Canaan had mostly disappeared.

The late 1200s and early 1100s B.C. were a time of great change and upheaval throughout the ancient Near East. Many societies collapsed, people migrated in large numbers, and centers of manufacturing and trade were destroyed or abandoned. On the Mediterranean coast, these changes may have been caused in part by the SEA PEOPLES, who are believed to have invaded the region and destroyed many coastal city-states. Following these upheavals, however, the Phoenician city-states experienced a period of renewal, great prosperity, and expansion. Many scholars date the rise of Phoenician civilization to this period.

Early in the first millennium B.C., the Phoenicians began to surpass other ancient peoples in maritime trade. As their wealth increased, the Phoenicians began to establish colonies in other areas of the Mediterranean. The drive for colonization resulted primarily from a search for sources of raw materials. The Phoenicians also sought to establish ports and SHIPPING ROUTES that would enable them to expand their control over Mediterranean trade. Fearless sailors, the Phoenicians carefully guarded the secrets of their TRADE ROUTES, and they became the undisputed masters of the seas.

The Phoenician city-states were fully independent at the beginning of the first millennium B.C., but this independence did not last long. Beginning in the 800s B.C., Phoenicia was dominated in varying degree by empires to the east. The first of these empires to threaten Phoenicia was

A lack of farmland forced the Phoenicians to turn to the sea to find their wealth. They became the greatest seafarers of the ancient Near East and dominated trade around the Mediterranean Sea for centuries. As the Phoenicians became more successful and wealthier, they also became great colonizers, establishing colonies in northern Africa, Anatolia, Cyprus, and Iberia (Spain).

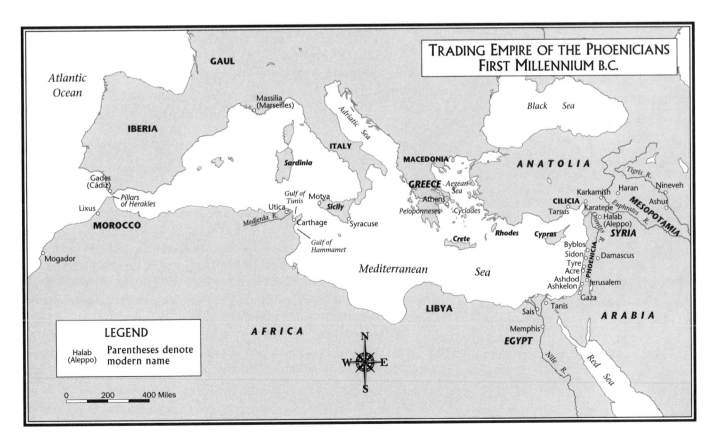

185

Phoenicia and the Phoenicians

* **vassal** individual or state that swears loyalty and obedience to a greater power

* **tribute** payment made by a smaller or weaker party to a more powerful one, often under the threat of force

* **Hellenistic** referring to the Greek-influenced culture of the Mediterranean world and western Asia during the three centuries after the death of Alexander the Great in 323 B.C.

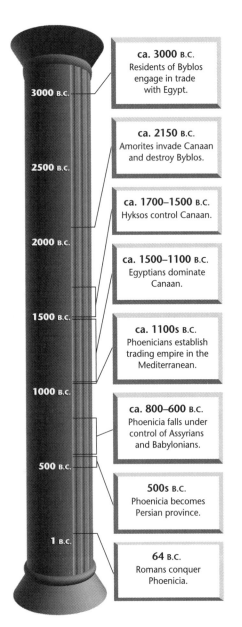

3000 B.C.

ca. 3000 B.C.
Residents of Byblos engage in trade with Egypt.

ca. 2150 B.C.
Amorites invade Canaan and destroy Byblos.

2500 B.C.

ca. 1700–1500 B.C.
Hyksos control Canaan.

2000 B.C.

ca. 1500–1100 B.C.
Egyptians dominate Canaan.

1500 B.C.

ca. 1100s B.C.
Phoenicians establish trading empire in the Mediterranean.

1000 B.C.

ca. 800–600 B.C.
Phoenicia falls under control of Assyrians and Babylonians.

500 B.C.

500s B.C.
Phoenicia becomes Persian province.

1 B.C.

64 B.C.
Romans conquer Phoenicia.

Assyria. Between the mid-800s and the 600s B.C., the Assyrians launched military campaigns on cities along the Mediterranean coast. Although the Assyrians did not attack the Phoenician cities, they made them vassals*. As long as the Phoenicians paid tribute* and taxes, Assyrian rule was mild, and the city-states were mostly independent.

In the late 600s B.C., the Babylonians gained control of Phoenicia and continued the Assyrian policy of collecting tribute and taxes while allowing substantial independence. Less than 100 years later, the Persians destroyed the Neo-Babylonian empire, and Phoenicia became a province of the PERSIAN EMPIRE. The Phoenician city-states prospered under the Persians, who encouraged trade and commercial activities.

The prosperity and peace enjoyed by the Phoenician city-states was interrupted from time to time by local uprisings against Persian rule, especially in the 300s B.C. These rebellions were often encouraged by the Egyptians and Greeks, who sought greater influence in the region. Although the uprisings were quelled, they made it more difficult for the Persians to control the region and helped pave the way for its conquest by the Macedonians under ALEXANDER THE GREAT in 332 B.C.

During the Hellenistic* period, Macedonian kingdoms competed for control of Phoenicia. In the 100s B.C., the region became part of the SELEUCID EMPIRE. Seleucid rule continued until 64 B.C., when the Romans conquered Phoenicia and incorporated it into their empire. Phoenicia remained under Roman rule for several centuries, during which time the remnants of traditional Phoenician culture disappeared.

Trade and Manufacturing. The Phoenicians became a great maritime trading people largely because of geography. Confined to a narrow coastal strip and with little farmland, they looked to the sea for their livelihood. As early as the third millennium B.C. (years from 3000 to 2001 B.C.), the local people were cutting timber from mountains in the interior and exporting it from the HARBORS of their cities along the coast. By the second millennium B.C. (years from 2000 to 1001 B.C.), their activities included manufacturing, and they became well known throughout the ancient Near East for their glassmaking, metalwork, carved wood and IVORY, and dyed cloth.

Some experts believe that the Phoenicians invented glassblowing around 100 B.C. They were perhaps most famous for their TEXTILES, particularly a purple-dyed cloth they manufactured. The purple dye for this cloth, which was produced from a type of shellfish, was more valuable than gold and thus became associated with royalty. By the time of the Roman Empire, the use of the dye was restricted to the most elite members of society.

The earliest records provide evidence that the Phoenicians were very successful MERCHANTS and traders. By the 900s B.C., they had established colonies all along the southern Mediterranean coast, and in the centuries that followed, they ventured farther, setting up colonies in many parts of the western Mediterranean region. Some evidence suggests that the Phoenicians also explored the Atlantic coast of Europe as far as Britain and perhaps sailed around the continent of Africa.

In addition to their colonies in the Mediterranean, they established trading centers in important cities of the Near East. Foreign merchants at

These coins, known as tetradrachma, were minted by the people of Carthage, the most important Phoenician colony. Like the Phoenicians, the Carthaginians engaged in trade throughout the Mediterranean. Over time, their economic ties were strengthened by their military. These coins, which show a woman's head and a horse being crowned by the goddess Victory, were probably minted to pay Carthaginian soldiers stationed in Carthage's province in Sicily during the 300s B.C.

* **artifact** ornament, tool, weapon, or other object made by humans

* **deity** god or goddess

* **pantheon** all the gods of a particular culture

Long Before the *Titanic*

In A.D. 1999, Robert Ballard, the man who located the wreck of the *Titanic,* found the oldest shipwrecks ever discovered—two 2,500-year-old Phoenician sailing ships containing cargoes of wine. The two vessels, probably bound for Egypt or Carthage from the ancient city of Tyre, sank about 30 miles off the coast of present-day Israel. Amazingly, the ships were largely undamaged, and the jugs holding the wine were still stacked together and intact. This was because the ships sank in deep water, where high water pressure, cold, and lack of sunlight helped preserve the vessels and their cargoes.

these centers conducted business under special arrangements between local and Phoenician authorities. In this manner, the Phoenicians controlled virtually all maritime trade in the Mediterranean, and many nations transported their goods in Phoenician ships. Not surprisingly, the Phoenicians made many advances in shipbuilding, including building ships that could make longer voyages.

Culture and Religion. The Phoenicians were influenced by many of the great civilizations that surrounded them. There is evidence of Egyptian cultural and religious influences starting at around 2500 B.C., and other evidence shows that the HITTITES, Assyrians, and Mycenaeans of Greece all influenced Phoenician art and culture.

Very little Phoenician art or architecture has survived to the present day. Among the finest surviving artifacts* are trade items such as jewelry, metalworks, small ivory carved objects, and glassworks. Many of these objects show a blending of designs and styles borrowed from other cultures yet combined to create a distinct new art form. Highly prized as trade items, such works were found throughout the ancient Near East and thus influenced the design of works created by skilled craftspeople in other societies as well.

Little is known of the Phoenician religion except that there were many deities*, most of whom were associated with individual cities rather than with a national pantheon*. Basic religious beliefs seem to have been shared, however, even though the specific local deities differed. Although the "chief" deity in all Phoenician cities was a god, the most important deity was usually a fertility goddess. Called Baalat Gubla in Byblos, she was named Tanit in Tyre and was known as Astarte (or Ashtart) in Sidon. The names of many Phoenician gods included the title Baal ("the lord"), such as Baal Shamem ("lord of the sky"). Historians are uncertain whether these were the actual names of the gods or merely titles used to refer to them and to their functions.

Scholars also know very little about Phoenician religious rituals or the priesthood. Rulers were probably considered to be earthly representatives of the gods, and in some cases, kings and queens served as high priests and priestesses. The Phoenicians cremated and buried the dead, and there

Phoenicia and the Phoenicians

* **cult** system of religious beliefs and rituals; group following these beliefs

* **cuneiform** world's oldest form of writing, which takes its name from the distinctive wedge-shaped signs pressed into clay tablets

See color plate 1, vol. 1.

is evidence that they practiced child sacrifice. Phoenician religious cults* and practices spread as a result of colonization, and temples dedicated to Phoenician deities sprang up in various parts of the Mediterranean world.

One of the greatest cultural legacies of the Phoenicians is their system of WRITING. The Phoenicians spoke a Semitic language closely related to Hebrew. Initially, the Phoenicians probably wrote in cuneiform*. However, by about 1400 B.C. they had developed an alphabetic system of writing consisting of 22 letters representing consonants but not vowels. This system of writing was eventually adopted by most of the societies in the western Mediterranean region. The Assyrians also used the Phoenician AL-PHABET to write the Aramaic language, which led to its introduction into all the areas controlled by Assyria. Ultimately, the Phoenician writing system was adopted and modified by the Greeks and then the Romans, whose alphabet became the basis for most of the modern European alphabets in use today. (*See also* **Economy and Trade; Glass and Glassmaking; Mediterranean Sea, Trade on; Mycenae and the Mycenaeans; Naval Power; Ships and Boats; Taxation.**)

A

Aba-Enlil-dari, 1:53
Abortion, 4:13
Abraham (Abram), 2:155, 3:24, 166–67
Absolute chronology, 1:166
Absolute dating (archaeological), 1:58–59
Abu Simbel, **1:1** (illus.)
Abydos, **1:1–2**, 3:157
Achaemenes, 3:171
Adad, **1:2–3**
  in Babylonian pantheon, 1:110
  Canaanite worship of, 1:139
  in Eblan pantheon, 2:130
  in *Enuma Anu Enlil*, 1:94
Adad-nirari, 1:86, 87
Adad-nirari III, 1:88
Addu. *See* Adad
Addu-yisci, 4:113 (illus.)
Adoption, 2:87
Aegean Sea, **1:3**
  earthquake belt in, 2:46
  Greek islands in, 2:139
  Mycenaean colonization of islands in, 3:122
  Thera, **4:123**
  volcanic belt through, 4:144
Aethiopia. *See* Nubia and the Nubians
Afro-Asiatic languages, 3:47–48. *See also* Hamitic (Hamito-Semitic) languages
Afterlife, **1:3–6**. *See also* Burial sites and tombs; Death and burial
  and Book of the Dead, 1:120–21
  cosmetics for use in, 2:11
  Egyptian beliefs about, 1:120–21, 2:63
  Hittite beliefs about, 2:170
  inscriptions as guide to, 3:4
  and letters to the dead, 1:4, 2:41
  Mesopotamian beliefs about, 2:29
  netherworld, 1:5
  offerings for the dead, 1:5, 3:151–52
  Osiris and, 3:157
  of pharaohs, 3:180
  pyramids and, 4:20
  resurrection in, 1:6
  and roles of dead in lives of the living, 2:86
  soul (portrayal of), 1:4 (illus.)
  underworld, 1:1
Agade. *See* Akkad and the Akkadians

Agriculture, **1:6–11**. *See also* Gardens
  of Akkadians, 1:20–21
  in Babylonia, 1:108
  calendars and, 1:135
  in Canaan, 1:138
  at Çatal Hüyük, 1:148
  cereal grains, **1:154–57**
  development of, 4:167
  as economic foundation, 2:47
  in Egypt, 1:9–10, 2:61–62
  farming methods, 1:8–10
  farmworkers, 1:10–11
  and flooding, 2:38, 98–99
  impact of, 1:11
  irrigation, **3:8–11**
  in the Levant, 1:8–9
  main crops, 1:7–8
  in Mesopotamia, 1:9, 3:94, 95
  Mosaic Law concerning, 3:116
  Nile River's impact on, 3:138
  nomadism and, 3:141, 142
  olive growing, 3:152
  origin of, 1:6
  peasants' role in, 3:168
  in Persian empire, 3:175
  state-run (in Akkad), 1:20
  in Syria, 4:110–11
Ahab, **1:11–12**, 3:15, 4:44
Ahhotep, Queen (Egypt), 1:12
Ahmose, **1:12–13**, 2:183
Ahriman, 1:6, **1:13**, 2:130, 4:179
Ahura Mazda, **1:14**
  on Behistun inscription, 1:116 (illus.)
  earth as battleground of, 1:13
  as Zoroastrian one true god, 1:6, 2:130, 3:114, 4:178–80
Akhenaten, **1:14–15**
  monotheism ordered by, 1:97, 3:113–1:114
  Nefertiti and, 3:133
  temple of, 1:15 (illus.)
  wives of, 4:25
Akhetaten, **1:16**, 1:31, 2:174
Akkad and the Akkadians, **1:16–22**, 1:19 (map), 2:79
  agriculture and trade, 1:20–21
  arts of, 1:21–22
  attack on Magan by, 3:153
  in Babylonian history, 1:102–3
  barus, 3:153–54
  cuneiform adopted by, 2:20–21
  and Elamites, 2:67–68
  fall of, 1:19

  government of, 2:132
  history of, 3:96
  language of, 1:16–17, 109, 2:34, 35, 3:47, 4:72
  literature of, 3:60
  naming in, 3:128
  Naram-Sin, 1:18, **3:129–30**
  poetry in, 3:59
  political organization, 1:20
  religion of, 1:21
  royal inscriptions, 1:164
  Sargon I, 1:17–18, **4:48–49**
  sculpture of, 4:57
  social institutions of, 4:88
Akrotiri, 4:123, 145
Alaca Hüyük, 1:38, 39
Alalakh, **1:22–23**
Albright, William F., 1:64
Aleph-beths, 1:27–30, 4:171–72
Alexander IV, King, 1:26
Alexander the Great, **1:23–27** (illus.)
  army of, 1:74–75
  and Darius III, 2:27
  empire of, 1:24 (map), 3:67
  and the Gordian knot, 1:26
  Lycian invasion by, 3:63
  Macedonia and Greece united by, 2:141
  Ptolemy I and, 4:19
  Tyre conquered by, 4:135
  use of cavalry by, 1:152
Alexandria, library in, 3:55
Alliance of the twelve kings, 1:52
Alloys and alloying, 3:101, 108, 4:54
Alluvial plains, 2:118, 3:9
Alphabetic numeration, 3:149
Alphabets, **1:27–30**, 4:172
  Greek, 2:142–43
  Hebrew, 2:157–58
  Phoenician, 3:188
Alyattes, King, 3:65
Amamet, 1:5
Amarna, **1:31–32**. *See also* Akhetaten
Amarna letters, 1:31
Ambassadors. *See* Messengers
Amenemhet I, 3:156
Amenemhet III, 3:36
Amenhotep III, 3:160–61
Amenhotep IV. *See* Akhenaten
Amharic language, 4:73
Amorites, **1:32–33**
  in Babylonian history, 1:103
  in Canaan, 1:138
  dynasties of, 2:44

Page numbers of articles in these volumes appear in boldface type.

189

Index

Index

Index

Index

Index

Index

Index

Index

Index

Index